Dudley Hardy, Alice Werner

The Humour of Holland

Dudley Hardy, Alice Werner

The Humour of Holland

ISBN/EAN: 9783743330375

Manufactured in Europe, USA, Canada, Australia, Japa

Cover: Foto ©Suzi / pixelio.de

Manufactured and distributed by brebook publishing software (www.brebook.com)

Dudley Hardy, Alice Werner

The Humour of Holland

THE
HUMOUR OF HOLLAND

TRANSLATED, WITH AN INTRO-
DUCTION, BY A. WERNER.
ILLUSTRATIONS BY DUDLEY
HARDY AND OTHERS

LONDON   WALTER SCOTT
1893   LTD

CONTENTS.

	PAGE
INTRODUCTION	ix
THE KING'S DREAM—*Frederick Van Eeden*	1
THE DOMINIE—*C. K. Elout*	6
MY HERO—*Conrad van der Liede*	35
NEWSPAPER HUMOUR	52
A RASCALLY VALET—*Multatuli*	55
DROOGSTOPPEL INTRODUCES HIMSELF—*Multatuli*	77
DROOGSTOPPEL PAYS A CHARITABLE VISIT—*Multatuli*	83
APHORISMS—*Multatuli*	90
OF SELF-DEPRECIATION—*Multatuli*	93
OF EDUCATION, WITH PRACTICAL ILLUSTRATIONS—*Multatuli*	94
GOING INTO BUSINESS—*Multatuli*	112
TWO PARABLES—*Multatuli*	113
THERSITES AND PLATO—*Multatuli*	115
EGOTISM—*Multatuli*	115
THE STORY OF CHRESOS—*Multatuli*	116
THE FAIRY TALE THAT FANCY TOLD WOUTER—*Multatuli*	119
HALF-AN-HOUR AT THE HAIR-DRESSER'S—*Anon.*	125
IN THE LITTLE REPUBLIC—*L. H. J. Lamberts-Hurrelbrinck*	139
NEWSPAPER HUMOUR	173

CONTENTS.

	PAGE
FICTION AT SEA—*A. Werumeus Buning*	174
NEWSPAPER HUMOUR	178
FARMER GERRIT'S VISIT TO AMSTERDAM—*J. J. Cremer*	184
NO SWORD—"*Humoristisch Album*"	197
A STUDENT'S LODGINGS SIXTY YEARS SINCE—*J. Van Lennep*	200
A COLONIAL PRIZE-GIVING—*Annie Foore*	205
HOW MATHIS KNOUPS TURNED "LIBERAL" AND THEN "CATHOLIC" AGAIN—*Emile Seipgens*	212
NEWSPAPER HUMOUR	232
THE CANDIDATE—*T. H. Hooijer*	252
EPIGRAMS	257
THE VILLAGE ON THE FRONTIER—*Van Lennep*	261
PROVERBS	290
A DUTCH PODSNAP—*Gerard Keller*	293
ROUGH DRAFT OF A NEW SET OF REGULATIONS—*Uilenspiegel*	346
THE STORY OF A BOUQUET—*Uilenspiegel*	347
UNBIDDEN GUESTS—*Annie Foore*	351
BIOGRAPHICAL INDEX OF WRITERS	393

INTRODUCTION.

THERE appears to be an idea abroad to the effect that the "Humour of Holland" could be most satisfactorily dealt with in a chapter resembling the famous one "Of Snakes in Ireland." As the average English reader, in the most favourable instances, knows little more of Dutch literature than a name or two (Rembrandt has introduced us to "the poet Vondel," and if Southey were not so little read in these days Bilderdijk and Cats would not be so unfamiliar), the subject offers a free field to the constructive imagination. Yet even so, one would think it must be obvious that the nation which has produced a Teniers, a Jan Steen, and—in some of his moods—a Rembrandt, could not be entirely destitute of humour. The estimate of its quality may be a question of taste; but—though many people practically do adopt this form of logic—we cannot make the fact of our not finding it to our liking a ground for denying its existence.

Of course, before determining what the humour of a nation is like, we need to know what is that nation's intellectual bent as a whole, and what forces have been at work to determine its character. On this point we may quote a paragraph or two from a Dutch writer, J. H. Hooijer, whom we shall meet again in the course of these pages. He is describing a village in North Holland, in the heart of the fat meadow-lands, famous for the production of Dutch cheeses.

"The same village which you find so depressing this November day,—so damp, so clammy, so dripping with water,—makes a very different impression when Spring, with full hands, has showered her blossom-snow over the orchards, or in the autumn, when the trees are hanging full of golden pears or rosy apples. Greener meadow-land is nowhere on earth, unless it be in the Emerald Isle itself. The rich green pastures have velvety lights in the sunshine, and the splendid cattle—their dappled skins smooth and shining as silk—show out to advantage against it—colour on colour. At such times there is a glow of colour in the whole landscape, which, strange as it may sound, reminds one of the South,—a glow one might almost think was stolen from the palettes of the Old Masters. Every breath you draw is perfumed with new milk and flowers, mingled with the salt smell of the sea. There is a fulness of outward life—a bubbling up and overflowing of vital juices,—for which they had an eye and a heart, those great old realists. The man who despises a rich clover pasture, speckled here and there with white-fleeced sheep; who cannot spare a look for the magnificent horned cattle that stand staring at you, with dreamy, half-sad gaze, over the fence, while Geertje's black eyes flash at you from behind the milking-pail,—well, he need not come to North Holland. Intellects of this sort, exclusively devoted to the contemplation of the sublime, will find everything ugly in these parts. To such an one our Old Masters have nothing to say; for him, Paul Potter's art is a mere waste of time, and many a racy bit of Vondel trivial nonsense. Happily the cheery sun is of another mind, and his smile falls well-pleased on the endless emerald plain. He nurses it, feeds it, warms it, —he sweetens the blades of grass for the palate of the pampered cow. And sometimes, just before setting, he draws along the horizon, with purple finger, broad streaks of crimson fire, and then the dykes flame out like ruby bands winding over the green velvet robe of the earth, and you wish for the power of wielding the brush, so as to throw on canvas what one might almost call these brutal effects of colour."

Here we have a fertile country, with the means of existence in plenty, but not one where it is easy to live without hard work. These rich meadow-lands have been wrung from the sea by the painful toil of centuries, and are only held by the tenure of constant vigilance. But the struggle for existence is not hard enough to exhaust the vital energies, and produce a stunted careworn race. There is abundance of rough but wholesome food, such as results in strong limbs and clear skins; there is leisure for dancing and play—rough horse-play though it may be—when work is done; that there is a recognised place in life for mere beauty and luxury, is shown in the gold head-ornaments of the women. There are no mountains to suggest the sense of remoteness and mystery; and the grey North Sea, with its sands and mud-flats, is rather a fact to be accepted, a foe to be struggled with, in a grim matter-of-course way from day to day, than the weird terror that the ocean is to more imaginative peoples. But within the narrow and well-ordered bounds of farm and homestead, there is a richness of colour to fire the painter's eye; the skies and sunsets are the glorious ones that flame over fen and marshland, and winter brings the joy of glittering ice and ringing skates. Life is and has been less bare and hard than of old in Scotland; but on the whole, the history of the two nations is somewhat similar, and they have many points of character in common.

Both learned thrift, endurance, and foresight in a hard school; both early acquired the inconvenient habit of thinking for themselves and dispensing with any mental spectacles save those of their own choosing; and both displayed a bull-dog tenacity in holding by their hardly won rights. But after the Reformation a marked difference becomes evident. Scotland only emerged from the troubles of that epoch to encounter the religious persecution of the Stuarts. The seventeenth century was fruitful of heroism; it tried the national character as by fire, and developed its sterner and deeper elements; it was not unfavourable even to tenderness, of a rugged and undemonstrative character, but the lighter side of life was left, for the time being, entirely in abeyance. In the quieter time which succeeded the Union, reaction soon became stagnation. The fiery earnestness, —call it fanaticism, if you like,—which had been so tremendous a force in action and endurance, now became a sour harsh bigotry, lying like a leaden weight on men's lives. It is one thing to be in such deadly earnest over an urgent crisis, that you have no time or inclination to admire a picture or laugh at a joke; it is another to forbid such enjoyment to other people, because it is inconsistent with the attitude of mind proper to the crisis that is over and past. We all have *les défauts de nos qualités;* and the mistakes of reformers include a tendency to regard the conclusions at which they have arrived as final, and an imperfect estimate of the relative value of means and ends—

in other words, the inability to see when a truth (that is to say, any particular statement of a truth) has done its work. This general state of flatness and dulness could only be ended by a volcanic outburst,—and such a one came in with Burns.

To return to Holland. The shaking off of the Spanish yoke was followed by a period of peace and prosperity. Dutch ships had for some time past been bringing home the wealth of the Indies. Dutch admirals were finding their way into unknown seas. Colonies sprang up in the Spice Islands, and the money gained by trade turned the swamps reclaimed from the sea into flower-gardens, or covered them with stately buildings. Wealthy burghers, even of the strictest Calvinist persuasion, did not appear to find their Protestant principles an obstacle to the encouragement of painters and poets. Roemer Visscher and his daughters, though members of the defeated and unpopular church, kept open house at Amsterdam for all who loved art and letters, and assembled round them the best wits of the time. Gerbrand Bredero, painter and poet both, belonged to a respectable burgher family, who—though grieved by the excesses of his riotous youth, and sorely troubled by his contemplated marriage with Alida Jansdoter, the pretty but characterless widow who kept the Toren van Monnickendam tavern—do not appear to have mourned over his choice of a vocation, or regarded his plays as anything to disapprove of. Joost van den Vondel, the tragic poet (in whose genius some have found an excuse for belittling that of our own Milton), was a deeply religious man; and though he seems to have suffered from the aspersions of the religious, it was not so much on account of his poems, as because he was a Baptist, and they Reformed Calvinists. No doubt there *was* religious bigotry in Holland, but there were also elements of healthy life which kept it in check. And there was a time when thought became dull and stagnant,—when the dead-weight of the commonplace, backed by the double sanction of social and religious orthodoxy, forced all individuality into its own prepared mould,—when the Dominie looked with suspicion on every independent expression of opinion, and the "Pious" kept a watchful eye on the Dominie, —but that time was not yet. Betje Wolff, who suffered in her youth from Cornelia Slimpslamp and Brother Benjamin,—and never forgot it,—came in for part of it; but the worst was not till after she and her friend Aagje had been laid to rest side by side. That was the darkness just before the dawn; for surely there never was such a world of dead forms and petty conventions, such a stifling atmosphere of cant and artificiality, as that in which Multatuli spent his childhood.

The humour of the Netherlands has, in common with that of Scotland, a certain canniness and practical shrewdness, characteristic of men and nations who have bought their experience at first hand and a heavy price. But, whether for want of that touch of Celtic fire which in Scotland has leavened the solid Teuton into a thing quite unique in the world, or what else, there is a notable lack of that dryness and terseness—that expressing more than the whole by means of less than the half—which comes out in the best Scotch anecdotes and sayings. It would be an insult to a listener of average intelligence, to explain, for example, "It's a puir shaw for Kirkintilloch." We are not sure that—supposing that the exact equivalent to this joke existed in Dutch—the Netherlander would feel the insult deeply; we rather think he would enjoy the story the better for a half page or so of comments in addition to the full explanation. Of this nature are many jocular poems by the revered Father Cats, and the "Zinne-poppen" of Roemer Visscher and his daughter Anna.

The Netherlander likes his fun pretty obvious, and not too concentrated. And the main characteristic of the said fun is its breadth,—or rather what the Germans call *Breite*, for the English word by no means conveys exactly the same idea. "Long-windedness" alone does not express it; Coleridge's "nimiety or too-muchness" (which he calls a characteristic fault in the German literary temperament) is much nearer the mark. It is long-windedness combined with infinite multiplicity of detail,—a gossipy, good-humoured, complacent triviality, which is the essence of boredom. Voss's "Luise" (which poem we doubt whether any British person now living has read through) is a shining example of the quality. Nothing is left to the reader's imagination—everything, and the reason for everything, is described and explained at full length, till the best ideas are swamped in floods of formless verbiage. In Holland, this kind of writing flourished most extensively in the seventeenth and eighteenth centuries, and **Father Cats**, already referred to, exhibits it in an excessive degree. He also shows an overpowering desire to be improving,—another point common to the Scot and the Batavian,—and the two things together made him, for two centuries, out and out the most popular writer in Holland.

As to "broad" farce, in the other sense of the word, Dutch literature possesses a good deal of it, of such extreme latitude, indeed, as to be for the most part entirely unavailable for this volume. Besides, it is not amusing. The *Sotterniëen*, or farces, of the Middle Ages, were of an extremely rough and ready type, to say no more, though Dr Jan Ten Brink accords them the praise of "accurate observation of Flemish low life, and a real comic gift." They mostly turn on matrimonial difficulties, in which a foolish husband gets the worst of it. More or less of the same kind, though of a somewhat higher type, were the farces (*Kluchten*) of what we may call the Dutch Renaissance (c. 1550-1650). They mostly turn on rough or even disgusting practical jokes; they are written in clumsy, lumbering verse, which has the effect of encouraging and intensifying the author's natural diffuseness; in short, whatever laugh-provoking power they may once have had, most of them are now quite intolerably dull. The best known are those of Coster, Vos, Jan Starter, Hooft, Huygens (who made one excursion in this direction—*Trijntje Cornelis*), and, above all, Gerbrand Bredero, whose genius had not yet reached its highest point, when his short and stormy life came to an end.

GERBRAND ADRIAENSZEN BREDERO was born at Amsterdam in 1585. His father was a wealthy tradesman, at first a shoemaker, and afterwards farmer of the taxes on wines and spirits. Adriaen Bredero was a generous patron of art, and intended his son to become a painter; but the latter, though he studied for a time, and appears to have shown some degree of talent, preferred to devote himself to literature. He became a member of the chamber, *In Liefde Bloeiende*,*

---

* The oldest "Chambers of Rhetoric" (or *Collèges de Rhétorique*—the name probably originated in the French influence introduced by the House of Burgundy) date back to about 1400, or some years previous. The oldest would seem to be the "Alpha and Omega," at Ypres, and the Antwerp "Violieren" (wall-flowers). The and soon formed the acquaintance of Spieghel, the didactic poet, and the genial Roemer Visscher, the scholarly author of the "Zinne-poppen" and "Brabbeling." An unhappy love for Roemer's younger daughter, Tesselschade, probably wrecked his life, the greater part of which was spent in noisy dissipation, alternating with intervals of deep depression. His work was both lyric and dramatic; his principal plays are the tragi-comedies of "Roderick and Alphonsus" (1611), "Griane" (1612), and "The Dumb Knight" (1618), to which may be added the unfinished play "Het daghet uyt den Oosten," the farces of the "Cow" (1612), the "Miller" and "Symen sonder Soeticheyt" (1613), and the regular comedies of "The Moor" (1615), and "The Spanish Brabanter" (1618). The last-named, his master-piece, was intended to satirise (under the name of Jerolimo) the Chevalier Theodor Rodenburgh, his rival in literature and in a second unhappy love affair. From this bitter disappointment Bredero never recovered. He died at the age of thirty-three, after a lingering illness, tended with devoted care by his mother, and comforted by the friendship of the gentle and earnest-hearted Vondel, whose religion was of a type to find easier access to the stormy soul than the gloomy Calvinism of Bredero's relations. For further particulars of the poet's life the reader is referred to the works of Dr Jan Ten Brink, among others an interesting historical novel (founded on contemporary documents) entitled "De Bredero's," which has appeared in "Elsevier's Geillustreerd Maandschrift" for 1891 and 1892. Bredero's farces are rough, and even coarse—a defect from which his more elevated work, such as the "Spanish Brabanter," is not free; but this is a fault common to the comic literature of

---

most famous, perhaps, is the Amsterdam association, "De Eglantier," better known perhaps under the name of its motto, "In Liefde Bloeiende" (Blooming in Love). They held poetical competitions, placed upon the stage (usually with great magnifi-cence) plays written and acted by their members, and arranged the most splendid page-ants and processions on the occasion of any festival or public rejoicing. They also celebrated festivals of their own, the most important of which were known by the name of *Landjuweelen*. In 1496 a great Landjuweel was held at Antwerp by twenty-eight societies, at which the Eglantier gained the first prize. But the most famous of all was the Landjuweel of 1561, also held at Antwerp, beginning on the 3rd August, when the chambers of Brabant and Flanders vied with one another in magnificence. The Brussels society, "The Book," was represented by 340 members, all on horse-back in crimson mantles. This festival was revived on the occasion of the jubilee of the Belgian Academy of Antiquities, August 1892.

all countries at that epoch. He was no scholar, and though acquainted with French, did not know Latin, a circumstance for which his writing is probably none the worse. His comedy, "Het Moortje" ("The Little Moor"), is an adaptation of a French version of Terence's "Eunuchus," and far inferior to the "Spanish Brabanter," which, though not absolutely original (the plot is to a great extent taken from the Spanish novel "Lazarillo de Tormes"), is as much so as most of Shakespeare's, and full of life and vigour. It is perhaps somewhat verbose, and the irregular kind of ballad-metre in which it is written lends itself to indefinite *longueurs;* but the character-painting is excellent. Indeed, Bredero's chief merit is the strong human sympathy shown in his broad, vivid pictures of popular life. He gives us the life of the street in Amsterdam as he knew it—the beggars, the scolding wives, the money-lender, the poor gentleman with his frayed velvet doublet and rapier showing through its worn sheath, the gossiping sexton, the boys playing at marbles. It is evident that Bredero was on the right track, and, had he lived, might have produced even better work than this play,—perhaps founded a new dramatic school, which might have repeated in Holland the triumphs of our Elizabethan writers. Dr Ten Brink compares him in his riotous enjoyment of life and noisy excesses to Greene, Marlowe, and Massinger. It is difficult to extract any single scene from the "Spaansche Brabander," far and away his best work; and, as, in fact, almost any attempt at translation could reproduce only the faults of the original, it seemed better to avoid courting inevitable failure.

English influence made itself felt in Holland during the seventeenth century in more ways than one. Huygens, who repeatedly visited England, and knew Donne, shows traces of the "Caroline" manner in his poems and epigrams. Intercourse between the two countries was frequent, and the connection, of course, became closer still with their temporary union under one sovereign. During the eighteenth century, Dutch literature appeared to be on the wane. Foreign works— English and French—were admired and read, and educated persons took a certain pride in neglecting their native language as a barbarous and uncultivated tongue. It was in a passionate impulse of patriotism that Mevrouw Betje Wolff and Mejuffrouw

INTRODUCTION.

Aagje Deken determined to enter into competition with the universally popular Richardson, and prove to the reading public of Holland that a Dutch novel, showing Dutch characters amid the everyday surroundings of Amsterdam, Utrecht, or the Hague, might be quite as interesting as any foreign importation. The result was the publication, in 1782, of the "History of Mejuffrouw Sara Burgerhart," which ran into a third edition in 1786.

ELIZABETH WOLFF and AGATHA DEKEN were two friends, affectionately spoken of by their compatriots as Betje and Aagje, who lived and wrote together, and collaborated so harmoniously that it is impossible to distinguish their respective shares in the works jointly issued by them. Elizabeth Bekker, born at Flushing, July 24, 1738, is described as "a little delicate woman, with penetrating dark eyes, twinkling with humorous mischief." Her lively spirit maintained a hard struggle against the harsh old-fashioned Calvinism of her Zeeland home, as represented by her elder brother Laurens. It was probably to escape from this that, at twenty, she married a "dominie" of fifty-two—the Predikant Adriaen Wolff. In the quiet of the country parsonage she lived, happily enough, from 1759 to 1777, devoted to her elderly husband, and with abundant leisure for literature. During this period she wrote chiefly in verse, and published several collections of poems; but, when left a widow in 1777, she invited her friend Agatha Deken to live with her. Agatha, three years younger than her friend, was an orphan, brought up in the Amsterdam "Weeshuis," who had been living as companion with an invalid lady named Maria Bosch, also given to poetry. The two friends first essayed themselves in prose, by publishing "Letters on Various Subjects," in 1780, after which they gradually developed the idea of a novel in letters, after the manner of Richardson. "The History of Mejuffrouw Sara Burgerhart," in spite of its somewhat repellent epistolary form, remains capital reading to the present day. The book is not so very long-winded, considering the epoch at which it was written; the characters are clearly conceived and sympathetically drawn; and there is a delicate humour which might almost be compared with Jane Austen's, but has a distinct flavour of its own. The portraiture of Sara's aunt, Mejuffrouw Hofland,

and the designing parasites who make her their prey—Cornelia Slimpslamp, and Brother Benjamin, the butcher's man turned preacher—reminds us of Betje Bekker's bitterness against the fanatical precisians (called by themselves "vromen," or pious, and by others "fijnen," or subtle) who had darkened her youth. "Sara Burgerhart," published in 1782, was followed by a longer work, "Historie van den Heer Willem Leevend," which in some respects surpasses it. In 1788 the friends left Holland, in consequence of political changes, and settled at Trevoux in Burgundy, where they remained till 1795, writing "Letters of Abraham Blankaart," and their third novel, "Cornelia Wildschut." Betje was robbed of her small property by a rascally man of business; and, at the time of the Terror, narrowly escaped the guillotine, being looked on as an aristocrat by the republicans of Trevoux. They returned to Holland in 1795, settled at the Hague, and set themselves to translating for a bare living. Their last years were spent amid great financial difficulties and privations, borne with their usual cheerfulness, and one cherished wish was granted them at last,—Betje died November 5, 1804, and Aagje only survived her nine days.

It is a pity that these books are not of a kind to show to advantage in extracts. To be appreciated, they must be taken in bulk, as the character-drawing, which is their chief attraction, only comes out indirectly, and point by point, in the course of the letters. Which of the two collaborators should be credited with the quiet humour—of the type recognised as peculiarly feminine—which flashes through them, is a disputed point, but it is usually attributed to Betje Wolff. Internal evidence, and especially the history of her early life, seem to point to her as having originated the character of Sara herself, the bright, lovable, merry-hearted girl, so willing to submit to loving guidance, but impatient of the gloomy restraint of Aunt Susanna's house, which called out all that was worst in her nature. Agatha Deken, we are told, was a large, fair person, of calm aspect and portly presence—somewhat prosaic and matter-of-fact—yet the description does not exclude the possibility of a certain "pawkiness,"—and probably there is no hard and fast distinction to be drawn between the two, as regards the humorous element. And, however that may be, "Sara

Burgerhart" is a charming book, and deserves to be much **more** widely known than it is. Lovers of "Evelina" would delight in its old-time quaintness, and even those without an especial *parti-pris* for the eighteenth century could not fail to appreciate the delicately finished pictures of Dutch life. Some points in this latter suggest the question whether many things which we **have** been accustomed to consider as purely American manners did not originate in the Dutch ancestry of the New-Yorkers. The comings and goings of the young ladies at the Amsterdam boarding-house, under the friendly (but to contemporary English notions very inadequate) supervision of the Widow Spilgoed, *née* Buigzaam, is one of those. Others suggest themselves to an attentive reader of the book. But this is only in passing. Decidedly, an English version of "Sara" with a loving and appreciative introduction by a capable hand, would **be an** addition to the pleasures of life.

It is no part of the plan of this brief **sketch—which aims** throughout at being suggestive rather than exhaustive—to furnish a comprehensive introduction to Dutch literature, or even to that part of it to which these pages are exclusively devoted. There is one point, however, which we must not overlook. This is not the place—and perhaps, indeed, the time has **not** fully come—to discuss the position which Multatuli holds, or ought to hold, in his country's literature ; but it cannot fail to strike any reader of this volume, that a large—perhaps disproportionately large—number of pages is assigned to the work **of** a writer cast in as un-Dutch, or even anti-Dutch, a mould as it is possible to imagine. In fact, Multatuli stands as much alone among the Dutch, as Heine does among the Germans ; and, by the same token, we might add, he is their only real humorist, in the highest sense. This apartness is not to be accounted for in Douwes Dekker's case, by difference of race ; but then, he was partly the product of reaction, and there were, after all, strong race-affinities in the deeper parts of his character. **He** had every quality calculated to **jar** upon the feelings of the Amsterdam *petits bourgeois* of his day : he had other ideals than theirs ; he would not be content to make money and abstain from shocking the neighbours ; he was nervous and imaginative in a stolid and prosaic generation—lavishly extravagant in a prudent, not to say parsimonious, one; but his passionate love of freedom, his intolerance of shams, his resolute refusal to utter the shibboleths of the age or bow before the idols of the market-place, proved him of one blood with William of Orange and Marnix de Sainte-Aldegonde. And, had he been as altogether isolated as he seems at first sight, he could hardly have become the force in national life that he now is. His "Max Havelaar" was like a volcanic outburst breaking up the crust of convention which had been slowly stiffening over Holland; but it gave voice to a cry which had been stifled in thousands of hearts. He spoke, and the younger generation answered him as one man. To-day, in Holland, Multatuli is a name to conjure with—a synonym for life, thought, progress, revolt against convention—for everything that may be called modernity.

He was a crude, formless, unmethodical writer. "Max Havelaar" is one of the most exasperatingly inartistic books ever written, and it must always remain matter for regret that he never seriously took in hand to complete and give artistic unity to the brilliant fragments that form the unfinished history of "Woutertje Pieterse." But there is life and red blood in everything he wrote—and that counts for far more than dead correctness of form,—though, of course, the perfect form *enshrining* the vitality gives it a chance to last longer.

There is something in "Wouter" that reminds one curiously of the "Story of an African Farm." Not that we would infer that the latter was suggested by the former,—it may well be that its author was, at the time, quite unaware of Multatuli's existence; and the agonies of isolated childhood are the same all the world over. But there are certain points of resemblance which make us think that a similar environment—the compound of dead Calvinism, Dutch pseudo-propriety, and crass ignorance—produced similar results. Though, perhaps it was natural that poor Wouter, dreaming on the bridge by the saw-mill at Amsterdam, should have less lofty visions than Waldo, dreaming on the open veldt under the stars.

Wouter began his career in the story with a crime. He wanted very much to read a book in the circulating library, but he had not the necessary twopence. His mother thought little boys had no use for pocket-money. Besides, circulating libraries did not enter into Juffrouw Pieterse's calculations from **any point** of view. But it was so deadly dull at home, where **there were** no interesting books left unread—and no one was supposed **to** want to read at all, except Stoffel, the elder brother, who was a pupil-teacher, and preparing for an examination,—and he did long, with an unspeakable longing, for the "History of Glorioso the Brigand." So he sold his Bible, with the paraphrases at the end, to a book-stall man on the Old Bridge (this particular is never forgotten in subsequent references to the misdemeanour, as though it had **been** an aggravation thereof), trusting **to** the fact that the volume was not likely to be inquired after on a week-day, to escape scot-free till Sunday. Which he did; but with Sunday came discovery and swift retribution. **But Wouter** did not mind that,—he had had his "Glorioso," **and was** willing to pay the price. That was not all, however;—this piece of juvenile depravity had far-reaching consequences; but what they **were will be discovered** from the **extracts given in the text.**

There is infinite humour, as **well** as infinite **pathos,** in **the** description of the **poor, starved** child-soul, to **which** even a **trashy sensational** novel could give some sort of outlook into the ideal—for **that was** what Wouter's (after **all very** innocent) glorification of crime practically amounted to. **No** better proof of the hold which Multatuli has **over the hearts of his countrymen** could be given than the **fact that many of his characters** have passed into proverbs. Juffrouw **Laps, Dominie Pennewip, the** Hallemans,—"who were so **very particularly respectable,"** —and others, **are** constantly to be met **with in current literature.**

And yet, curiously enough, his views **are almost entirely** negative. **He is a** preacher **of revolt—a revolt often blind,** illogical, inconsistent with itself, **and** which, from **our point of** view, seems curiously out of **date—so** that one is apt **to forget** he has only **been** dead **six** years,—and he is seldom, if ever, a teacher of anything else. It proves how greatly the revolt was needed, and **what** was the power of that Dagon of convention against which he directed his blows.

One word about the drama* **from** which an extract has been

---

* The plot of the "Bride in Heaven" is briefly this:—Many years before the opening of the play, Major Huser had killed Baron Van Bergen in a duel. There was no personal enmity between the men,—indeed they were intimate friends; it was only

given. It was one of his earliest works, being written at Padang (Sumatra) in 1843, when he was little more than a youth; and public opinion and a barbarous etiquette that forced on this ending to a trifling dispute. Huser was broken-hearted at the way it ended: he accepted the charge of Van Bergen's only son as a sacred trust; and when he died, shortly afterwards, made his own son, Gustaaf, promise to be a friend to young Van Bergen at any sacrifice. Van Bergen turned out wild and dissipated, and Gustaaf redeemed his promise by taking on himself a forgery committed by his friend when in desperate straits for lack of money at the university. No one knew the truth of this affair but himself, Van Bergen, and the latter's worthless valet, Frans. The proofs of the whole were contained in certain letters in Van Bergen's possession. Huser disappears from society, and is supposed to have fled the country. As a matter of fact, he is getting his living as a music-master, under the name of Holm, and as such he is introduced to us in the play. His principal pupil is Caroline, daughter of a high government official named Van Wachler,—a shrewd, honourable, and upright man, of simple tastes, meeting with little sympathy from his fashionable and affected wife, with her would-be French manners, and the aristocratic connections she will not allow him to forget. Mevrouw Van Wachler is young Van Bergen's aunt, and exceedingly anxious to marry her daughter to the scapegrace, who, for his part, is not unwilling to accept such a way of escape from his embarrassments. Her husband is less dazzled by the match, and declares his intention of letting his daughter choose for herself. He questions her, and finds that her affections are set on Holm. Holm, who has meanwhile awakened to the fact that he is in love with Caroline, has made up his mind that he must leave without a sign; but Van Wachler's genial kindness wins his secret from him, and, finding that the statesman respects him for himself, and is willing to take his position and his past for granted, and that all he has to do is, to consent to the engagement, he can only shut his eyes for the moment, and accept the offered happiness. In the second act, which, with a few unimportant abridgments, is given entire in the text, General Van Weller, brother to Mevrouw Van Wachler, and the elder Huser's old friend and comrade, returns from the Indies, determined to clear up the mystery of Gustaaf Huser's disappearance, and is unwittingly helped on to the right track by Frans. In the third act, Holm and Van Bergen meet—the best side of the latter comes uppermost, and he has a passing mood of repentance and reconciliation. But Frans' influence is too strong; he is persuaded to take a base advantage of his rival, and tells the Van Wachler family, in Holm's presence, that the latter is not only passing under a false name, but is an outlaw and a convicted felon. Holm (who had previously made up his mind, for the sake of their old friendship and his promise to his father, to renounce Caroline, in the hope that her love—could he succeed in winning it—might save Van Bergen) is stunned and driven to despair by this treacherous attack, goes home to his lodgings, and is about to commit suicide, when he is interrupted by a visit from a man whose children he saved from a fire a year ago, and who has now brought them to see him. This man (Wolf) discovers his purpose, and does not leave till he has persuaded him to forego it. Scarcely has he gone, when Caroline comes in. She tells Holm that she has come to bid him farewell, but that nothing that has happened can make any possible difference to their love. If she may not belong to him on earth, she will be his bride in the other life, and wait for him there. So they part.

Van Wachler is full of indignation at the way in which he considers himself to have been deceived by Holm, but Van Weller arrives in time to explain everything,—tells the whole story, sends for Holm, or Huser, and sees his old friend's son triumphantly righted, while Van Bergen retires in disgrace. (See *A Rascally Valet*, p. 55.)

he himself in later years, was sarcastic enough at the expense of its "lachrymose sentiment" and emotional idealism. Perhaps it **does** err by excess in this direction, especially in Holm's interminable monologues,—perhaps, also, the comic scenes force the note a little, and are not free from the trick of catch-words,—but the play, as a whole, is a capital one, and was, we believe, very successful on the stage. He wrote another serious drama, in verse, the "Vorstenschool," which has never been acted, but perhaps for political rather than dramatic reasons. It seems a pity that he did not make more sustained efforts in this style **of** writing, which would have chastened the formlessness above alluded to as marring his work; but he seems to have been too impatient in getting his thoughts on paper to submit to the necessary restraints.

It will be noticed **that this** selection includes specimens from both Dutch **and Belgian** writers. **The** fact is that Belgium, **from a literary point of view, scarcely exists.** The written language is the same for both countries, the differences being mainly local and dialectical. After Brabant and Flanders had ceased to be Spanish provinces, and prior to the Revolution **of 1830,** the two portions were respectively known as Noord and Zuid Nederland. After 1830, the national language was, for a time, entirely **discredited, and** Belgium threatened to become a mere imitation of France, if not actually **an appendage** to that country. Of late years a **reaction** has set in. **A knowledge** of Flemish is required by **law of all** Government **officials, except in** those districts exclusively inhabited by the **Walloons, who are** supposed to speak **French,** though in fact, **they discourse in a** tongue which no mortal **but themselves** can understand.

There is an increasing **number** of Flemish papers,—the comic ones especially **doing valiant service** on the national side. **In** 1883 a law was **passed rendering** the teaching of Flemish (or "Netherlands," **as both Dutch and** Belgians prefer to call it) **obligatory in all intermediate schools.** At **Ghent University,** moreover, all **lectures are now** delivered in that language, as well as some of the courses at the Universities of Brussels and Louvain. Straws show which way the wind blows; and, though a trifle, it is a significant one, that the streets of Antwerp are now labelled in Flemish, as well as French, and that public notices, advertisements, &c., when not bi-lingual, are usually Flemish.

The time of this linguistic reaction has also been one of revival in the national literature. Maeterlinck, it is true, writes in French; and a small coterie of less-known writers, calling themselves *La Jeune Belgique*, have chosen that language as the vehicle of their inspirations; but these do not represent the main current of the national life. For a long time, Conscience stood almost alone as a Flemish writer, and he was only known to the outer world through the medium of French translations. Now we have, of poets, Pol de Mont, De la Montagne, Hilda Ram, and Hélène Swarth, who, had she written in a more widely known language, would be recognised as one of the world's greatest lyrists;—of prose-writers, Stijns, Virginie Loveling, Segers, Smits, Van Cuyck, Anton Moortgat, Emile Seipgens, and many others. Not all of them are available for our present purpose,—but some, as will be seen, have been selected from.

In conclusion, I would express my indebtedness for valuable information kindly given by Mr Frans Van Cuyck, of the Public Library, Antwerp, and author of "Twee Huwelijken," "Sinoren," and other works.

A. WERNER.

THE HUMOUR OF HOLLAND.

THE KING'S DREAM.

"I STROLLED THOUGHTFULLY ALONG THE BEACH."

King Bilbonzo. It is well. We ourself now desire to make an important communication to you.

Palaemon (*Prime Minister and Chancellor of the Kingdom*). We are all attention.

King Bilbonzo. It pleased us to have a very strange dream last night.

Courtiers. Aha!

King Bilbonzo. I dreamed, gentlemen, that I was on an island in the midst of the ocean. My royal palace, surrounded by luxuriant gardens, stood in the centre of the island. My whole retinue was assembled there,—they were all laughing, dancing, and feasting. On all sides, smiling faces, rustling silks, and waves of sweet dance-music. Meanwhile, I strolled thoughtfully along the beach, reflected on the bounties of nature, and picked up shells.

Courtiers. Ah!

King Bilbonzo. But suddenly the ground trembled under my feet. I looked up, and perceived that the whole island was moving under me. It heaved, rocked this way and that, rose and fell on the water, and, finally, shot swiftly over the surface of the foaming sea. The beautiful island, my lords and gentlemen, was a living, terrible sea-monster!

Courtiers (in horror). Ah!

King Bilbonzo. My courtiers clung to me in terror. My head swam. Suddenly the monster dived, and the sea at once destroyed the palace and gardens. I myself, with a few faithful ones—you, my lords, among the number—remained bobbing up and down, holding to an empty cask. But the monster came once more to the surface, lifted a huge dripping mouth out of the water, and swallowed us all.

Courtiers. B-r-r-r!—most horrible!

King Bilbonzo. However, after a short interval of oppressive darkness, it cast us out again uninjured—and I found myself in my bed!

Courtiers (drawing a long breath of relief). Eh!

King Bilbonzo. What is your opinion, my lords? Is this a prophetic vision?

Palaemon. It is a fact that the prophet Jonah, some time

since, had the honour of experiencing something very like what your Majesty has just dreamed.

King Bilbonzo. Does any of you think himself in a position to explain this dream to me? [*All shake their heads.*]

Palaemon. Sire, I have been told that there is, at this moment, a Spanish magician staying in our capital. Perhaps he might be able to comply with your wish. I have already given orders to have this person searched for—probably he has already reached the palace. . . .

King Bilbonzo. Why! this is exceedingly interesting! Be so good as to bring the man into our presence at once.

[*Exit Palaemon.*

Enter PALAEMON, *and* DON TORRIBIO, *a Spanish magician.*

Palaemon. Here is the man.

King Bilbonzo. Come nearer, my friend.

Don Torribio. Who told you that I am your friend? Are you in the thought-reading business too?

Homaris (*3rd Minister*). This is an unmannerly customer.

Palaemon. Do you know you are speaking to the King?

Don Torribio. Why, yes,—I thought so. I presume no one else would wear such a head-gear.

King Bilbonzo. Silence, my lords!—this is evidently an eccentric man. Let him alone. Magicians, fools, and poets have ever been allowed a certain familiarity with princes.

Don Torribio. You forget to add *fleas*, my prince.

Ministers. Hush!—shame!—shame!

King Bilbonzo. Decency! decency!

Don Torribio. I assure you they are very decent well-behaved little beasts, O King. They have never bitten you in your absence! They are the most honest of your subjects. They have never taken anything from you without informing you of the fact. There are not many like that. And they are not at present suffering from hunger. Not many like that either.

King Bilbonzo. Silence, now! Do you know wherefore you have been summoned hither?

Don Torribio. Certainly. We are going to act a little play together. You are Nebuchadnezzar, and I am Daniel.

King Bilbonzo (*to Palaemon*). I see your Excellency has already enlightened him.

Palaemon. Certainly not, your Majesty

King Bilbonzo. Ah! this is indeed surprising Listen then, and I will tell you my dream.

Don Torribio. No, no—you need not let me off any of my part. I mean to play Daniel entire—but I am not going to let you off the grass-eating, either! Do *you* listen to me, and I will interpret the dream.

King Bilbonzo. Well—this is astonishing!

Ministers. Think of that, now!

Homaris. All pre-concerted!

Don Torribio. Gathering shells is an innocent and even laudable employment,—but it should be carried on on a safe shore, and not within reach of hungry sea-monsters.

Every man—and more especially a king—ought to know what his house is built on.

If your house happens to stand—not on a rock foundation, but on the back of a sleeping whale, you must not dance too vigorously, or you will probably wake the brute.

It is safer to swim about in the sea on the back of a shark, than to be king of a famished people.

The conclusion of your dream I will interpret to you after the grass-eating. Now it is your turn.

King Bilbonzo. This is really going too far! Our toleration has reached its limits. Can you be wanting to sow discord between Us and our beloved people? Out of our sight, impious liar!—this very moment!

Hyacinthe (*the Poet-Laureate—seated next to the King*). Majesty!—look out for your crown!

King Bilbonzo. Oh!—thanks! [*Sets his crown straight.*]

Don Torribio. Omen accipio. How do you wish me to disappear, O King?

Palaemon (to a footman). Fetch the lictors to remove **this** person.

King Bilbonzo. My lords, you will agree with me that **a** man like this is very dangerous to the State.

Homaris. I had feared as much, Sire! He is a clever quack, and what he sells is poison for the people.

Lepidus. But his knowledge was something wonderful.

Homaris. Tricks!—most likely there's bribery at the **bottom of it.**

Hyacinthe. Or else **atheistic** magic.

King Bilbonzo. In any case, **my Lord** Palaemon, you ought to have taken measures somewhat earlier to **prevent his doing** harm.

Palaemon. **He** shall be thrown into chains **at once.**

Amenias (4th *Minister*). **It is** really **a** case for **capital** punishment.

King Bilbonzo. No—our delight is to show mercy. **When** the judges have condemned him to death, we will **commute** the sentence into penal servitude for life.

A Footman. Your Excellency!—the lictors.

[*Torribio has suddenly vanished during the previous conversation.*]

Palaemon. Let this man **be** strictly **confined.**

Footman. What man, your **Excellency?**

Palaemon. Here—what! **Where is he?**

Ministers. What! Where is he? Gone?

King Bilbonzo. This is unspeakably insolent!

Amenias. He was standing here when I last saw him.

Palaemon. He was standing here.

[*They search all over the room.*]

King Bilbonzo (to *Amenias*). What is that on the floor?

Amenias (*picking it up*). A tuft of grass, Sire!

King Bilbonzo. This is infamous ribaldry.

Lepidus. It is very mysterious.

Homaris. Jugglers' tricks! We have all been made fools of.

Footman (opening a door). Breakfast is served, your Majesty!

King Bilbonzo. Come, my lords,—search no further! It is not worth while. Follow me! [*He retires with dignity.*]

Hyacinthe (follows, improvising)—

> Shall hate and envy dim its lustre—
>   The crown on royal brows that glows—
> And rob the People of their father,
>   And lead both parties by the nose?
> La, la, la, la—no, never! no, never!
>   La, la, la!

[*Exeunt omnes, following one another in a solemn procession.*

FREDERICK VAN EEDEN.

(*From the Comedy of "Don Torribio."*)

THE DOMINIE.*

"It is a very serious matter," said Gerrit Rond, the burgomaster, to Kobus.

"Very serious, indeed," replied Kobus, the *veldwachter*.†

"It is a disgrace to the whole parish!" continued the burgomaster.

"An everlasting disgrace!" repeated the veldwachter.

Then followed an ominous silence, in the course of which the burgomaster, with gloomy countenance and wildly

---

* Strictly speaking, "Dominie," in Holland, is a title reserved for ministers, the old-fashioned designation of the schoolmaster being simply "Meester." But as the former title has, with us, become inseparably attached to the latter profession, it has been thought best to use it as the translation of "Meester."

† Equivalent to the French *garde-champêtre* and the German *Feldschütz*,—an official who is something between a gamekeeper and a policeman. His duty is to patrol the fields and orchards with a gun, and see that nothing is stolen.

rolling eye, attentively followed the movements of a fly which was leisurely walking about the stately expanse of his waistcoat; while the veldwachter kept a watchful eye on his superior's features, that he might not fail to mould his own accordingly. In the meantime, he knit his brows, and provided himself with a half-expectant, half-threatening expression.

"IT IS A DISGRACE TO THE WHOLE PARISH!"

At length the reverend head of Gerrit, the burgomaster, solemnly rose upright, and his reflection opposite did the same.

"Kobus," said Gerrit, "it *must* be seen to."

And Kobus replied: "It *shall* be seen to, if your worship pleases."

"Very good, Kobus; and I *do* please—of that I assure you. . . ."

"I think I've got something," said Gerrit, with an astute smile, and rubbed his nose with a civic forefinger, in a satisfied way.

"Ha!" cried Kobus, triumphantly.

"Yes, surely, . . . surely, . . ." said Gerrit, as though thinking aloud,— still, astute, smiling, and rubbing his nose, . . . "But let us at least go over the whole thing once more—at least the main point."

"Shall I tell your worship once more, exactly?" asked Kobus, with a self-satisfied laugh.

"Well, yes, it will be just as well. I can then weigh the importance of the whole matter so much better. Just go on," said the burgomaster, with the lofty attitude of one who is quite sure of himself, and can afford to wait for anything, seeing that his resolution is already taken.

"I will therefore tell your worship, once more," began Kobus, "that on Saturday week—a fortnight ago to-morrow —Jan o' the Wood came running into my house with a face —with a face . . ."

"Like Balthasar Gerard's,"* the burgomaster helped him out, with a certain gloomy majesty befitting the dignity of his position and his historical knowledge.

"That would be just about it," said Kobus, with deep respect, and then went on. "He rushed into my house with a face like—h'm, h'm—it's sinful to think of—what a face the man had! And first he dropped down on a chair, and couldn't speak a word—not a letter—your worship! My wife gave him a glass of water, and she said, says she, 'Come, Jan, just drink a little, and then you'll come to yourself again, and then you can tell us what's the matter.'

---

* Readers of Motley will not need to be reminded that this was the name of William the Silent's murderer.

That's what she said, your worship,—for them women-folk are always so curious, and she was just on fire, I tell you. Jan soon got his breath, and then it came out—how, that night—last Saturday week, a fortnight ago to-morrow—two baskets full of pears had been taken away from his trees— **two** whole baskets, your worship!"

Gerrit Rond, the burgomaster, the principal resident, and the respected head of his parish, stroked his plump chin complacently, and **looked** at his factotum, quietly smiling.

"Well; and what more, Kobus?"

Such imperturbable calm must surely conceal a great plan, thought the veldwachter; and he was several seconds recovering from his consternation. Then he stammered,—

"And . . and . . nothing more, your worship. I reported the matter to you at once; I drew up the *procès verbal*. But though I have done my best to find out . . . ."

The honest veldwachter completed his sentence by shrugging his shoulders, extending his arms, and dropping them again,—illustrating the whole pantomime **by a** face expressive of the utmost helplessness.

But now Gerrit Rond, burgomaster, the principal resident, **and** respected head of the community, arose from **his** municipal arm-chair, and spake,—

"Kobus, I know **it!**"

Kobus listened in breathless excitement.

"Kobus," the burgomaster went on, looking round him with vigilant eyes, as though he suspected that pear-thieves might be hidden in the corners of his sitting-room,—"Kobus, did he steal *all* the pears?"

The veldwachter was silent, and looked questioningly at the burgomaster. He could not make out what the latter was driving at.

"I mean," explained the father of the citizens, "whether Jan **o' the** Wood has not got a single pear left on his trees?"

"Well; no, sir. Two baskets the rascal made off with; but how many baskets there were to be had in that orchard, I don't know. It's quite terrible the way Jan's trees bear, and everything prime quality, large-sized, and juicy. I think Jan's father had them before him, and he must have brought them...."

"That will do, Kobus," the burgomaster interrupted his subordinate; "but that's not the point.... So the pears have not *all* been removed? I mean, by this, that the thief has not unlawfully possessed himself of the *whole*?"

"Why, no, your worship."

"Now, Kobus, look here."

Kobus listened respectfully, understanding that the critical moment had now arrived.

"My father, Kobus, was a man of sense, and when he had enjoyed anything, he always used to say, 'This peach tastes of more.'"

"Oh, yes!" exclaimed Kobus, as though suddenly enlightened,—whereas, in truth, he was more puzzled than ever.

"And, look you, Kobus, the apple can never fall far from the tree. My father was a sensible man; and I, too, say, 'This peach tastes of more,' and ...."

Here the burgomaster looked through his half-closed eyelids with an air of infinite sagacity, and added, slowly dragging out his words, one by one,—

"... And—that—I suspect—the thief—will—say—too."

"O-o-oh!" bellowed the veldwachter; "I understand—the thief will want more pears. He will come back, and then we'll catch him?"

The burgomaster looked at his factotum with a paternal air of approbation.

"Kobus!" said he, "something may be made of you yet!"

"Does your worship think that?" cried Kobus, in an

ecstasy,—and a rosy prospect instantly appeared before his mind's eye—chief agent in a large town, commissioner of police, nay, perhaps,—but that he would not have dared to say out loud for any money in the world,—perhaps, one day, even burgomaster!

"But now to business, Kobus! This very night we will try to catch the thief; and my name is not Gerrit Rond if we don't succeed. We'll hide in Jan's orchard, and when he comes we'll collar him, and then . . . ."

Here the burgomaster-detective pointed downwards. Under the tower of the court-house there was a vault or cellar of masonry, which usually served as a receptacle for old iron and thieves; the latter destination, however, was unknown, save by tradition, for only the very oldest inhabitants of the village dimly remembered an evil-doer being imprisoned there.

Kobus then suggested that it might be as well to take his son Hannes with him on their expedition, a suggestion which might have been unkindly interpreted by outsiders, for there were unpleasant reports current about the brave *garde-champêtre's* reluctance to pursue criminals alone. The suggestion, however, found favour in the eyes of the magistrate, as it would enable them to take forty winks while the boy watched for the appearance of the thief. This being settled, Kobus withdrew, to reappear at the appointed time that evening. But he had not been gone long when a loud knocking startled the burgomaster out of an incipient reverie.

"Come in!" he cried, somewhat ungraciously, and the opening door revealed Kobus's bearded face; but this time with so scared an expression, and such wildly rolling eyes, that Gerrit turned rigid with terror and, pale as death, held on to the back of his chair for support, as he stammered,

"Wh—wh—what is it, Kobus?"

"*Burrgemeesterr*," rolled out Kobus, hoarsely, making as much as possible of the *r's*, and putting his head round the door without coming into the room, "the thief of the apples that were stolen from Piet Stein a year and a half ago, and this thief of the pears . . . ."

"The same," sighed the burgomaster, struck with consternation.

"Your worship," said Kobus, "it is a conspiracy! Shall we—should we—go and ask the Dominie?"

But scarcely had Kobus uttered this fatal word than he darted out of the door and up the street, and it was long before his mind's eye had lost sight of that frightful picture: the burgomaster, purple in the face, and boiling over with indignation; and the voice of his superior thundered in his ears with all the annihilating force of contempt.

"The Dominie!" was all he had said.

The village schoolmaster was an old man of sixty-three, who, ever since his twentieth year, had stood, day after day, Sundays excepted, behind the same desk, leading the peasants' children from the spelling of s, p, a—spa, to the four elementary rules of arithmetic. Every year a few left him, being found ripe for forgetting at the plough-tail what they had learnt in the schoolroom, and every year fresh aspirants for s, p, a—spa, appeared on the scenes. So he had grown old at his work, and his work with him. For he belonged to the pre-examination days—he was a "*schoolmeester,*" not an "*onderwijzer.*" The new generation looked on him rather as a curiosity, a touchstone of progress, a souvenir of old times, than a living being, a wheel in the world-machine of the nineteenth century. Other men of his age had gone with the stream, and followed its capricious windings; he had landed on the bank, and followed his own old path; his mind had rusted into the old groove, and he could not extricate it.

He had already received hints that he ought to retire, to ask for his pension, so as to make way for modern forces; but the idea of ceasing to stand before his class and behind his desk was too strange to the old man—too new!

So he remained on for the present, till his resignation should no longer be a matter of choice.

The elder children were busy doing sums; the younger ones were being attended to by the Dominie himself.

But how strange he was to-day! It sometimes seemed as if he heard nothing of the lesson the children were droning over,—saw nothing of the tricks the older ones were up to in the background,—as if, in fact, he were thinking of something entirely different. He had such fits, sometimes. How funny it was, now, when he dipped his pencil into the inkstand, instead of a penholder, and, shortly afterwards, abstractedly put it into his mouth! What a face he made when he found it out! The whole school had simply yelled at the joke, and the Dominie had got very angry, and put the whole lot of them in detention. Later, however, he almost laughed at the matter himself, and allowed them all to go home. Such foolish and absurd things he used to do every now and then; and the reason for this was, as the burgomaster said, because the Dominie was "an obstructive fellow," and "not practical."

And when the burgomaster said so, every one believed him, for the burgomaster was considered a very clever man.

But, after all, the Dominie was cleverer still.

For, indeed, there were sometimes things that the Dominie himself did not know,—of course, for no man can know everything. But, in those cases, he always said, "I'll just look it up." And then he looked in his books, and kept on looking till he found it; and he always did find it, because he had such piles of books! For, after all, that was where things were to be found—in books! For this reason the burgomaster was not so clever as the schoolmaster; he had scarcely any books at all. This was one cause of the burgomaster's dislike. He was Gerrit Rond, *the burgomaster*, the first man in the village; and the Dominie was just the schoolmaster.

And, naturally, the former could not endure being looked on as less clever than the latter. But he did not utter this opinion aloud; he sometimes needed the Dominie's help in "just looking up something," and swallowed his dislike as best he could; but people could see it all the same.

Yes, indeed! the Dominie was particularly clever!

Once it befell that Piet Stein's son came home from the city, where he had "studied" with a view to becoming assistant-teacher; and on that occasion he had said, in the presence of his father, "All the Dominie's cleverness is worth nothing; he is antiquated, and doesn't know French." Piet Stein, junior, was well acquainted with the French language; he had just learnt it. But Piet Stein, senior, seized his promising son by the collar, and dealt him a well-intentioned thrashing, "to knock these new-fangled notions out of him once for all."

For the schoolmaster was a knowledgeable man. He lived with his books, and—which was less obvious to the eyes of the world—with his instruments and his medicine-chest. For years past he had been practising on his own account, and had acquired a certain medical reputation among the peasants of the neighbourhood as well as within the village. He had, in truth, treated several cases within the last few years with great success; but it might be better not to inquire how many earlier trials had failed. Then came the new ideas—the laws against unlicensed doctoring were strictly enforced, and he received warnings from various quarters, of which, however, he took no notice. He could not understand why he might not try to lessen people's sufferings, as well as other men, who usually did not succeed any better than he. It had become to him a passion, an aim in life, a vocation.

So he obstinately went his own way, in spite of warnings, till the doctors, whom he injured in their practice, at last lost patience, and prosecuted him. He was convicted and fined,

and from that time his medical career was over,—at least so it was universally reported. It seemed strange, however, that **now** and then a sick person made a wonderful **recovery**, without having been treated by the doctor.

Now, one evening it happened that old Klaas, the shepherd, was seriously ill, and had asked for the schoolmaster. The Dominie had said "No," but he had meant "Yes"; for though no longer allowed to do any doctoring, he could not keep from it. So he meant to wait till it was dark, and then slip out unnoticed to Klaas' cottage.

In Jan o' the Wood's orchard three figures were crouching down behind three low dwarf pear-trees, and each of the three had his head full of thoughts that were not those of his neighbour. The burgomaster was chiefly tortured by the idea that on the good or ill success of the evening's undertaking depended the preservation of his official dignity; for, seeing that he had enjoined the strictest secrecy on the veldwachter, and his promising son and heir, the only question was which of the two would most speedily spread abroad the whole story through the village. But, over and above this, the respected head of the community was trembling like an aspen-leaf, for before his mental eye there arose a vision of a robber—yes, truly and literally, *a robber*,—a man with a long beard, bristling hair, and bloodshot eyes,—a man who goes about with jemmies and murderous weapons on his person, and—and—who might kill you if you came in his way, you see!

The veldwachter was, before all things, eager to behold the heroic feats of the burgomaster, for he was firmly convinced that the mere presence of the great man was sufficient to compel the miscreant to run into the snare. For terror there was *now* no room in his martial spirit,—for, after all, he had Hannes with him!

Hannes was a big sturdy chap, who at fifteen might well

have been taken for eighteen,—a fellow with fists like engine-buffers, and a face which, for shrewd intelligence of expression, was about equal to that of a sheep. Hannes was burning with impatience to hammer away at the malefactor; hitherto he had only tried his strength on mere vagabonds, but now he was to have the opportunity of measuring himself with a real thief. That would be something to boast of!

Thus the three would-be thief-catchers sat in the greatest excitement behind three of the smallest dwarf pear-trees that any one can imagine.

A considerable time elapsed, during which even the strained senses of the triumvirate could perceive nothing which, in the remotest degree, resembled even a fraction of a thief. At last Hannes' patience was exhausted, and with it his capacity for silence. "Dad," he began in a whisper, "if he comes, am I to take him by the throat and choke him, or shall I punch his head till he falls down dead?"

"I don't know," replied the veldwachter, in an equally cautious whisper, at least as low as his love for gutturals and sibilants would allow, "I'll just ask his worship." Thus did Kobus, and repeated the gruesome question to the burgomaster, thereby sending a shudder through the latter's limbs.

"Tell him," said the heroic man to his heroic subordinate, who was squatting between his superior and his son, "that he must seize him by the legs, so as not to come within reach of his hands; the thief is sure to have daggers and pistols to defend himself with if he is attacked." Thus spake the wise man; but the real reason for his caution was that he felt there might be disagreeable consequences for himself if Hannes received the thief in too heavy-handed a manner.

The veldwachter passed on the message in a whisper to his son:

"Hold him by the legs, Hannes!"

"All right, dad," replied Hannes, though he did not understand why he was to treat the criminal so gently. But the burgomaster had said so,—in other words, the oracle had spoken, and so——

It was very quiet, in the dark, behind Jan's pear-tree. The burgomaster dropped his venerated head, and slept. When Kobus heard the low sound of snoring beside him, he turned to his son, and said :

"Hannes, his worship is off; I think I'll have a nap too; keep a good look-out, and give me a push if you see anything wrong."

"All right, dad," said Hannes, and he sat bolt upright, and opened his eyes still wider than before. But the duet at his side, the darkness all round him, and the weariness in his eyelids, made him close them now and then. He struggled bravely against sleep, but there was no one to help him. And he was only fifteen, and it was so late and so dark, and Hannes fell into a doze.

Now and then he was awakened for a moment or so by the uneasy thought that he was the one who had to watch. On one of these occasions, he thought he saw a dim figure pass right before him in the dark, and to hear steps—hurried footsteps. He rubbed his eyes, and—yes—there was some one carefully opening the gate and leaving the orchard.

Hastily Hannes awakened his parent, in the gentle manner prescribed and told him, in a whisper, what he knew. The awful tidings were then reported to the burgomaster, and a moment later the trio were on their way to seek the thief, who surely, as the veldwachter supposed, was just carrying away his booty. Hannes went first, the burgomaster followed, and Kobus formed the rearguard. This order had been determined by the burgomaster. "For," said he, "as head of the community, I ought to have the most protection."

In this way the police force wandered aimlessly about for some time. Hannes did not know for certain what direction the thief had taken after leaving the orchard; and, besides, there was scarcely any light. It really seemed as though the moon were taking upon herself to play at bo-peep with the most worshipful the burgomaster, for she chose not to show up at all. Yes, perhaps, indeed—oh! scandalous thought!—she was making faces at the great man behind her thick curtain of clouds! Who knows?—there are such queer stories told about the moon.

The expedition, then, returned to the orchard unsuccessful, and once more took up its position behind the dwarf pear-trees. That the miscreant might yet return seemed probable, as Hannes assured them that he had indeed seen him carrying something under his arm, but not a large sack or anything of that sort. He could not, therefore, have taken *much* with him. And they waited—waited—waited. . . .

Meanwhile the schoolmaster had quietly gone on his way. The better to escape observation, he did not take the nearest way, along the main street, but went out into his back garden, opened a little gate which led into Jan o' the Wood's orchard, struck right across the orchard, and so reached a lane leading round to the other side of the village. Here he turned into a wood, and, following a small winding footpath, came at length to a lonely cottage, seemingly forsaken, hidden away among the tall trees. Here he seemed a habitual visitor. At least he lifted the latch without first knocking, opened the door, and found himself in an apartment serving at the same time as bedroom and kitchen.

A close, heavy air, and an ominous stillness, seemed to oppress him as he entered. But the Dominie was not easily daunted. He felt about till he found a lamp standing on the table, and lit it. With the light, life seemed to come into the dead silence of the room; at least a low moaning was heard from a corner where there was a bedstead, and a broken voice asked, "Who's there?"

"It's I, Klaas, the schoolmaster," announced the visitor;

and, bending over the sick man, he went on, "How is it with you?"

"It's all up, Dominie, it's all up," gasped the voice. "Oh, Klaas is no great loss—not much; oh no!"

There seemed to be reason enough for such an estimate; at least the man who lay there dying did not give the idea of one whose loss society would feel very keenly. The flickering lamp-light showed the bed-place, let into the wall like a ship's berth, in an indefinite half-darkness, except the head, on which a dull yellow gleam was cast. There lay, on an unsightly grey, greasy bolster, a head that at first sight seemed more animal than human. The thin face was made still more angular and hollow by the strongly projecting cheek-bones, and the pointed chin with its bristly beard. The upper-lip, and indeed the whole mouth, was almost covered with stiff hair; the nose was broad, flat, and turned up; while a quantity of lank, tangled hair fell over the projecting forehead and deep-set eyes. But these eyes glittered fiercely, every now and then, in their dark sockets, and then again looked anxiously, almost entreatingly, at the schoolmaster.

The Dominie tried to answer him cheerfully. "Come, come, Klaas! What foolish talk is this? You may not have been a king or a great man, but you have been of use for all that. Shepherds are wanted just as much as kings."

"No, sir," said Klaas, moving his head restlessly. "Every day so many finer lights are blown out, and Klaas is only a rushlight. Oh, Lord, yes!"

The old schoolmaster tried to comfort him, but Klaas still seemed to have something on his mind.

He had stolen Jan's pears a fortnight ago, he told the schoolmaster at last.

The old man remained with him till a late hour, and then started homewards by the same way as he had come.

"Father, father!"

"What is it, Hannes?"

"I hear the gate creak."

"So it does. . . . Your worship, here he comes back again."

"Really? Yes, I see him. . . . Kobus, stand firm, my man. Let Hannes hold him fast by the legs. No, not yet —wait till he passes! Oh, do be careful! Look out for his weapons!"

"Hannes, be ready!"

"I'm quite ready, dad."

"Not before I speak, and then by the legs—do you hear?"

"Yes, dad. Hush now!"

—The shuffling of approaching footsteps in the grass of the orchard . . . suddenly a figure disengages itself from the darkness.—

"Now, Hannes, now!"

Hannes creeps forward along the ground, seizes the figure, according to instructions, firmly by the ankles—a good pull —and the thief falls forward at full length. Hannes seizes his wrists, and lets himself fall flat on the top of his prey.

The veldwachter, for greater security, incontinently throws himself upon his two predecessors; and the burgomaster crowns the human pyramid, and the successful thief-hunt, by sitting down, with all his burgomasterly weight and a heavy bump, upon the three others, triumphantly shouting the while, "I've got him,"—which is answered by, "Oh my ribs, your worship!" from the uppermost stratum, "What in thunder!" from the midmost, and a smothered groan from the lowest.

"Hannes, have you got a hold of his hands—tight now?"

"Yes, your worship, but I can't do anything myself like this."

"Well, I'll get up, but keep a good hold of him—do you hear?"

"All right, sir."

The burgomaster arose. "Kobus, put the handcuffs on him at once. In heaven's name make haste about it then."

The veldwachter bustled up from the ground, and set about securing the prisoner as closely as possible. While he was thus occupied, and Hannes was holding the persistently silent criminal, the burgomaster kept walking round and round his captive in order to see what sort of a fish he had got in his net. In this he would probably have been unsuccessful, had not the moon, in a sudden caprice, shone out brightly once more. When the triumvirate saw the pale face, paler than ever with the fright and the cold moonlight, and perceived it to be the face so well known to them, all their astonishment uttered itself in the simultaneous cry—

"The Dominie!"

The school was empty, and the children had a holiday, for the Dominie . . . was sitting in the vault under the tower.

Under the tower sat the Dominie, amidst pieces of old iron and other rubbish. Light and air stole in shyly, in small quantities, through the little, square, grated window, in which a single scrap of glass, dusty and weather-stained, remained in one corner, to show there had once been a pane. As the court-house was surrounded by a paddock, which again was enclosed by a low wall, the sounds from outside only penetrated indistinctly, as a vague murmur, into this chamber. Sometimes it was quiet,—deadly still, there, especially of an evening, and then life came into the place, for the rats and mice began their games. The Master was an old man, and nervous, and he could not sleep much. He thought over the whole matter in his wakeful hours, and it gradually became clear to him that he had been arrested by mistake. Klaas had stolen Jan van 't Hout's pears,

"SITTING IN THE VAULT UNDER THE TOWER."

and he, the Dominie, had been taken for the thief returning for a second load. But it would not be difficult to prove his innocence. Only it was lasting a long time; he ought surely to have been tried before now. Four days had passed without his hearing anything. Even the veldwachter, who, as a rule, could not be with him two minutes without wanting to relate some story or other, was now silence itself, when he brought the Dominie his daily rations. What was the meaning of this delay?

Yes, the delay had well-founded reasons! The burgomaster had indeed caught the fish, but he did not exactly know what he was to do with him. It was a ticklish business. Was he to hand over the prisoner immediately, without the form of a trial, to the authorities in town? or was he first to hold an inquiry, and send up the *procès-verbal* along with the prisoner? Supposing the latter to be the case, how was he to set about it? It was a most unfortunate circumstance that there had never been any thieves in the parish, for now the burgomaster was most certainly at his wits' end. The secretary—a poor, infirm old man, almost in his dotage—was consulted in vain. The same result attended a conference with the "law-holders."* Finally the burgomaster called Kobus to his assistance. He reflected for some time, and said at last:

"Doesn't it say in the communal bye-laws?"

"This case is one for which no provision is made in the *Gemeentewet*," said the burgomaster, with admirable composure,—the truth being that the greater part of the Gemeentewet was Greek to him, and that he had gradually picked up, by practical experience, what knowledge he possessed of his official duties. Kobus, however, was very far from suspecting any such subtleties, and believed his

---

* "Wethouders:" corresponding to the "selectmen" of a New England village.

superior implicitly. His invention being now exhausted, he confined himself to remarking, with a sigh, "If it hadn't been the Dominie himself, now, we might have asked him—he could surely have looked it up somewhere."

Yes, that would have been too absurd. They could not have brought the Dominie all his books in a wheelbarrow, and requested him to "look up" information as to what was to be done with himself! No—that would not do. But all at once an expedient occurred to Kobus. There was an old, old man in the village—a grey-beard of ninety or more. Perhaps in his young days there might have been such a thing as a malefactor in this rural region. Yes, the idea was not such a bad one, and Kobus was sent as a delegate from the government to this oracle of antiquity. In fact, the old man had a suggestion ready. He remembered that some sixty years ago an analogous case had occurred, and then the burgomaster had first examined the culprit himself, and then sent him to town for trial. He added, however, that the burgomaster on that occasion had not been quite certain of what he ought to do. That, however, did not matter so much—the precedent was there in any case. The schoolmaster then must be examined; and, as Mulders had once been present at a trial in court, the forms of justice presented no such great difficulty after all.

On the fifth day after his arrest, the schoolmaster was haled forth from the dungeon under the tower, and—of course, heavily handcuffed—taken to the council-chamber. That was an event. The whole village formed a long procession, which accompanied the prisoner; and when he was taken inside, his train remained hanging about the doors. Then followed a buzz and clatter among the crowd, as though it were a swarm of bees, or a duck-yard.

"It's too bad," said a little old woman; "an old white-haired man like that. What may not a man come to? Only yesterday he was teaching my daughter's children

"THAT WAS AN EVENT."

their lessons, and to-day the poor lambs are running after their master, because he's been in jail just like some nasty vagabond. And I can't believe it of him, do you know—anything but that. He has always been much too kind to every one. I'm not the only one here whom he has helped for nothing—nothing at all—without your having to pay a cent for it."

"Yes, but, mother," began a rich farmer,—with a face and attitude in which the most condescending amiability could not altogether hide the lowest greed, and a stupid arrogant conceit,—"you must understand that there are well-founded reasons—I say, *well-founded reasons*—for the man to have been taken up—eh? That's surely self-evident—eh? No one is put into handcuffs without important reasons; there must be a ground for such a motive—I say, *for such a motive.*" And then the mighty orator looked round him with a "What do you think of me now?" expression, and enjoyed his victory over the old woman. But the latter was not to be driven from the field so easily.

"You go along with your French talk. I know nothing about that,—and yet I think I know quite as much as you do yourself. But this I know, that it doesn't look well for you, of all people, to abuse the schoolmaster anyway. Even though it were as clear as a post above the water that the Dominie had stolen, *you* ought to stand up for him! Do you understand me—eh?"

The rich farmer understood quite well. When his youngest boy had been lying ill some months ago, he had been too mean to send for a doctor, though he could well afford it, and had called the schoolmaster to his assistance. Then, as at other times, the Dominie had said "No," to keep up appearances, as he was not supposed to practise any more; but he had thought "Yes," and acted on his thought. And the rich farmer had paid him nothing. This was why he now hurriedly turned away from this covert attack, muttering something about "old creatures getting quite childish," but abstained from **further** contradiction.

But the old woman could not be everywhere at once to take the Dominie's part, and the conclusion of most conversations was this: "Yes, you see, folks don't call a cow piebald, when **there's not a spot** about her."

Suddenly, however, all voices were hushed before the reverently-uttered magic formula, "The Burgomaster!"

The crowd parted to let him pass, and he went up to the council-chamber, where the faithful Kobus, in his Sunday suit, was awaiting him. He was already going to meet the burgomaster, in order to tell him that "they" were all there; but the great man was looking straight in front of him, as stiff as a poker, **and making, in a** direct line, for his official chair, like a **guest who, on being ushered** in, looks neither to right nor left, but makes straight for the lady of the house.

This was "the proper form." Kobus was so **impressed** by this ceremonial that he stared with open mouth and eyes, and remained immovable, like a masculine counterpart of Lot's wife. The burgomaster had elegant manners, that **he** had.

"Are all present?" asked the burgomaster, suddenly.

Kobus awakened with a start from his ecstatic trance. "Yes, your worship," he answered, regaining his composure.

"Then the trial **may** begin," said the President **of the** Court. "And you, Veldwachter, do you caligraph it!"

"I—I don't altogether understand, your worship."

"Caligraph, Veldwachter!"

"**Oh!—ah**!—hm—yes, I don't understand——"

"**Write it down, Veldwachter.** Caligraphy—that is the art of writing, you know."

"All right, your worship." **Kobus sat** down at a table, took up a pen, and bent over a sheet of paper. But the paper was destined to remain unsoiled. For, all of a sudden, the burgomaster looked round him, and, probably struck by the emptiness of the room, inquired, "Veldwachter, are all the witnesses present?"

"All the witnesses are present, your worship," answered Kobus, indicating, with a majestic wave of the hand, his solitary son Hannes, who sat so forlorn, that, looking at him and the schoolmaster, it would have been hard to say which was witness and which defendant; for the Dominie had his handcuffed hands on his knees under the table, and you would not have guessed from his calm features—pale and worn with the fatigues of the last few days—that he was accused of any crime.

"But," pursued Kobus, "your worship has just said something that gives me an idea. Ought there not to be some other witnesses?"

"Other witnesses?"

"Yes, I mean witnesses to witness *for* him, do you see? I mean to say, Hannes sits here, for instance, to speak against—I mean against the Dominie,—but ought there not to be some witnesses to speak for him as well?"

The burgomaster began to think. This was a difficult question, one of those ticklish and delicate problems, the solution of which forms the principal *raison d'être* of a burgomaster's career. If only this miserable trial had never begun! He cast a furtive glance at the defendant. If only he could consult the Dominie, and ask him to look up his books about the matter! But away with such humiliating thoughts! No; better, if it must be, to manifest his ignorance in a more becoming way: "Veldwachter, is that what they do in town? It was different in my time."

"They do it that way now, your worship."

"Then we had better move with the times, and adapt ourselves to the new usages. But where are the—the *for*-witnesses to come from?"

"Oh! there's a whole crowd outside the door, your worship—perhaps you might find one among them. And if there's no one to be had—well, **at any rate, we've done** our best to find one."

"Go outside, then, and proclaim a summons, on **my** behalf."

Kobus went **and did so, wording the** "proclamation" **as** clearly as **he** knew how. But **a** deathly stillness was all the answer he received. For though many a simple soul was honestly convinced of the defendant's innocence, and though here and there **a** solitary voice had been raised in his favour, —to go in there, into the council-chamber,—*to stand before the tribunal*,—that was more than **those** timid folk could undertake.

Suddenly, however, **a** shrill voice cried, "**Well, if no one else will do it, I will.**" And the little **old woman who had** already taken up the cudgels for the **Dominie, forced her** way hastily to the front of the crowd.

"Look'ee there; Auntie's going to speak," cried various voices. Every one repeated, laughing, "Auntie's going to speak!" for under this name the old lady was known **to** all the village.

Auntie cared neither for **laughter nor** tears, but **went** straight forward, climbed the **court-house** steps, and then suddenly turned round, **waved her thin** old arms, and cried as loud as she could, "**You're a pack of** cowards, the lot of you,—do you hear, **you** great **loobies?**" Then she disappeared inside. **And** though she **was** a funny figure enough as she stood there, **no** one thought of laughing,—they all **felt** the truth of Auntie's words too deeply.

Auntie was conducted inside by the veldwachter, and her eye immediately fell on her client. The Dominie remained seated in the same attitude, discouraged and dejected— deeply humiliated by the thought that, **at** his age, with his aspirations and such a past behind him, he should have to bow his head beneath the weight of a criminal accusation! The trouble dimmed his thinking powers, and drove the blood

"YOU'RE A PACK OF COWARDS."

through his veins at lightning **speed**. What a **hammering** in his pulses—what **a** thumping in his temples—what a rushing in his ears! He felt like a swimmer who has been long under water, and finds it press more and more crushingly on him, and hears its noise in his **ears**. That was the fever— the fever that was rising higher and higher in his blood, and brought that unnatural flush to his usually pale cheeks.

Auntie looked at the sad spectacle he presented, and her indignation rose, and craved for immediate utterance.

"Burgomaster!" she began, "don't you call **it a shame** that the Dominie——"

But her flow of words was immediately interrupted by **the** burgomaster: "Silence! witness, this is not as it should be. You have come here to give your **evidence voluntarily, and** to do this effectually all the forms must be observed. **Witness**, what is your name?"

"Well, I never—my name! Just as though the whole village didn't know me? Come, come, Burgomaster, every one knew my name long before yours was ever thought of; and do you want to pretend that you **don't know me?** No, man, that won't do. All those grand manners won't go down with old Auntie. All the same, I can tell you plainly why the poor fellow could not have stolen the pears; and so you are quite out of it, with all your fine forms and speeches, do you see? Now just let me ask you, If he took the pears, where did he leave them,—say?"

And Auntie placed her arms akimbo, and **assumed** an attitude which seemed to say, "Your turn now—come on!"

But the opposite party remained passive. The burgomaster, as it happened, was seized with a violent fit of coughing, which seemed as though it could not come to an end. It was a pity, for, but for that, surely, the wise man would have answered the conundrum with Solomonic **perspicuity**. The veldwachter-clerk said, "Hm, hm—yes, yes," and covered his beard with his hand. The witness for the prosecution yawned with *ennui* and hunger. The defendant sat still, and looked at the old woman with rigid eyes.

But all things come to an end, and so did the presiding judge's cough. However, he seemed to have coughed away all his judicial sagacity, for he remained silent. Not so Kobus Mulders, who awakened from his reverie after this fashion—

"Yes, yes,—where did he leave them? I only say, your worship,—where did he leave the pears, if he stole them?"

"Oh, yes, that's what I should like to know," said Auntie, shortly, and closed her lips with a look of firm conviction.

Another pause.

"Yes," resumed Kobus, "he can't have swallowed them all down at once." This joke appeared to him so inexpressibly funny, that he burst into a loud hoarse laugh, which was echoed by no one except Hannes. But suddenly the joker's features became rigid, and he looked at every one present with a face whose expression plainly said, "How is it possible that I did not think of it before?" and exclaimed, "I know! Your worship, the little chest that we found in Klaas's cottage the day after he died——"

"Well, Kobus?" asked the burgomaster, in great excitement—so much so that he quite forgot to speak officially.

"It is the Dominie's, and now I understand everything. The Dominie *didn't* steal, and Auntie is quite right. It could not be, either. Just listen. The Dominie has been at his doctoring again. He went to see Klaas when he was dying, and forgot to take his medicine-chest away with him when he left. I am quite sure it is his medicine-chest, because it is the same thing I used to see in his hands in the old times, when nobody minded his doctoring folks. And the time just corresponds. On the day after we arrested the Dominie, I went to see Klaas, and found him dead. It's as plain—as—well, it's quite plain!"

Every one had listened with the greatest attention, and the explanation seemed to have made a deep impression on all. The Dominie, however, seemed to feel it **most.** He suddenly started up out of his apathy, leaned his handcuffed hands on the table, and tried to speak. Everything melted into a dull roar inside his head—the light turned to scarlet—he had fainted.

All of them hastened up to help him—Auntie foremost, in spite of her old legs. Slowly he came to himself again, and then he tried to think. **He** remembered what had happened, in a dim sort of way. What now? What should he answer if they asked him whether Kobus's supposition was correct? It was—and yet, **if he acknowledged that he** had gone to Klaas on that particular evening to give him medical help, then he would have to expect for the future so strict a supervision of his forbidden practice, that it would thenceforth be almost impossible to carry it **on. And he** could not give it up—he could not, and would not. But **to** be looked on as a thief! Oh, if he could only think—think quietly and calmly. But this fever! this fever! No, it was his duty, his calling, and he must be true to it, though he should be crushed by the contempt of the whole world—the world he longed to do good to. And wildly, as a wave of delirium swept over him, he said, "**No**! no! no! I didn't do that! The chest is not mine! **I** know nothing **about** it, and wish to **know** nothing—do you hear? **I am no** doctor; I am only a poor schoolmaster! I am much too stupid to be a doctor, and I have never done anything of the sort! I'm a thief—a wretched thief—a thief!" He cried shrilly once more, with all his strength, "**A thief!**" and let his burning head drop on his heaving breast.

His hearers looked at each other. Not one of them now believed in his guilt, and even in the burgomaster—who was only narrow-minded, not bad-hearted—every hostile feeling now gave place to pity.

"Come, Dominie," he said, laying his hand on the old man's shoulder, "come, you mustn't make so much of it as all that. We all understand the whole business now; and as for the medicine-chest, I forbid every one here present to say one word about it!" At these words the burgomaster looked round him with such a solemn air of command, that Kobus cast down his eyes, and Hannes shuddered with sheer reverence. But the great man, mindful of his duties as presiding judge, went on—"Now, defendant, you are acquitted; you may go."

But Auntie flew up in a storm of indignation. "What! go? My patience, me! Burgomaster, don't you see the poor soul can hardly sit in his chair? Come, Hannes, you great lout, what are you loafing about there for, you great long booby, you? Run out, and tell them to send some menfolks to carry the Dominie home. Quick now!"

This classic oration produced a visible impression on Hannes, and, before long, he came back with several men, who carried the schoolmaster away, Auntie walking behind, and saying, from time to time, "Take care! take care!" When it became known outside that the Dominie's innocence was established, every one set up a loud cry of joy.

Inside, however, the burgomaster and Kobus were looking at each other with serious faces. "I haven't written down anything, with all the confusion," said Kobus. The burgomaster considered. If the matter were reported in town, he would probably get well laughed at for his mistake. And what about the forms in which such a narrative, if reported, would have to be clothed? No; it was best to put the whole thing aside, and say no more about it.

"Veldwachter, it seems to me that this matter is not now of sufficient importance for us to communicate it to the judicial authorities of the *parquet*; so you may go too."

Without understanding half of this speech, Kobus was able to catch the burgomaster's drift,—the matter was at an end. So he went home, reflecting how frightfully learned the burgomaster was.

C. K. ELOUT.

MY HERO.

I was a boy of twelve or thirteen, and, just like other boys of that age, full of life, mischief, ideals, and illusions.

A good-for-nothing little **scamp** out of school, **I was,** under the master's eye, **a** queer **mixture of the genuine** mischief-loving boy and the zealous pupil. **If I found no** attraction in the dry **science** of arithmetic and the rules of grammar, all the more did I feel **attracted by the history** of all nations in general, **and ours in particular.**

Yet not altogether; **it was only the warlike Spartans and** Romans, our own crusading **knights, and the fierce and** enterprising Gueux,—in short, **only those whom I looked** upon as heroes **who could arrest my** attention.

Frequently it vexed me that **my lunch-slice of bread** and butter did not **consist of** black, **coarse bread;** sometimes I felt a deep disdain **for my clothes, so different from** those in which the Roman **legions marched to victory;** all peaceable merchant-vessels were an **abomination to me,—I** knew but **one** ideal—to be **a hero.**

What I understood by **a hero was not quite clear, even** to myself,—only **this** was certain, that no **one could** be a hero unless he had won many great battles **over** stronger adversaries, or had blown up his ship in order to save the flag, or ended his glorious life covered with **wounds in** the breast (never in the back, of course!). In short, my idea of **a hero was** somewhat complicated; **but this much was certain,** that a great hero ought to be able to show a large number of wounds and scars, and that his bravery should be equalled by his **generosity.**

I wished to **be a hero** myself, but as I quite understood that **I was too young** for the position at present, my great desire was, **at** least, to see and know a hero.

I sought everywhere for this superior being, and thought at last that I had found my ideal in our new "odd man," who had been a soldier, and had a large scar on his cheek.

From this one outward and visible token of his bravery, I argued that he must have more hidden about his person, under his clothes. These wounds, alas! I could never hope to see, as he did not live in the house, but came every day to clean boots and run errands.

I was, however, firmly convinced that they existed. The only drawback to his greatness was the fact that he had both his arms and no wooden leg. I would much rather it had been otherwise, but managed to content myself with his many unseen wounds.

I was still seeking an opportunity of asking him how and when he had become a hero, when I was suddenly bereft of my illusion.

Our kitchenmaid was beforehand with me.

One day, when I had furtively slipped out to the kitchen, in order to question Frans, I heard Mie, our maid, say—

"I say, Frans, have you been in the wars, that you have such a mark over your face?"

Then he replied—

"In the wars! I believe you! We've nothing more to do with wars in this country, now! No,—when I was leaving the service, I treated my chum one night. But he got drunk and outrageous, and chucked me through a window, so that I cut my face open. No—I didn't get it in the wars—and jolly glad of it, too!"

I stood thunderstruck—the tears rose in my eyes.

No wounds on his breast! Even the scar was a delusion and a snare. I no longer believed in living heroes. They no longer existed.

But I was going to be a hero all the same. And till I was able to re-introduce the breed, I would content myself with the dead heroes of the past.

"I HAD FURTIVELY SLIPPED OUT TO THE KITCHEN."

But there were so many of them—and I wanted a special hero all to myself. Where should I find him?

De Ruyter was a hero, killed by the enemy's shot—but I had nowhere read that he had many wounds.

Bayard!—but I knew so little of him—and besides, he was not a Dutchman.

Cæsar — Napoleon — Blücher! — but how about the wounds?

Besides, every one knew that these were heroes; and I wanted one for myself—for my own special worship—not one of the universally famous ones.

My search, however, was not to be fruitless long. I found my hero in the following way.

There were to be drains laid down round the old church in our city; and the ground being dug up for that purpose, a number of skulls and bones were found in the black earth.

All the boys of the school went to look as soon as they could get away, and it may be supposed that I did not remain behind. We were all inspired with a frenzied enthusiasm for relics of antiquity. We grubbed about in the earth of the opened graves, to find coins, pots, or even potsherds if we could get nothing else. We envied the town workmen, who were allowed to keep on digging and finding all day long; and scarcely had it struck twelve when we flew to the Kerkplein, to see what these greedy persons had left us, and to discover anything that might have escaped their search.

But we found nothing—neither did the diggers. Most of the boys, therefore, gave up the search—I, alone, did not. I was seeking a dead, unknown hero,—while they were looking only for coins and nicknacks. I knew for certain that I should find something, when there were not so many eyes on the watch, and therefore I remained away from school one morning in order to go to the old churchyard.

For a long time nothing **at** all had been found—not even bones or mouldering boards; so that all the other boys too—those who did not belong to our school—had grown tired of coming.

Luck, however, was with me!

On one particular spot, at some distance from the church, pieces of skeletons again began to be dug up. The workmen examined the earth to see if it contained anything **of** value, but found nothing. My eager eye, however, spied among the clods a lump of a different colour. I loosened the earth from it, and found, to my great joy, a flattened **bullet.**

That was a discovery!

I turned over the heap of earth, and thus **came into** possession of six bullets, and a little copper plate covered with earth and rust.

The bullets!—My hero was found!

Reverently I picked up some bones which had been thrown aside, and carefully packed the remains of my hero in my school satchel.

My hero!—a real hero now!—not an imaginary one, like Frans, the odd man.

When I came home, in a tumult of joyful excitement, I secured my treasure safely in my play-box, to which I had a key. And then I had my hero safe—all to myself!

At dinner, I looked round triumphantly, and felt the deepest disdain for my parents and sisters. They had never made such a discovery! They could not **even** understand what it is to possess the very remains of a hero—the hero himself! I scarcely ate anything for pride and joy, till my mother said—

"Why, Con, you're not eating. Are you not well?"

I could only stammer a few words, and then thrust a whole potato into my mouth in order to prove my appetite, which, happily, reassured my mother.

As soon as dinner was over, I darted to my own room to assure myself that I had not been dreaming, and that my hero existed in very truth. The bones and bullets, and the little metal plate, were there still.

I contemplated them all once more, with a look full of love and reverence, and went downstairs again, so as to arouse no suspicion.

Never had I been a better-behaved boy than on that evening. I played with my little sister as nicely as possible; I was obedient as I had never been before,—all for fear that some unlucky circumstance might lead to a discovery of my hero on the part of my parents.

At last it was time to go to bed. At last I was alone with the sacred relics of the man who had stood six bullets, without reckoning the innumerable wounds—to be taken for granted—on his breast!

I gazed at the bones, brown and dirty as they looked—at the flattened bullets, and rusty bit of metal, with deep reverence. The plate probably bore his name; but if so, it was illegible with the dirt. Should I clean it? I burned with eagerness to know his name, and felt half inclined to do it; but desisted, thinking that, being rusty, and covered with earth, it would prove its age much better than if it were bright and polished up like new.

At last, after long contemplation of my treasures, I locked them up, and put the key under my pillow, for fear of burglars. Once in bed, however, I could get no sleep. All sorts of ideas relating to my hero crossed and recrossed my brain.

In the first place, I resolved to make a secret of him. It is a glorious thing to have a secret all to one's self—and such a secret!

It was settled, then—no one was to see or hear anything of him. I alone was to possess my Hero, and be able to worship Him.

MY HERO.

Then I began to wonder who he could have been, and when he had lived, and where he had fought and died.

It was quite clear to me that the six bullets represented but a small part of his wounds, for it was not possible that he had been killed on the field of battle by the sixth of those bullets. I knew that the fallen are always buried on the field of honour. Therefore he must have died of other wounds,—probably sword-cuts, lance-thrusts, or the like. . . . Then I fancied all sorts of biographies for my hero.

I should have liked best of all for him to have been a Crusader; but I was forced to give up that idea, seeing that in those days there were no guns, and therefore no bullets.

I therefore resolved to seek in more modern times.

A Water Gueux slain in fight? That, too, would not do. *They* were wrapped in a flag, and with a "One, two, three—in God's name," let down into the sea.

I weighed all possible cases—to reject them again immediately.

At last I hit upon the following, which satisfied me pretty well:—My hero had fought in Napoleon's wars, and was for his valour promoted by the great Emperor to the rank of general. In all battles he had been foremost, and many a wound bore witness to his courage. Napoleon had even chosen out a kingdom for him; when fortune changed, and all nations rose to free themselves from the power of the great conqueror.

Then my hero had left his place in the army, and his exalted offices, and had ranged himself under his country's flag to serve her as a private soldier.

After giving numerous proofs of courage, he was so severely wounded at the battle of Waterloo,—where he defended the colours of his regiment, single-handed, against a large number of the foe,—that he felt his end approaching.

And when he knew that the victory was won, he dragged himself home to his native town to die.

His funeral was a splendid one, and the fallen hero was buried in a spot apart from others, who were not thought worthy to be near him, even in death.

This last circumstance I added, after long consideration, to explain the isolated position of my hero's grave.

Another difficulty, however, presented itself. Why was there no monument erected to him?

The solution of this question cost me no little trouble. In our church there were two splendid monuments, with beautiful Latin verses on them; and the men who slept under them were of far less importance than my hero. But here, too, there was an explanation. My hero himself had said on his deathbed that he did not wish for a monument, but preferred to rest simply under the green grass;—his name would live well enough without one!

This, however, raised a new difficulty. I had never heard of any hero buried in the former burying-ground close to the church. Happily, however, I remembered to have read somewhere that "ingratitude is the world's reward."

He was forgotten!

That grieved me deeply; but I determined with myself to revive the memory of his name, when I should be somewhat older, and could write in the papers, and become a member of the Useful Knowledge Society. Then I would tell people how great my hero had been, and how ungratefully the world had treated him. Till then, he should remain my secret.

Of course I had adorned him with all sorts of chivalric qualities. I had seen him in my thoughts as the protector of helpless women, as the avenger of wrong; I had seen him risk his life at the command of his superiors, and in order to win one look from his lady.

And I had ended by endowing him with the crowning

grace of modesty. Of this I was not a little proud. I knew for certain that all the other boys' heroes would be brutal and arrogant, and set upon getting monuments for themselves.

Mine, however, was modest . . . and his reward was oblivion. . . . Yes—till I should arise . . . *then* my hero should be greater than all others.

Happy that now I knew *all* about my hero, youth and excitement were too much for me, and I fell asleep.

Next morning I arose, no longer a boy—not even a man. I was a great man. I had a task before me. I must give back to my hero his just fame and honours.

I had even assumed a new manner!—marbles and suchlike games were now beneath me,—and I thought the other boys uninteresting and childish. They, on their part, soon found that I had become tiresome and pedantic, and asked me if I had come in for a fortune, and was now too much of a swell for them. I only laughed, and wrapped myself once more in my own glory.

This lasted a few days, and then I began to find out that the solitary enjoyment of glory and a secret was not so great a pleasure as I had thought. Happily I had two bosom friends—Wil and Ed.

I resolved, after many heart searchings of heart, to share my wealth with these two. After I had sworn them to secrecy, and also exacted a solemn promise that they would not endeavour to appropriate my hero to themselves, I told them of my discovery, and all I knew of him,—for what I had myself imagined now seemed like truth to me. I enjoyed their evident jealousy, and, still more, their admiration and reverence for me.

"But, Con," said Wil at last, "what is the hero's name, really?"

I stood aghast. I had never thought of that! But they shall never exult over me because I did not know the name

"AFTER I HAD SWORN THEM TO SECRECY."

of my own hero. So I mentioned the first name that came into my head—"Jan Liller."

Happily, they believed me.

From that day forward there was a constant whispering among us, a mystery in our conversation, even on the most unimportant subjects, which drove all the other boys wild with curiosity. But we revealed nothing. We had even determined, for fear of discovery, never to speak of my hero otherwise than as "L. J."—even when we were alone. J. L. seemed to us much too dangerous.

Sometimes little boys were sent out to listen to us, under pretence of carrying on their games in our neighbourhood. But we were on our guard, and only talked all sorts of nonsense when the small spies were within hearing. Thus my secret did not leak out. Yet we could not be silent altogether.

In school, when the master told us about the great men of our country, from Claudius Civilis to William the Silent, we smiled pityingly, and said to each other, afterwards—

"L. J. could have done better than that!"—or, "They ought to have tried L. J.; he could have taught them something!"—and the like—so that we began to be called "L. J.'s." But we took great care that no one should find us out, and were very proud of our secret.

I say *our* secret,—yet, after all, it was really mine, for I had shown the bullets, the metal plate, and the bones neither to Wil nor to Ed. They thus only knew the half—and no more than I had thought fit to tell them. The finest and most important part of all was unknown to them. Of course they acted as if they had been *au fait* in the whole thing; but they were nothing of the sort.

At home, my changed behaviour began gradually to attract general attention. I had assumed a mysteriousness of demeanour, from which my father—judging from long experience—argued that there must be some special piece of mischief on hand.

As I frequently remained lost in thought, and no longer cared for games as I used to do (I thought them childish since the discovery of my hero), my mother came to the conclusion that I was not well; while my little sister, of course, was as curious as a girl can be. Therefore the three, each for his or her own reason, were constantly at my heels. I soon noticed this, and it was no small hindrance to my doings and projects.

I scarcely dared to produce my hero, for fear some one should come to my room unawares and surprise me in the midst of my relics, and so discover my secret.

My plans, more especially, were in danger!

I wished—as a homage to the glorious Jan Liller—to make an elegant little casket, lined with precious bits of silk, plush, and lace, to preserve therein his precious relics, and the glorious evidences of his heroic existence. I intended to make the fret-work casket myself,—but I durst not do it in the general sitting-room. Whenever I could, I stole away to my own little room, and went to work there. Once I was surprised by my mother when very busy; but when she saw my work, she pretended not to have noticed anything. My conscience reproached me bitterly; for I understood that my dear mother had thought I was working at a present for her approaching birthday.

But, for the moment, my hero took precedence of everything. I hoped to be able to buy something for my mother's birthday, trusting to the ready aid of my father's purse.

On a certain day, when I was out for a walk with my father, he suddenly said to me, "Well, Con, is the digging in the Kerkplein all over? I have not been there for some time. I suppose you have been there to see whether anything in your line has been turned up?"

Did my father suspect anything? and was he fishing?

I answered evasively.

"I have not been there since last week."

"DID MY FATHER SUSPECT ANYTHING?"

That was true—for just a week ago I had found my hero—and after I had found him, I was satisfied. The charm of rooting about among the graves had vanished. There was nothing more to find now.

"I only thought," said my father, jokingly, "that you had found a treasure—you are so mysterious lately. Say, my boy, have you grown rich, and are you going to keep your money all to yourself?"

"I have never found anything, father," I stammered, full of shame at the lie, and yet full of satisfaction at my courage—in daring to tell a falsehood to save my hero from discovery.

Happily my father changed the subject, by asking me if I had any present in view for mother's birthday. To be honest, I had to answer no, for my hero had taken up all my thoughts and energies. But just as I was thinking what to say, a great, a glorious idea rose up in me. What could be a better present for my mother than my hero?

At the sacrifice of my secret,—of my own discovery,—I would surprise her with the revelation of my find, and share my hero with her! It was a hard struggle, but, once resolved, I could say with cheerful assurance, "Yes, father, I have something very, very nice!"

"That's good, my boy!" said my father, as he patted me approvingly on the shoulder. "Do your best to make it so, for your mother deserves it."

Since the old churchyard had been mentioned, I was eager to find out if my father knew anything about my hero. Therefore I asked, with as careless an air as I could assume—

"Say, father, who used to be buried in that place round the church?"

"Why, my boy, I don't know. It must be at least fifty years since that burying-ground was used. When I came to live here the new cemetery was already opened, and I really do not know who was buried in the old place."

"But, father, did you never hear of *any* one that was buried there?"

"No," said my father; but, after thinking a little, he went on: "Yes, I do, though! they buried Kees Van Assen there. I heard so the other day from Notary Van Tefelen."

Could that be my hero? It might well be, why else should the old burying-ground have been mentioned at the notary's?

Surely, then, he must have been a great-uncle or distant cousin of that odious Alfred, whom we always called "the Muff," because he never would join our games for fear of getting bruised and scratched, or soiling his clothes and hands.

"Was Van Assen a hero, father?" I uttered the words with difficulty.

"A hero, my boy? No, certainly not. No, quite the contrary!"

"A coward, father? I thought as much."

"Indeed, and why?"

"Because that stupid boy of the minister's is Van Assen too, and he *is* a coward!"

"That does not follow. This Van Assen was not in any way related to the minister's family. At least I believe not. But he was not a coward, he was far worse. He was a traitor to his country. He betrayed the town to the French."

"And what did they do to a low fellow like that?" I asked, full of pain and indignation that a countryman of mine could have betrayed his native town to the enemy.

"At first, nothing; for at that time he was protected by the French. But when they were gone, his fellow-townsmen razed his house to the ground, and he was shot."

"Then he was buried in the churchyard?"

"Well, yes; because his family was a rich and dis-

4

tinguished one, they consented to bury him in the churchyard; but, of course, it was done without show or splendour. I know no more about it."

"Don't you know in which corner he was buried?"

"Yes, the corner by the baker's shop."

Now there were two corners of the churchyard which had a baker's shop near them. Near one of them, I had found my hero; but he was called Jan Liller, and not Van Assen! I resolved never more to buy tarts or buns in the corner where the traitor was buried,—that was accursed from henceforth. We had been in the habit of going there, because we got far more for our money than elsewhere.

It now at once became clear to me that this baker knew of the traitor's neighbourhood, and was afraid of losing his customers unless he sold his goods very cheap!

I had not thus gained much information by my inquiries. Only I had found a new point of comparison, my hero *versus* Van Assen! Jan Liller was dearer to me than before, now that I could contrast him with a contemptible Van Assen! My hero had become greater than ever!

As soon as I reached home, I ran to my own little room, in order to gaze my fill on his relics—to steep my soul in his greatness.

On the stairs I felt for my key.

What was that? It was not in my pocket! I had not lost it—I was certain of that. Then I must have left it sticking in my box, and in that case my secret—my hero was lost!

A terrible fear overcame me. My steps dragged on the stairs. With a sinking heart I opened my door,—my presentiment had not deceived me!

There stood my little sister before the open box!

"You horrid girl—what are you doing with my things? Keep off!" I screamed, when I saw my secret revealed.

"But, Con! you had left the key in the lock, and I just looked in!" cried my sister, terrified.

MY HERO.

"DASHED THEM ON THE GROUND!"

"Yes—it's just like girls—always bothering about things that don't concern them. You're always meddling with everything, and spoiling other people's things!"

"Oh, Con! don't be so angry! I only just wanted to look! And, just see,—I've been cleaning up this dirty little brass plate that was inside. I've made it look quite nice—and there's some writing on it."

At the same time she thrust the now glittering brass plate into my hands.

I looked at it.

Everything seemed to turn round with me. Everything was black. I could see nothing but the glittering yellow plate, and the name engraved on it :—

KEES VAN ASSEN,

1813.

I dropped the brass plate, seized the bones and the bullets out of the box, and dashed them on the ground.

There lay my hero!

CONRAD VAN DER LIEDE.

NEWSPAPER HUMOUR.

To keep apples from spoiling, they should be placed in a cool room in the house occupied by a family with eight children.

Florist. "Look at the blush on these roses, sir."

Bachelor (*with a look at his purse*). "I see. They must be blushing at the exorbitant price you charge for them."

FLORIST: "LOOK AT THE BLUSH ON THESE ROSES, SIR."

Domestic Morality.

"You have not been looking sharp, Bet; the butcher has given you more bones than meat again."

Bet. Well, I told him so at the time. I said, *if it was for myself I wouldn't take it.*"

Actor. "When I was last acting here, the public were so enthusiastic, you can't imagine. Why, they insisted on *carrying* me back to the hotel, when I left the theatre."

Critic. "Man, man, you don't mean to say you were so far gone as *that?*"

Patient. "Doctor, I think I have had an attack of the gout."

Doctor. "Stuff and nonsense! if you had really had one, you couldn't *think*—you'd know it."

"Father," inquired a small boy, "what does a 'Paradise' mean?"

"A Paradise, my son, is the corner by the fire when your mother has gone to stay with her friends for a few days."

A Harmless Insect.

Traveller. "Waiter, how can you give me soup like this?—there's a fly in it."

Waiter. "Oh! *that* won't hurt you—it's quite dead."

A LADY having engaged a new man-servant, answering to the name of Joseph, told him that she would always ring once for him, and twice for her maid.

A short time after this, she rang the bell, but Joseph failed to appear. She grew impatient, and pulled the bell-rope again. The maid entered.

"I did not ring for you; I wanted Joseph. Why does he not come?"

"Joseph," replied the maid, "is sitting by the fire, reading Madame's paper. When Madame rang the first time, he told me to look out, for he should not wonder if you were to ring again. And when Madame did so, he turned to me, and said, 'See? that's for you.'"

"Why, ma'am," said the housemaid, when she heard that her mistress had been very unwell during the night, "why didn't you tell me when you felt ill?"

"I didn't want to wake you, you had been working hard all day, and——"

"Oh! that's nothing; you might have called me all the same. I sleep so sound that you would never have waked me."

A RASCALLY VALET.

A room in a hotel. Tables and chairs **are** *covered with portmanteaus, carpet-bags, clothes, &c. On a table (L.) is an open jewel-case, (R.) a sofa; in the background a bed. Frans (Jonker Van Bergen's man) is discovered, half-reclining on the sofa, smoking a cigar.*

Frans (sings).
"Mon maître est un filou,
Et moi j' n' suis pas bête, la, la . . ."

That was indeed a barbarous idea—leaving me at home. "Charité bien ordonnée commence par soi-même," as we used to say at Paris. My gentleman's gone out a-courting, and I may just sit and grumble in these confounded lodgings! He hasn't the smallest grain of feeling. Why couldn't he remember that while he's busy making love to his silly cousin, and flattering his cracked old aunt,—that is, making fools of both of them,—I might, in the meanwhile, very appropriately amuse myself with the maid!

Pretty little thing, that Sophie! Just a little bit *bête*, still —but that will come all right in time—I'll educate her fast enough. We haven't been to Paris for nothing. I had views on her already, when we were here eighteen months ago. She was then a mere child, and I had not yet seen Notre Dame and the Pont-Neuf. In point of fact, come to think of it, I was still very young, and not *au fait* about life. I can clearly remember getting quite confused when the postman's flaxen-haired daughter scolded me for . . . come, Frans, let those things rest . . . she's at rest herself. . . . How could I help it, if the girl was so gone on me? Why didn't her father take better care of her? What is a father for, if not to look after his daughter?

What a difference, when I think of those days! Confused! ashamed!—why, I don't know the meaning of the words. The only thing I'm ashamed of now, is that I ever had the *faiblesse* to be ashamed of anything. And now that, thanks to my education in the *guinguettes*, I have become quite a *jeune homme accompli*,—now that I might have begun a nice diversion with the *suivante* of my master's intended, . . . now I'm got rid off with a gruff, "Frans, stay and look after the room!"

He'll talk in a different tune when he finds he needs me again to get him out of some scrape or other. Then it is, "Frans, dear Frans, save me; I don't know what I'm to do!" Frans is good enough for that. But besides this, *au fond*, it's unjust to leave me here indoors. A man is a man, and has reason and freewill. Jonker Van Bergen goes out courting. So we see that beings with reason and freewill do go courting. But I too am a man; I have freewill and reason—therefore I ought to go out courting **too**. That is clear and undeniable.

Glorious **logic**! Precious philosophy! Invaluable gift of Heaven, **which** is scattered with generous hand at Paris. Beloved nurse of all that . . . that . . .

And with all that I'm sitting here indoors, like Job, on his ancient sofa. It is annoying; it's very annoying! It's the most annoying thing in the world! It could not possibly be worse; it's *ennuyant, étouffant, embêtant!*

[*Jumps up angrily, and walks backwards and forwards, smoking.*]

I'm curious to know whether he'll get through with his business, and succeed better than last year. The devil grant he may! Otherwise it's all up with him—all up—and **he's** ruined! If he hasn't made his lady-cousin his own, with all that belongs to her [*goes through the gestures of counting money*], within a month, he's a dead man! Physically dead, financially dead, civilly dead,—dead in every possible way! Dead to *chambertin, baronfayol*, and champagne; dead to the *bouillotte* table; dead *pour tout ce qui porte un jupon* . . . *enfin*—burst up!

This wouldn't really matter so much if these gentlemen hadn't the disagreeable habit of dragging down every one about them in their fall. [*Makes a wry face.*] The cheques! the cheques!

I am anything but *à monaise*, as we used to say at Paris. We have only a month before us. Before that time **we** must have money to pay up, or the whole thing will go smash. And then he's quite capable of saying that it was I who forged the cheques. Then come examinations and cross-examinations, witnesses *à charge* and *à décharge;* reply, duplicate, triplicate, or whatever they call **it**; and the end of it is that the President puts on the black cap—grim fashion that!—and has a sentence read out, in which poor Frans is very badly used on the score of . . . complicity!

I might indeed get hold of a lawyer who has studied the *circonstances atténuantes*, as we used to say at Paris; but what's the good, when the stupid bench don't understand them? Civilisation is at such a low ebb in this land of ours. Quite otherwise over there. I attended a trial in France ... a woman who had committed the *sottise* of hacking her child to pieces, chopping it up small, and cooking it ... what further could you have? It would have been a bad look-out for her in this country. Over there, she simply had to take the precaution of providing *circonstances atténuantes*, ... and she got off all right. That's what I call philanthropy—civilisation! Just look for civilisation *here!* there's nothing of the sort. Everything is taken ill here. If your scales or your weights are not quite right, they take it ill of you! If you call a man a thief or a scoundrel, in the friendliest way in the world, and can't produce your proofs on the spot, they take it ill of you! Just as if those were not the biggest scoundrels of all against whom nothing can be proved! If you happen to swear falsely, they take that ill too! Why, not long ago I heard of a man undergoing very unpleasant treatment in public, because he—it seems incredible—because he had set his own house on fire! Stupid nation this! Not the faintest notion of the universal rights of mankind! The house belonged to him; what business was it of people's what he did with it? Why shouldn't he make a bonfire of it as soon as smoke this "light brown"? (Good cigar, too!) Yes, they say, but ... his *next-door neighbour!* Stuff and nonsense! Am *I* not to illuminate, because somebody else prefers to sit in darkness? If my next-door neighbour has cat's eyes, he had better go and live somewhere else.

No, no,—that delicate feeling,—that tact,—that talent for making black white with all the facility in the world, and without fear of contradiction,—and above all, the glorious *circonstances atténuantes*,—*all these* you find only in France!

Splendid invention, those *circonstances atténuantes!* They are the lightning-conductor of the Procureur du Roi's wrath, as we used to say at Paris. They are galvanism applied to the Code Napoléon. They are . . . in short, they are anything you please.

Oh, pleasant France! beloved France! When I say France, I mean Paris. Paris, with its *bals-musard!* Paris, with its *rendezvous* on the Boulevards and in the Bois de Boulogne! Paris, with its *limonadières, fruitières,* **bouquetières**, and all other *ières!*

[*Begins to recite, with exaggerated action.*]

"O France! O precious land! O paradise o' the world!
I greet thee, though the marsh and mud . . . marsh and mud. . . ."

. . . well, never mind; I shall hit it some other time. How is one to find a rhyme to "world"? I ought to have begun differently. But what I mean is, that if ever I find myself mixed up in this *fâcheuse* affaire of the cheques, I shall at once make my native country a present of my citizenship, and take shares in France. Then I shall have the right of being attended to by a French court, take a few *circonstances atténuantes* with me, and Frans is all right—quits the court without a stain on his character!

A greater fool than that young Huser I never saw in all my born days. Who ever heard of a man letting himself be ill-treated in the place of another? I never could understand that story. The imbecile! I wish I knew where to find him; I should go to him, and say, "Huser, my dear boy, we've made a mistake again about a signature or two; do make yourself responsible for the error—there's a good fellow." I believe, upon my soul! the man would be fool enough to do it over again. I can't explain the matter, but I dare swear that Huser, in spite of his sour face, was the most faithful chum in the world. I would bet something that he had been brought up at Paris, or at least had a

French nurse or a Swiss *bonne*. Sacrifices like that it would be vain to look for elsewhere . . . [*A knock at the door.*] Ho, hey! *entrez*.

[*Sits down on a chair in the middle of the stage, stretching his legs straight out in front of him.*]

Look here now, Frans, you must represent your master, the noble and honourable gentleman, Jonkheer Karel Bernhard Anton Jozef Delmare Van Bergen Van Wiesendaal! (*Raises his voice.*) *Entrez!*

Enter GENERAL VAN WELLER, *in undress uniform, with a riding-whip in his hand.*

Frans (*without looking round*). Who's there?

Van Weller. Look round, and perhaps you'll know.

Frans. I'm just like Louis Napoleon's knights—I do well, but I don't care to look round.*

Van Weller (*looks round with displeasure, then approaches and gazes fixedly for a few moments at Frans*). No, you are not he. You are too low-looking a fellow to be my nephew. Who are you?

Frans (*without changing his position*). In the first place, or, as we used to say at Paris, *primo*, I must request you to allow me to express my thanks for your very flattering opinion with regard to my physiognomy; *secundo*, it would be the proper thing for you to do me the favour of informing me of *your* name.

Van Weller. Insolence personified!—my nephew cannot

---

* *Doe wel en zie niet om* (Do well, and don't look behind you), was the motto of the Knights of the Union. King Louis of Holland (Napoleon I.'s brother) was but an indifferent Dutch scholar, and the tradition goes, that, having to preside at a chapter of the above Order, he was provided with a French phonetic version of their motto, as follows: *Doux lainsi nid d'homme.* With the aid of this guide to pronunciation he is said to have acquitted himself all right; but on another occasion he came to grief by describing himself as the "friend and rabbit" (Konijn, *quasi koning*, king) of his audience.

"ENTREZ."

be far off. (*To Frans.*) My name is Jan Weller. Who are you?

Frans. I don't know.

Van Weller. It is surely your place to know.

Frans. Alas! who in this corrupt age does know himself? At Ephesus, it was written——

Van Weller. That does not concern me, or you either. What is your name?

Frans. That's another matter. My late master used to call me . . .

Van Weller (*impatiently*). Well?

Frans. . . . when he was in a good humour, "You vagabond!"

Van Weller. Pretty! very pretty! If you keep up this game much longer, I shall be tempted to write that name on your back with my horsewhip!

Frans. Don't do that, please. It would cause confusion, as it is not my name at present.

Van Weller (*smiling*). Well, tell me your name, then?

Frans. Girls who don't know me call me "Angel," or something similar. Others,—of earlier date,—" scoundrel, wretch, miscreant," and I don't know what all . . . mostly words that are not to be found in the *Dictionnaire de l'Académie*.

Van Weller. Tell me, in the devil's name, who you are, fellow!

Frans. My mother used to call me Levi . . .

Van Weller. Well then?

Frans. Yes, but . . . that is not my name. She only called me so, because there was a Jew of that name who sold vegetables down our street, and I could imitate him so well.

Van Weller. It is enough to exhaust any man's patience! Speak out, once for all, in whose rooms am I?

[ANDRIES *puts his head in at the door.*]

Andries. Are you here, **General?**

Frans (springs to his feet). General? **Your** obedient servant!

Van Weller (to Andries). **Come in!** [*Enter Andries.*] Ask this fellow his name. If he does not answer briefly, **and to** the point, as soon **as** I give the word " March!" you take him by the collar and throw him out of window.

[*Andries salutes, turns on his heel, and marches up **to** Frans. Frans approaches the bed.*]

Van Weller (to Frans). What are you going to do?

Frans. With your permission, General . . . I have always been a lover of military exercises, but being only a **civilian** I am not at all well up in window-throwing drill, **and so,** I thought, a couple of pillows on the pavement . . .

Van Weller. Andries, bring the fellow **here!**

[*Points to **the floor** with his riding-whip. Frans escapes Andries, who walks toward him with a stiff military step.*]

Van Weller. Quick march! Seize him, and bring him here!

[**Sits down.** *Andries seizes Frans, and drags him roughly to the spot indicated, but in such a manner that Frans stands with his back to the General.*]

Van Weller. Right about face!

[*Andries turns Frans round by the shoulders, forcing him to face **the** General,—then takes **a** step backward, and remains standing at attention.*]

Van *Weller (throws the riding-whip to Andries).* **Take it!** Now, attend! When I say "Out!" you begin to thrash him till the **word is** given to stop. (*To Frans.*) What is your name?

Frans. I have already told **you,** sir, that my mother—

Van Weller. Out!

[*Andries lays on with the whip.*]

Frans. No—no— oh!—my name is Frans Varel, General!

Van Weller. Leave out the "General!" for the future. And the "oh!" also. Answer briefly what I ask you—no more, no less. What is your profession?

Frans. Valet, or rather secretary, to——

Van Weller. Enough! Who is your master?

Frans. Jonkheer Van Bergen.

Van Weller. Just so, that must be the right man! Has he any other name besides Bergen?

Frans. My master's full name is Jonkheer Karel Bernhard Anton Jozef Delmare Van Bergen Van Wiesendaal. (*Aside.*) Oh! how miserably I'm representing him!

Van Weller. How old is your master?

Frans. I think he is twenty-eight.

Van Weller. The same! the same! How long have you been in his service?

Frans. We grew up together.

Van Weller. Then you knew his father?

Frans. Certainly. It was he who used to call me "vagabond," when——

Van Weller. That is not what I am asking. How long is it since the old gentleman died?

Frans (*considering*). Fifteen or sixteen years.

Van Weller. Did he die of an illness?

Frans. He certainly did not die of health.

Van Weller (*impatiently*). Speak out—what did he die of?

Frans. Of . . . of . . . an exaggerated sense of honour.

Van Weller. Speak plainly, fellow, or I'll give the word! Relate what happened shortly before his death.

Frans. Shortly before his death . . .

Van Weller. Well—be quick!

Frans. He was still alive.

Van Weller (*angrily*). Out!

   [*Andries lays on with the whip.*]

Frans (*quickly*). Stop!

Van Weller (to Andries). Why are you not thrashing him as I told you? **You hear him trying to make a** fool of me!

Andries. The word was given to stop, General.

Van Weller. He gave it, not I!

Andries. There was nothing about that in the orders, General.

Van Weller. I am in sole **command here, of course**. Now speak, you scoundrel, quickly! *Out*——

Frans. Oh, sir! I'm beginning! The next day——

Van **Weller. What?** What **day?** I know nothing yet!

Frans. Monsieur Socrates also knew nothing. The recognition of this fact **is** the source of all wisdom, General. I am telling you the story in my own way, beginning at the end. I belong to the school of M. Dumas and M. Sue.

Van **Weller.** Don't **wear** out my patience any longer, fellow! Relate consecutively what took place on the last day of Mr Van Bergen's life.

Frans. He got up at half-past four in the morning, and put on his socks and boots. **I** did **not see** this, but **I am** induced to believe it, as he appeared, a little later, with his boots and spurs on. It is thus **a** fair inference that he had just put them **on,** unless, like M. Charles Douze, he **had** been sleeping **in** them—in which case . . .

Van Weller. **Are you quite** incorrigible? Don't tell me the story like that!

Frans. Am *I* **to blame?** *N'est pas conteur* **qui veut.** I did not profess to be a good story-teller, General.

Van Weller. Silence! I ask you for the last time whether you are willing to relate, in a proper manner, what you know of the affair?

Frans. About Charles Douze? **He was** born——

Van Weller. Out!

[*Andries strikes Frans with the whip, several* **times.**]

Frans. Ai! ai!—oh! General!—I'll tell you everything!

5

Van Weller. Stop! (*To Frans.*) Now go on, and think of your back.

Frans. The old gentleman had come back from an assembly at Court, the evening before, very much put out. They said he had had a quarrel, and was to fight a duel next day. I only know this by tradition, as you may say, because I and the young master were under arrest, locked up in the summer-house, because we had stolen apri——

Van Weller. Never mind the apricots, and tell me about the duel.

Frans. Well, then—my master must have slept very badly that night. This, too, I only know by way of tradition; and since tradition represents the border-land between the dark region of myth and the daylight of history——

Van Weller. Out——

Frans. Ow!—wait—listen! Next morning he went out at five o'clock, and came home at half-past six, mortally wounded. He had a bullet in his left breast, whence I infer that he had been shot. But I cannot with certainty——

Van Weller. Silence! Who was his adversary?

Frans. That I do not know. The coachman who drove the master out, said . . .

Van Weller (*impatiently*). Well?

Frans. Said he did not know either.

Van Weller (*stamps his foot*). Did your master die soon after?

Frans. Yes—at half-past one that afternoon . . . as near as I can guess. For, you see, as the young gentleman had fastened a frog to the pendulum of the big clock that stood in the hall——

Van Weller. To the deuce with your frogs and your clocks! Answer me—did any one come to see Bergen before his death?

Frans. Yes; three officers, one of them a major.

Van Weller (*aside*). Ah! that was Huser. (*To Frans.*) What happened then?

Frans. They were admitted to see him, but the servants were sent away. But as I have always been very fond of tragedy scenes, I managed to peep through the keyhole; and I saw that the Major fell on his knees beside the bed, and cried. The kneeling was very well done . . . his *contenance* was simply perfect . . . I was all attention. Old Mr Van Bergen held out his hand to him, and said——

Van Weller (*rising quickly*). That is just what I want to know—go on!

Frans. That he was thirsty.

Van Weller (*sits down again, as if disappointed*). That's not what I meant. Go on!

Frans. They gave him something to drink. Then he sat up in bed, and put his arms round that officer. "Let us part in peace," he said, "*sans rancune!*" The officer kept on crying, and said, "Can you ever forgive me, Bergen?" The master smiled, and said, "Gladly! gladly!—*sans rancune*, dearest——"

Van Weller. Well—dearest *what?*

Frans. I couldn't catch the name. And I never saw that Major again. I heard that he died about six months later.

Van Weller (*aside*). It must have been Huser—not a doubt about it! (*To Frans.*) And then? What happened next?

Frans. The wounded man asked one of the officers to call his little Charles—that was the young master, who was still in the summer-house—*I* had got out . . . The young gentleman came up to the bed, and, instead of being pleased at getting out sooner than he expected, he began to cry too.

Van Weller. Go on, go on!

Frans. After being silent for some time, the master said to the Major——

Van Weller. Go on, do, fellow! I've been waiting for that about an hour!

Frans. He said,—" Don't distress yourself over my death. It was in fair fight. My fate might have been yours. Only —be a father to my poor Charles!"

Van Weller. What next?

Frans. The Major began to sob again, and cried, "I swear to you I will!" Then Baron Van Bergen smiled pleasantly, held out his hand to him once more, and died. [*V. W. remains lost in thought.*] It was a touching scene, General. The old gentleman died almost as naturally as M. Furneau of the Théâtre Royal. I should have been quite overcome with emotion if the other two officers had possessed any knowledge of the stage. They seemed to be novices, who had never been in Paris. Not the faintest idea of tragic action—they didn't even wring their hands! Of course that of itself gave them a stupid attitude——

Van Weller. Will you hold your tongue? How was it that you never saw this officer again?

Frans. They said in the kitchen that he was abroad with his son, and that when he came home he was going to take Master Charles with him. But he never came back.

Van Weller. And his son?

Frans. I never heard anything about him.

Van Weller. Have you ever seen him?

Frans. Never.

Van Weller (*aside*). I think the fellow is lying. (*To Frans.*) Did you ever know a man by the name of Huser?

Frans. Huser? Yes, very well indeed. He was the young master's greatest friend. Or rather—for they weren't exactly friends—he was . . . he did . . . he gave . . . well, I never quite knew what to make of that Huser.

Van Weller. Now we're getting near it! What became of Huser?

Frans. H'm!—nothing much! . . . he did not turn out

anything to boast of, General. **He** was careless,—he was **fast**
... that is **to say,** he wasn't exactly that. He gambled
... at least, no, he never gambled. But ... in short, I
don't know anything about it. All I know is, that he came
to smash in the **end.**

Van Weller (*aside*). **Poor** Gustav! poor boy! (***To Frans.***)
Go on, man, tell me all you know.

Frans. He had a difference of opinion with the Procureur
du Roi, as we used to say at Paris. He had been imprudent
—(*whispers*)—forged cheques!—people took it ill of him,—
and—you know the law, General!

Van Weller (*aside*). Poor boy! (***To Frans.***) But how
was that possible? Was **he in debt**?

Frans. On **the** contrary, his father **had** left him plenty
of money, and he lived very economically.

Van Weller. **And** he **did** not play, you say?

Frans. **Never. He had** old-fashioned notions on that
head.

Van Weller. Was he, perhaps, given to courting?

Frans. Oh! no—he was too stiff and solemn for that. **He**
always looked sulky and discontented. He was a tiresome
sort of fellow. I think, even, **that he used to** make verses.

Van Weller. And he **was your** master's friend?

Frans. No, and ... yes! **He was** always with us, and
at our rooms. He always helped the young master when **he**
had the chance; but afterwards **he used** to give it **him like**
blazes.

Van Weller. Strange, very strange! And how long ago is
that?

Frans. Four years.

Van Weller. What was your master doing then?

Frans. Nothing.

Van Weller. How? I thought he was at the university.

Frans. Well—studying, and doing nothing—that comes
pretty much to the same thing.

Van Weller. And this Huser?

Frans. Before that *fâcheux évènement* I spoke of, he was studying too. I think he wanted to be a lawyer . . .

Van Weller. Silence! Nothing but what I ask you! Is your master a good sort of man?

Frans. He might certainly be better.

Van Weller. Silence! You deserve a good thrashing. He is a bad servant that speaks ill of his master. If I ask you any question that you would injure your master by answering, then you are to hold your tongue. Do you understand? I don't want to make any traitors. Remember this carefully, or I shall give the word. Did your master play high at the university? [*Frans is silent.*] . . . So—he's silent . . . therefore our young gentleman *did* play . . . therefore he is betraying his master by his silence . . . Out!

[*Andries strikes him.*]

Frans. Oh! my dear good gentleman, what *am* I to say? No, no, the young master never gambled.

Van Weller. He lies! Yes—I forgot to say that if you don't tell the truth, I shall give the word too. Did your master gamble at the university? Out!

[*Andries again raises the whip.*]

Frans (*points to the window*). Fire! fire! for heaven's sake!—save yourselves! . . . fire!

[*The General hastens to the window. Andries remains rigidly at his post. Frans runs to the door.*]

Frans. I should have done that sooner. (*With a low bow.*) General, your humble servant.   [*Exit.*

Van Weller (*returning from the window*). I see nothing, absolutely nothing. Where is the fellow?

Andries. He's run away, General.

Van Weller. Why didn't you hold him?

Andries. That was not in the orders, sir.

Van Weller. The scoundrel has been making a fool of me! Never mind—I know enough for the present. Do you know him, Andries?

Andries. Yes, sir, he's a good-for-nothing fellow.
Van Weller. Of course—like master, like man!

Enter SOPHIE, *with a note.*

Sophie. You here, Andries? (*Looks at General V. W.*) Who's this man?

Andries. Hush—sh!

Van Weller (to Andries). Silence! (*To Sophie.*) What do you want here, my girl?

Sophie (looks hard at him). I have a note for young Mr Van Bergen's man. (*To Andries.*) Hasn't Frans been here? Surely this is the gentleman's room? He said number four, and——

Van Weller. Just give me that note.

Sophie. Are you Mr Van Bergen's man too?

Van Weller. Yes. Give it here.

Sophie (to Andries). Will it be all right if I give it to this man? [*Andries does not answer.*] Good gracious! what's the matter? Why are you standing there as glum and stiff as if you were on parade?

[*Tries to seize his hand, but he pushes her gently back.*]

Andries (nodding towards the General, who is watching them with an air of amusement). Eh!

Sophie (shakes him by the arm). Do speak! What is it?

Andries. Eh!

Sophie. Has he made you like that? (*To Van Weller.*) What does this mean? I don't like it. It doesn't suit me at all. May I ask you, for the last time, to tell me what it means? [*Van Weller laughs heartily.*] Still better! He thinks he's making a fool of me. [*Turns to Andries and shakes his arm again.*] Andries, Andries, do speak, or I shall be angry!

Andries (under his breath). Do be quiet! It's the General!

Sophie. Oh! (*Turns to Van Weller.*) Please, sir, may I

"ENTER SOPHIE WITH A NOTE."

ask why you wouldn't let Andries go **out on leave the other day**? That was not nice of you. I'd——

Van Weller (*to Andries*). Who is this pretty child?

Andries. She's Mam'zelle Sophie, Freule Van Wachler's maid.

Van Weller. Why, that's fortunate! (*To Sophie.*) Well, and how is my sister Koosje?

Sophie (*surprised*). Your sister Koosje, **sir?**

Van Weller. Yes—Mevrouw Wachler!

Sophie (*curtseys*). Very well, sir. (*To Andries.*) **Think of** that—I never knew that the mistress's Christian **name was** Koosje. Why, that's a name any one of us might **have**!

Van Weller (*to Andries*). **Are you** in love with this charming creature?

Andries. With your permission,—yes, General.

Sophie. That's nice of you, Andries! *I* never asked any one's permission. And supposing the gentleman were to **say, No?**

Van Weller. Well, well,—you may make your mind easy, —I won't say No! (*To Andries, calling **him aside.***) Something has just occurred to me. I don't want that rascal to tell his master that I have been questioning him. Does he care about . . . ? [*makes the gesture of drinking*].

Andries. **Yes**, General.

Van Weller. And try to persuade your sweetheart to **stay** here a little. **I should like to** talk to her.

Andrew. Yes, General. (*To Sophie.*) Just give your note **to** the General, Sophie, and answer him nicely if he asks **anything**, and be as pleasant and polite as you can. Remember, he can let me off on leave!

[*Salutes, and turns to go, but comes back.*]

*Van **Weller**.* Well—what is it now?

Andries. Am *I* to be drunk, too, General?

Van Weller. No need for that! March! [*Exit Andries.*

Sophie. Do you wish to take the note, sir**?**

Van Weller. Just lay it down here.

Sophie. But I think there's some hurry about it. The young gentleman said I was to bring a key back with me.

> [*Van Weller takes the note, and reads it, with gestures of astonishment. Looking round, he sees the casket. He goes up to it, and stands still, lost in thought. At last he takes the key out of the lock and gives it to Sophie.*]

Van Weller. There's the key, my girl. You have done your errand well—so go now—just go.

Sophie. But Andries said you wanted to talk to me.

Van Weller. Yes . . . no . . . it's hardly needed now . . . Or . . . (*hesitating*) How are things going, Sophie?—is there to be a wedding soon?

Sophie (*confused*). Yes—if Andries . . .

Van Weller. I'm not speaking of Andries now—I mean in the Van Wachler family.

Sophie. Ah! I think there will, indeed! for the young lady has three lovers.

Van Weller. That's enough to begin with. I had only heard of one. And who are they?

Sophie (*counts on her fingers*). First, Jonkar Van Bergen,—then the music-master, Holm,—and the third is old Mr Buys.

Van Weller. What do you say?—a music-master?

Sophie. Oh, don't laugh at him, sir—he's such a good man! It's only a pity that he's always so sad.

Van Weller. And why do you think he is one of the young lady's lovers?

Sophie. Why—because Mr Van Wachler said so himself.

Van Weller. Surely you misunderstood him, my good girl.

Sophie. Why so? For my part, I should prefer him to Jonkar Van Bergen. Mr Holm is less merry and cheerful, but then one can see that he has had his troubles. They say he is a prince, who has for some reason or other turned music-master,—but I'm not sure of that.

Van Weller. And Jonkar **Karel?**

Sophie. Jonkar Van Bergen is—but please don't say I said so, sir—I don't think he is to be trusted. This morning, he had been talking to Madame about the young lady and Mr Holm—Madame is very much opposed to the music-master . . .

Van Weller. That I can well believe!

Sophie. Well . . . he put his arm round her neck and kissed her, and when she was **out of** the room he made fun of her, though she had just been calling him "*charmant garçon.*" Later on, I heard him say, "Just as silly as ever! She'll choke with her affection some day!" Now, do you call that a man to be trusted, sir?

Van Weller. No, not exactly. [*Chucks her under the chin.*] But old Buys **now?—how** did you come to think of him?

Sophie. I don't quite understand how it is. I never used to notice **anything.** He is nearly as old as you, sir—and one can't love a **man like that,** can one?

Van Weller (*with a start*). Ah!

Sophie. I mean love like—love as one——

Van Weller. Yes, yes, I understand. I'll make you a present of the explanation.

Sophie. Well—I know nothing about it—but, the other day, when **I went up to her** sitting-room—now don't say I told you, sir!

Van Weller. No, no—just go on.

Sophie. She was sitting on his knee, and he kissed her.

Van Weller. Well, I'm surprised at my niece!

Sophie. Oh! don't think any harm of her, sir! The three lovers is the only thing, and I don't think the worse of her for that! If I were a man, I'd want to **be her lover too,—** I'm sure I would!

Van Weller (*aside*). I think I must be on the track. (*To Sophie.*) Look here, can you hold your tongue?

Sophie. Yes—when I've nothing to say.

Van Weller. When you get home, don't mention having seen me. I have just returned from Java, and want to surprise the family. Give young Mr Karel the key, and say you had it from Frans.

Sophie. But—that would be a story.

Van Weller. Did you never tell a fib in your life?

Sophie (after thinking a while). Only once—when Andries asked me whether . . .

Van Weller. All right, my child. Say whatever you like.

Sophie (coaxingly). Please, sir, if Andries asks for leave——

Van Weller. He shall get it! If I were Andries, and had a sweetheart like you, I should have deserted long ago!

[*Exit Sophie.*

Van Weller (alone). I shall find him—I must find him!—on my soul I *will* find him. [*Starts, as if remembering something.*] That note!—there was something about Huser in it. [*Takes it up and reads.*] "Frans, lock the casket at once,—I forgot it. There are letters from Huser in it that concern us alone. Send me the key." Why is he so anxious to keep these letters secret, as if the existence of the State depended on the publication of a student's correspondence? I left the box open—but it's not honest, Weller! [*Walks up and down, as if in doubt.*] It's not honest. But, Gustaf!—perhaps it will help me to trace him! I *will* read them! [*He goes up to the box, takes out some papers, looks at them, and lays them aside. At last he comes to one which he appears to recognise.*] That's Gustaf's hand. [*Sits down, reads, and seems much disturbed. At last he jumps up.*] Andries! Yes, my presentiment did not deceive me! Oh! my noble boy, where are you? Gustaf! Gustaf! But that scoundrel—that Karel Van Bergen,—who, Heaven mend it! calls himself my nephew. I must see him! He shan't have that girl of my sister's, though she were ten times as much of a coquette, and had twenty lovers instead of three! She would still be **too good** for him! Andries!

Enter FRANS, *intoxicated.*

Frans (sings).

"Mon maître est un filou
Et moi j' n' suis pas bête ... la ... la ..."

Ah! good morning! good morning! *Mon maître est un filou.* Oh, yes! but we've had *circonstances,* splendid *circonstances*—to begin with.

Van Weller. Andries!

Frans. Andries is a good fellow, a downright good fellow **—but just the least bit** *bête.* Never been to Paris, sir? Are you coming to Paris? *Allons mourir pour la patrie.*

[*Approaches the General.*]

Van Weller (*pushes him away roughly, so that Frans falls on the sofa*). Lie there, beast! Andries!

Frans (*muttering*). *Mon maître est un filou* ... [*Falls asleep.*]

Enter ANDRIES.

Van Weller (*stamps his foot*). Where **the devil** have you been all this time, fellow? Get the horses—at once—I must see the king immediately! [*Exit Andries.*] My poor boy shall be righted, or they shall never hear the last of it!

MULTATULI.
(*From* "*The Bride in Heaven.*")

DROOGSTOPPEL INTRODUCES HIMSELF.

I AM a coffee-broker, and live at No. 37 Lauriergracht. It is not my custom to write novels, or any such thing; so it was a long time before I made up my mind to order a couple of reams of paper and begin the work which you, dear reader, have just taken up, and which you ought to read if **you are** in the coffee business,—or, in fact, if **you** are anything else. And not only have I never written anything which was in the least like a novel, but I don't hold with even reading anything of the sort, because I am a man of business. For several years past, I have been asking myself, what is the use of such things? and I am perfectly amazed at the impudence of poets and novelists in palming off upon you things which have never happened, and, for the most part, never can happen. Now, in *my* business,—I am a coffee-broker, and live in the Lauriergracht, No. 37,—if I were to send in to a principal (a principal is a man who sells coffee) an account containing only a small part of the untruths which are the main point in all poems and romances—why, he would at once go to Busselinck & Waterman. (Busselinck & Waterman are coffee-brokers too; but it is not necessary for you to know *their* address.) So I take good care not to write any novels, or send in wrong accounts. I have always noticed that persons who let themselves in for that kind of thing generally get the worst of it. I am forty-three, and have been at the Exchange for twenty years, so that I have every right to put myself forward when a man of experience is in demand. I have seen plenty of firms fail in my time! And usually, when I examined into the causes of their failure, it seemed to me that they must be sought for in the wrong direction given to most people in their youth.

I say, "truth and sound sense!" and that I stick to. The mistake comes in, in the first place, with Van Alphen;[*] and that in his very first line about the "dear little creatures." What on earth could induce this old gentleman to call himself an adorer of my little sister Truitje, who had sore eyes; or of my brother Gerrit, who was always biting his nails? And yet he says that "he sang these verses, compelled by love." I used often to think, when I was a child, "Man,

---

[*] The Dr Watts of Holland.

I *should* like to meet you, just for once—and then, if you refused me the marbles I should ask you for, or the whole of my name in chocolate letters" (my name is Batavus), "then I should consider you a liar." But I never saw Van Alphen. I think he was already dead when he used to tell us that my father was my best friend. I thought far more of Pauweltje Winser, who lived next door to us. And that my little dog was so grateful for kindness! We never kept dogs, because they are dirty.

That is the way children are brought up; and, later on, come other lies again. A girl is an angel! The man who was the first to discover that, never had any sisters of his own. Love is bliss! One is going to fly, with one object or another, to the end of the earth. The earth has no ends; and, besides, love is madness. No one can say that I do not live happily with my wife,—she is a daughter of Last & Co., coffee-brokers. I am a member of *Artis*,*—she has a shawl that cost ninety-two florins,—and yet there was never any question between us of a foolish love like that, which insists on living at the very end of the earth! When we were married, we made a little tour to the Hague, she bought some flannel there, and I am wearing under-vests made of it to this day,—but love never drove us out into the world any farther than that. Thus, it is all madness, and lies together! . . . It is not verses alone that seduce the young into untruthfulness. Just go into the theatre, and listen to the falsehoods that are being spread abroad there! The hero of the play is pulled out of the water by some fellow on the point of going into the bankruptcy

---

* A society at Amsterdam, which, besides fulfilling the usual functions of a club, holds picture exhibitions and gives concerts, and founded the zoological gardens in that city (hence often referred to as "Artis," *tout court*), to which its members have free right of entry. Membership in "Artis," as implied in the text, is a trustworthy guarantee of respectability.

court. Then he gives the fellow half his fortune. That cannot happen! Not long ago, when my hat was blown into the Prinsengracht I gave the man who brought it back to me twopence, and he was quite satisfied. Of course, I know I should have had to give something more if it had been myself that he pulled out, but certainly not half what I possess. Why, it is quite clear that, on this principle, one need only fall into the water twice to be ruined! But the worst of it is, with such things represented on the stage, the public gets so accustomed to all these falsehoods, that it thinks them fine, and applauds them. I should just like to throw a whole pit full of such people into the water, and see whose applause was sincere. I, who hold by the truth, warn every one that I am not going to pay so high a salvage for the fishing up of my person. Any one who is not satisfied with less, may just let me stay where I am. On a Sunday, however, I should pay rather more, because then I wear my gold watch-chain, and my best coat.

Yes! the stage ruins many—still more than the novels. It looks so well! With a little gold tinsel and paper lace, things can be made so attractive. For children, that is to say; and for people who are not in business. Even when they want to represent poverty on the stage, the picture given is always a false one. A girl, whose father has gone bankrupt, is working to keep the family. Very good! There she sits, then, sewing, knitting, or embroidering. But just count the stitches that she takes in the course of the whole scene. She talks, she sighs,—she keeps running to the window,—but she does not work. The family who can live on such work as this, must have few wants indeed! Of course a girl like this is the heroine. She has thrown several villains down the stairs. She continually calls out, "Oh! my mother! my mother!" and thus represents virtue. What sort of a virtue do you call that, that takes a year to finish a pair of woollen socks? Does not all this

"AND HE WAS QUITE SATISFIED."

give people wrong ideas about virtue and working for their living?

Then her first lover — he was formerly a clerk at the copying-book, but now a millionaire—suddenly comes back and marries her. Lies again. A man with money will never marry a girl from a house that has failed. . . . And then—virtue rewarded! I have had plenty of experience in my time; but still it shocks me terribly when I see truth perverted in this way. Virtue rewarded! Isn't it just like making a traffic out of virtue? It is not so in this world, and a very good thing it is that it is not. Where is the merit of being virtuous, if virtue is to be rewarded? Now, I am as virtuous as most people, but do I expect to be rewarded for it? If my business goes on well,—which, in fact, it does;—if my wife and children keep in health, so that I have no worry with the doctor and chemist;—if, year by year, I can put away a little sum for my old age . . . ;—if Fritz grows up a good man of business, so that he can step into my shoes when I retire and go to live at Driebergen, . . .—well, if all these things are so, I am quite content. But all that is a natural result of circumstances, and of my attention to business. I don't ask for any special reward for my virtue.

That I am virtuous, is quite evident from my love for truth. This—next to my attachment to our orthodox belief—is my ruling passion. And I should like the reader to be quite convinced of this, because it is my excuse for writing this book.

A second passion, which rules me quite as much, is my devotion to my business. And it is these two which have caused me to write this book. I am now going to explain how this happened.

MULTATULI.
(*From "Max Havelaar."*)

DROOGSTOPPEL **PAYS A** *CHARITABLE VISIT.*

Droogstoppel had undertaken to publish a volume selected from the MSS. of his old schoolfellow Havelaar—*alias* "Sjaalman,"—who had returned from the Indies in great poverty. He was preparing it for the press with the help of his son Fritz and his German clerk Stern. He soon found that the work involved difficulties.

BESIDES the difficulty of selecting and arranging what **was necessary** out of such a mass of **materials, there** were **constantly** occurring **in** the MSS. words and expressions which **Stern could** not understand, **and** which were new even to **me.** They were mostly **Javanese or** Malay. Moreover, **many** abbreviations were used, **which** were difficult **to decipher.** I saw that we needed Sjaalman, and as **I do not** think it **good for** a **young man to pick** up undesirable acquaintances, I was **unwilling to send either** Stern or Fritz. I took with me some **sweets that** had **remained over** from our last party,—for I am always one **to think of things like** that,—and **I set** out to look for his abode. **It was not a very** brilliant one,—but there is no such thing as equality among people, so how can **they** all expect **to live in the same** sort of houses? He says something of the same kind himself in **his** essay on "Claims to Happiness." Besides, I don't think anything of people who are always discontented.

It was in the Langeleidsche Dwarsstraat, in a back-room upstairs. The ground-floor was occupied by a second-hand **dealer,** who sold all **sorts** of things—cups and saucers, furniture, old books, glass, pictures **by Van** Speyk, and I don't know **what else. I was terribly** afraid of breaking something; for in such a case **the** people always charge **you** more than the things are worth. A little girl was sitting **on** the steps, dressing her doll. I asked her whether Mr Sjaalman lived **there.** She ran away, and presently her mother came.

"A SECOND-HAND DEALER, WHO SOLD ALL SORTS OF THINGS."

"Yes, he lives here, sir. Just you go upstairs to the first door, and then up the next floor to the next door, and then another flight of stairs, and then you can't miss it. Mijntje, just run up and say there's a gentleman. Who shall I say is asking for them, sir?"

I told her I was Mijnheer Droogstoppel, coffee-broker in the Lauriergracht, but that I would announce myself. I climbed up as high as they had told me, and heard a child's voice singing inside the door on the third floor. I knocked, and the door was opened by a woman—or a lady. I really did not quite know what to make of her; she looked very pale, and tired, and the look in her face made me think of my wife on washing-day. She was dressed in a long white shirt or jacket, without a waist, that hung down to her knees, and was fastened in front with a black pin. Under this, instead of a proper skirt or petticoat, she wore a piece of dark flowered linen, wound round her several times, and rather tight at hips and knees. There was no trace of folds, width, or fulness, such as there ought to be in any decent woman's dress. I was glad I had not sent Fritz, for I thought her costume very indelicate; and what made it still stranger was the case with which she moved—as if she felt quite comfortable like that. The creature seemed quite unconscious that she did not look like other women. Moreover, she did not seem in the least embarrassed at my coming. She hid nothing under the table, and did not push the chairs about, or do any of the things you always see people do when a respectably dressed stranger comes in.

She had her hair combed back like a Chinese, and fastened behind her head in a sort of twist or knot. I have heard since that her dress was a sort of Indian costume, which they call *sarong* and *kaabai* out there, but I thought the whole thing very ugly.

"Are you Juffrouw Sjaalman?" I asked.

"Whom have I the honour of speaking to?" she said, in

"A LONG WHITE SHIRT OR JACKET."

a tone that seemed to convey that I ought to have said something about *honour* too.

Well—I don't hold with compliments. A principal is a different matter, and I have been in business long enough to know what I am about; but I didn't think it necessary to use much ceremony in a third-floor back. So I said, without more ado, that I was Mijnheer Droogstoppel, coffee-broker, Lauriergracht, No. 37, and I wanted to see her husband. Well—and why should I have made any more fuss about it?

She offered me a rush-bottomed chair, and took a little girl on her lap, who was sitting on the ground playing. The little boy, whom I had heard singing, looked full at me, and stared at me from top to toe. He, too, did not seem in the least embarrassed. He was a little chap of about six, as queerly dressed as his mother. He had on a wide pair of knickerbockers that did not come down to the knees; and his legs were bare from there to the ankle. Very indecent, I think. "Have you come to talk to papa?" he asked, in a way which showed me at once that his upbringing was not at all what it ought to be. But because I did not quite know what attitude to take up, and also wanted to talk a little, I answered, "Yes, my little fellow, I want to talk to your papa. Do you think he will be coming in soon?"

"I don't know; he's gone out to look for some money to buy me a paint-box."

"Hush, my boy," said the woman. "Play with the pictures a little, or with your Chinese puzzle-box."

"Why, you know the gentleman came and took all the things away yesterday."

So that was the way he spoke to his mother—h'm! . . . and there had been "a gentleman," it appeared, to "take everything away." . . . Cheerful visit, this! The woman, too, did not look in good spirits; she turned away and wiped her eyes, when she thought I could not see her, as she put the little girl down on the floor beside her brother. "There," she said, "now play with Nonnie a little." An extraordinary name for a child.

"Well, Juffrouw," I asked, "do you expect your husband in soon?"

"I cannot say for certain," she answered.

At this the little boy suddenly left his sister, came up to me, and asked,

"Sir, why do you call mamma Juffrouw?"*

"Why, what then, youngster?" said I, "what ought I to say?"

"Why . . . just like other people. The Juffrouw lives downstairs—she sells saucers and tops."

Well—I am a coffee-broker—Last & Co., Lauriergracht, 37—there are thirteen of us in the counting-house, and, if you count Stern, who gets no salary, fourteen. And yet my wife is simply called *Juffrouw;* and does any one expect me to go and say *Mevrouw* to *that* person? Certainly not. Every one ought to keep his place; and what's more, the sheriff's officers had been there the day before, and taken away the furniture. So I thought it quite the proper thing to say *Juffrouw,* and stuck to it.

I asked why Sjaalman has not come to my house to fetch back his parcel. She seemed to know all about it, and said that they had been away—at Brussels. He had been writing for the *Indépendance* there, but had been obliged to give it up, because the paper had so often been refused admission into France on account of his articles. They had returned to Amsterdam a few days since, because Sjaalman had heard of a situation there.

"At Gaafzuiger's, I suppose?"

Yes, that was the name. But it had come to nothing,

---

* The hierarchy of Dutch etiquette is as follows, beginning from above :—*Mevrouw, Joffrouw, Vrouw.*

after all, she said. Well, I knew more about that than she did. He had dropped the bound volume of *Aglaia*, and he was lazy, pedantic, and in bad health ... just so; that was why they discharged him.

She added that he meant to come and see me one of these days,—perhaps he was even now on his way to my house,—to ask me for an answer to the request he had made to me.

I said that he could come when it suited him, but that he was not to ring the bell, because that gives the servant so much trouble. If he waited a little, I told her, some one would be sure to come out sooner or later, and he could go in then. And then I departed, taking my sweets with me, for, to tell the truth, I didn't like the look of things at all. I did not feel at my ease there. Why, a coffee-broker is not a crossing-sweeper, or a street-porter, I should think; and I am sure I look respectable enough. I had on my fur-lined overcoat, and yet she sat there as calmly, and talked as unconcernedly to her children, as if she had been alone. Besides, she seemed to have been crying, and if there is anything I cannot put up with, it is discontented people. Besides, it was chilly and unsociable in the place,—I suppose, because the furniture had been taken,—and I like a room to look cosy and comfortable. As I was going home, I thought I would try and keep on my old clerk Bastiaans a little longer,—because, after all, I don't like turning a man into the street.

MULTATULI.

(*From* "*Max Havelaar.*")

APHORISMS.

I think so much of Heine that I am glad I never met him.

Two people are never at the same moment equally angry with one another.

The assertion that we prefer other work than that given us to do, frequently implies a dislike to any work whatever.

Two left-hand gloves do not make a pair. Two half truths do not necessarily constitute a truth.

A horseman once fell from his horse, and since then every one who is thrown calls himself a good rider.

Every one has thoughts. Only with a few persons does the *thought* become an *idéa*. Still fewer are those who know how to reproduce the form and colour of their ideas. And to those who do, people continually say, "Just what I was thinking!" Just so—except for the outline—except for the colour—except for the light and shade. That is—except for a great deal.

He who has gone farthest astray is best able to find the right road. I do not say that much straying is necessary to know the way. Nor yet that every one who has gone astray knows it.

When a swift runner breaks his leg, the crawlers have a *bal paré*.

"TWO PEOPLE ARE NEVER AT THE SAME MOMENT EQUALLY ANGRY WITH ONE ANOTHER."

TAKE one piece of advice. Don't be advised by any one.

BETWEEN soul and speech lies the length of a trumpet. I think—I almost believe—that few trumpets are as short as the Dutch.

IN the hospital at Amsterdam a sailor was to have his leg amputated. The professor—I mean Tilanus—took it off for him. The man calmly smoked his pipe, clenched his teeth now and then, but kept the upper hand of the pain.

Professor T. admired his spirit, and spoke in praise of it while he was putting on the bandages.

Suddenly the courageous patient gave a yell. The Professor had pricked him with a pin.

"How! *you* calling out like this? You, who just now——"

"That's true; but look here, Professor, *the pin was not in the bargain!*"

The sailor was right.

PROFESSOR Z. was a friend of Apothecary Y.'s. He invited him to tea one day by means of a note, which got lost.

The note was picked up by a man who knew the signature, and deciphered the rest. He read it as a prescription for convulsions in cattle.

Moral: Not a day passes but the public surprises me with a reading of my writings which is still wilder than the interpretation of Professor Z.'s note.

MULTATULI.

OF SELF-DEPRECIATION.

Now I **am going** to tell you **how** humility came into the world.

Pygmee was small of stature, and liked looking over other people's heads. In which he was seldom successful, because he was so **very** small.

He went on a journey to look for people smaller than himself, but he could not find them. And his longing to look down on them became more and more intolerable.

At last he came to Patagonia, where people are so tall that even the children just born look **down on their fathers**.

Pygmee did **not** like this—in **other** people. But in his despair of finding any **smaller than himself, he** bethought himself of **a** plan. He invented a virtue, which proclaimed **as its** first principle, "*Whosoever is taller than Pygmee must stoop till he comes within Pygmee's line of **vision**,*"—and the novelty made **its way**. All the Patagonians became virtuous. When any one, by walking upright, sinned against the "first principles" of Pygmee's virtue, he was punished in **a** peculiar way. Every **one** who was bowed down and virtuous jumped up and caught him round the neck till his head reached the level of Patagonian **good** conduct. And the **man** who was strong enough to carry all Patagonia on his shoulders, without becoming virtuous, was set in the pillory, **with** a collar round his neck, and a word inscribed thereon **in** the Patagonian tongue, which, being literally translated, signifies—

"THIS **MAN** MADE HIMSELF **OBNOXIOUS TO PYGMEE**."

People have tacitly agreed, however, **to** express it in our language by—"*Pride*."

MULTATULI.

OF EDUCATION, WITH PRACTICAL ILLUSTRATIONS.

... I am positively forced to tell you that I think Dominie Pennewip's lot might have been counted an extenuating circumstance had he been convicted of eight deadly sins at once.

I have noticed that a considerable number of great men began their careers as swineherds (see all biographical dictionaries); and it seems, therefore, as if this employment called out the elements of all the qualities needed to govern men—or to enlighten them. Which is not quite the same thing. ...

... As for comparing human beings and pigs, let the reader remember the connection between coal and diamonds, and every one will be satisfied—even the theologians!

But, since making this observation on the splendid prospects which await any one who has spent his tender youth in the society of the grunting coal-diamonds of the animal kingdom, I have several times thought it strange that, in the biographies of great men, there should be so few examples of ex-schoolmasters. For, after all, all the elements which seem to constitute a pig-pasture the nursery of genius are abundantly present in the schoolroom.

The reverse process frequently occurs. Every day we see exiled princes giving instruction to idle youth. Dionysius and Louis Philippe are not the only ones; and I myself have attempted to teach French to an American. Which proved impossible.

If elective monarchies should come into fashion again, I should like to see the people's choice confine itself, by preference, to persons who had studied mankind from models in miniature, just as one learns geography from portable globes and atlases. All virtues, inclinations, passions, errors, misdeeds,—all points which have to be studied in human society,—are found in a small and comprehensive scale on the benches of the school; and the boasted diplomacy of many a statesman only amounts, when looked at carefully, to the tricks of which our Machiavels of three feet high **make** the warp and woof of their tactics.

The schoolmaster's profession is not an easy one; and I have never understood why it is so poorly paid, or, since it seems that this is an inexorable law of nature, how it is that people are always found to fill it, instead of drawing the same pay as drill-instructors, and showing soldiers **how to** load their guns, which is less perplexing to the mind, and gives you more fresh air, with oxygen in it.

Or else, I should prefer to be a minister. For **the latter has to do** with people **who are** quite **at one with** him **as to the matter** in hand, **and come and** listen **to him of their** own free choice; while the teacher has to keep up a constant fight with reluctance on the part of the pupils, and also with a highly dangerous set of rivals, in the shape of tops, marbles, and paper dolls—not to mention sweets, changing teeth, scarlet fever, and weak mothers.

Pennewip **was a** man of the old school,—at **least so** he would appear to us if we saw him now-a-days, in his grey coat, long waistcoat, and knee-breeches with buckles, the whole figure crowned with a brown wig, which he was constantly pushing hither and thither, and which was always curled just so at the beginning of the week—if there was no rain in the air. For curls cannot stand damp; and it was on Sundays that the **man came** with the curling-tongs.

Yet the *old-fashionedness* is, perhaps, only relative. Who knows whether it was not counted new-fangled in its day; or how soon the same thing may be said of us. However that may be, the man was addressed as "*meester*," and his school was called a *school*, and not an *institution*. In his school, where, according to the simple fashion of the time, boys and girls sat side by side, you learned—or you could learn, if so minded—reading, arithmetic, writing, the history of your own country, psalm-singing, wool-work, knitting, marking, and religion. All this was in the ordinary curriculum; but any pupil who particularly distinguished him or herself by talent, application, or obedience, received, over and above, lessons in verse-making,—an art wherein the soul of Dominie Pennewip greatly delighted. He "finished" the boys to the point of complete fitness for "acceptance";* and, with the help of his wife, brought the girls the length of a sampler, with a red text on a black ground, or a spitted heart between two flowerpots. Then their education was complete, and they were quite fit, if so minded, to become the grandmothers of our present generation of citizens.

The school was empty, and the forms looked as though the pupils had left all their weariness behind them there. The map of Europe looked ill-temperedly down on the pile of copy-books, next to which lay the quill pens, worn down to the gums, so to speak, in the pot-hooks and hangers which have opened the gate of access to all learning so long that the memory of man goeth not to the contrary. The difficult sum in fractions was still visible, in all its glory, on the blackboard; but yet, the school was no school; its spirit had fled—it was a corpse.

Yes, the informing mind had departed with the children. For that these carried about with them a large quantity of the above article shall speedily be made evident.

It was the great day on which Dominie Pennewip was to judge of the fruits of his pupils' poetic genius. There he sat. His much-moved wig shared in the emotions which

---

* *I.e.*, confirmation.

filled him on reading the poems; and we will be indiscreet enough to look over his shoulder, so as, in our turn, to be touched by impressions of never-sufficiently-to-be-appreciated artistic enjoyment.

Wig to the right, and at rest.

TRYNTJE FOP, ON HER CAP.

"My name is Tryntje Fop,
I have a cap on my head atop."

"Not bad; but—let us see—yes, that is better. The superfluous words, 'on my head,' weaken the impression of the whole."

He scored through the superfluous words, and now Tryntje Fop has simply a cap on, without a head.

"This is the sort of terse and concise style I like."

Wig somewhat to the left.

LUCAS DE BRYER, ON OUR COUNTRY.

"Fatherland, cake, and almonds also,
In the moonlight I a-walking go;
Cake, Fatherland, and brandy-wine,
I go a-walking in the moonshine.
Five fingers have I upon my hand,
In honour of our dear Fatherland."

"Melodious," said the master; "it runs quite melodiously. And there is depth in the cake and the brandy, with the Fatherland in between them."

Wig to the right.

LYSJE WEBBELAAR, ON HER FATHER'S TRADE.

"The cat fell downstairs to-day;
My father, he sells pota-
Toes and onions."

"Original; but I do not like her dividing the word potatoes."

Wig to the left.

Jannetje Rast, on a Weathercock.

"He stands on a chimney, all soot below,
And shows the wind the way it must blow."

"This is not quite accurate; for, strictly speaking———, but, as a poetical license, it may pass."

Wig to the front.

Grietje Wanzer, on a Caterpillar.

"The little caterpillar, without fear,
Jumps round upon the trees, both far and near."

"Descriptive poetry. There is a certain boldness in the idea of the caterpillar fearlessly jumping about."

Wig at rest.

Leendert Snelleman, on Spring.

"In the spring all is bright and gay;
My brother's birthday is in May;
But now he has chilblains on his feet.
So we'll praise the spring, as it is meet.
Then we'll go for walks together,
And look for eggs at Easter."

"It is a pity that the rhyme is so very careless. His ideas are really uncommon, and well developed. The transition to the egg is quite characteristic."

Wig pushed down to the back of his neck.

Keesje, the Butcher's Son—Eulogy of the Dominie.

"My father has killed many an ox with his knife,
But Master Pennewip is still in life.
Sometimes they were lean, and sometimes fat,
And he wears a wig underneath his hat."

The wig was pushed to one side—very far to one side.

"H'm—strange—what shall I say about it?"

The wig went back again to the extreme right.

"What have I got to do with the oxen?"

The wig protested, with some impressive movements, against all such bovine relationships.

"WIG PUSHED DOWN TO THE BACK OF HIS NECK"

"H'm—could that be what these new-fangled writers call *humour*?"

The wig was drawn forward to Dominie Pennewip's eyebrows, which denotes doubt.*

"I must take that boy in hand one of these days."

The wig came to anchor on the zenith, by way of expressing its satisfaction at the Dominie's intention of taking Butcher's Keesje seriously in hand.

LUCAS DE WILDE, ON RELIGION.

> "Religion's a good thing indeed,
> Of which all people have great need."

"The fundamental idea is correct and beautiful," said Pennewip, "but it ought to have been further developed."

The wig nodded assent.

TRUITJE GIER, ON MRS PENNEWIP.

> "The path of virtue she does show,—
> Who would not gladly with her go?
> And at odd moments, as is fit,
> She teaches us to darn and knit."

The wig gave a leap of joy, and its curls embraced one another. The master could not refrain from calling his wife to share in the enjoyment of Truitje Gier's effusion, which was pasted on a piece of cardboard, and hung up above the mantelpiece in honour both of the poetess and her subject. . . .

LOUWTJE DE WILDE, ON FRIENDSHIP.

> "Friendship is a good thing indeed,
> Of which all people have great need."

The wig did not appear quite satisfied. Lucas de Wilde's

---

* Erroneously so. For, even though this is *not* humour, it is quite true that jokes of this sort are given out as such; and Master Pennewip's question can only have referred to this. The wig's doubts are therefore unfounded, and I would recommend to it the attentive perusal of Professor Oosterzee's treatise, "De Sceptici mo caute Vitando."

"Religion" was brought to light, and placed for comparison beside Louwtje's "Friendship."

"H'm ... well ... it might be possible. Instances do occur of the same idea springing up simultaneously in two different minds. ... It might ... or could ... be so ..."

WIMPJE DE WILDE, ON ANGLING.
"Angling is ..."

"How! What is that?"
Yes, indeed! there it was—

> "Angling is a good thing indeed,
> Of which all people have great need."

The wig was in perpetual motion; it seemed as though it too were taking part in the angling operations.

Master Pennewip hastily turned over the papers he had not yet examined, sorted out the productions of the whole Wilde family, and ... yes, indeed! Mietje de Wilde, Kees de Wilde, Piet and Jan de Wilde, declared, with touching unanimity, that religion, friendship, fishing, dreaming, cauliflower, and conjuring are good things indeed, of which all people have great need. It was an overwhelming flood of good things and human need!

What was an honest wig to do? It did the best thing that could be done under the circumstances, and more cannot be required of any one. After perceiving the fruitlessness of its efforts to find out any difference between fishing and friendship, conjuring and dreaming, cauliflower and religion, it behaved as though the matter did not concern it in the least, and assumed a neutral position, with an air, on the part of its little curls, of looking forward with interest to the sequel—as the reader is no doubt doing.

"ANGLING IS A GOOD THING INDEED."

LEENTJE DE HAAS, ON ADMIRAL DE RUYTER.

"He climbed to the top of a tower,
    And twisted ropes on the same;
Then he went to sea in a vessel,
    And was crowned with eternal fame.

"He did great **deeds** and glorious,
    And overthrew Sallee;
The States named him victorious,
    Our hero **of the sea.**

"Then to marauding England
    He went in wrath so dire,
The same he, most intrepid,
    Besieged and set on fire.

"How many Christian captives
    He freed from slavery's chains!
Then Netherland's valiant warriors
    Broke all his window-panes.

"For terror of all traitors
    What time he sailed the sea,
His title it was '**Daddy**'—
    His wife was 'Granny,' she!

"**He** gave the Lord the **glory,**
    A Christian life he **led,**—
Then got he through his garments
    A bullet, and was dead!"

The wig clapped **its** curls applaudingly. It seemed delighted. Alas! the joy **of such a wig does not last long.** This, too, was soon to—— **But we will not anticipate.** . . . We shall know only too **soon.**

"WOUTER PIETERSE—THE SONG OF THE BRIGAND."

"Hey! **What's this?** And Virtue—where is Virtue?"
Dominie **Pennewip** could **not** trust **his own eyes.** He

"ADMIRAL DE RUYTER."

turned the sheet over and looked at the back, to see if the Virtue he had given Wouter as a subject was hidden there.

Alas, alas! there was no trace of virtue in Wouter's composition.

Poor wig!

Yes—poor **wig!** For after having made it to undergo what no wig ever underwent before,—after having tugged, plucked, ill-used, and tormented it to an extent which would have taken more than the imagination of the whole De Wilde family to conceive,—Dominie Pennewip tore it from his head, doubled it up between his convulsively clenched hands,—stammered, "Heaven and earth! Gracious goodness! where in nature did he pick that up?"—banged it down on his head again, clapped his venerable three-cornered hat atop of it, and flew out of the front door like a man possessed. He went straight to the Pieterses' house.

Juffrouw Pieterse, Wouter's mother, had been entertaining a few of her friends and neighbours at a "little evening," with tea and cake.

"Good evening, Juffrouw Pieterse; I am your obedient servant. I see you have company,—but——"

"Don't mention it, sir! Just come in and sit down! . . . Will you take a cup with us—sage-milk?"

"Juffrouw Pieterse," replied the master, solemnly, "I did not come here to drink sage-milk!"

"But please sit down, Dominie——"

It was not easy, under the circumstances, but the ladies shifted their chairs a little, and the Dominie was finally installed in his. He was coughing with overwhelming seriousness. He looked round on the company, drew out a roll of papers, pulled his wig to one side, and spoke:

"Juffrouw Pieterse! you are an honest, respectable woman,—and your late husband—sold shoes——"

Juffrouw Pieterse cast on Juffrouw Laps a glance of vindictive triumph.

"Yes, sir, he did!"

"Don't interrupt me, Juffrouw Pieterse. Your deceased consort sold shoes. I have had your children at my school, from the time when they were *so* high, to their confirmation. Is not that true, Juffrouw Pieterse?"

"Yes, sir," she replied, somewhat uneasily, for she began to be frightened at the impressive solemnity of Pennewip's tone. "Yes, that's true, Dominie!"

"And I ask you, Juffrouw Pieterse, whether you, so long as you, through the means of your children, have had anything to do with my school, have had any complaints—I mean, well-founded complaints, Juffrouw Pieterse—to make of the way in which I—with the help of my wife—have given your numerous offspring instruction in reading, writing, arithmetic, Dutch history, psalm-singing, sewing, knitting, marking, and religion? That is what I ask you, Juffrouw Pieterse."

A ghastly silence. The neighbour in the back-room downstairs, who had repeatedly complained of the noise during the evening, had every reason to be satisfied.

"That is what I ask you, Juffrouw Pieterse," repeated the Dominie, putting on the *pince-nez*, which was considered antiquated in those days—destined, as it was, to become the height of fashion some decades later.

"But, Dominie——"

"No buts, Juffrouw Pieterse. I ask of you—or I ask you,—for it is quite allowable, Juffrouw Pieterse, in this case, to omit the preposition,—I ask you if you have any complaints to make—I mean, of course, well-founded complaints—of the instruction given by me in reading, writing——"

"Goodness, no, Dominie!—I have no complaints; but——"

"Is that so? No complaints? Well, then, I declare to you—— Where is your son Wouter?"

"Wouter? **Why—oh**! he went out, so he did! Hasn't he come in yet, Trui? Wouter is out **for a** walk, Dominie, with the little Hallemans—very nicely-behaved children, Dominie,—and they live——"

"Eh! what?—with **the** Hallemans, **is** he?—the Hallemans who go to the French school? **oh!** indeed—yes! So it's from the Hallemans he learns such things—it must be—— . . . loose morals . . . utter depravity . . . the French school . . ! Well, in short, Juffrouw Pieterse,—I say that your son——"

"Eh?"

"I tell you that **your** son Wouter——"

"Well—what **has Wouter** been **doing now?**" asked Juffrouw Laps, rejoiced, pious person **that she was, at the** new misdeed she was to hear of.

Just as Pennewip was about to open the indictment, there was another ring at the bell,—and the unfortunate delinquent entered the room.

"Juffrouw Pieterse," Pennewip began, "my school is known as a good school even so far off as Kattenburg *—do you hear that, and understand it?"

"Oh yes, Dominie!"

"I repeat it,—well known; and more especially so **on account of the** good moral tone which prevails there,—I mean, of course, in my school. Religion and virtue **are** put foremost. I could show you verses on **such** subjects that—but I will pass over that for the present. Let it suffice you **to** know that my school is known as far as . . . what do I say?—I have even taught the son **of a** resident in Wittenburg,*—a block-maker he was—and once, indeed, I was consulted in writing **as to** what was to be done with a boy whose father lived no nearer than Muiderberg!"

"Very good, Dominie!"

---

* **Two** outlying districts of Amsterdam.

"Yes, Juffrouw Pieterse! I am still in possession of the letter—which I could show you if I chose; the man was a sexton, and the youth had fallen into a sad habit of drawing unseemly figures on the tombstones—but just on that account—I mean for the sake of the religion and virtue for which I am so well known—I feel it my duty to take this opportunity of informing you that I do not choose to see the good name of my school ruined by means of that good-for-nothing rascal of a son of yours, who stands there!"

Poor Wouter was aghast. That sounded very unlike the appointment he had been dreaming of—brigand-in-chief to the Pope of Rome,—which, however, he no longer desired, having thought of a different position which would suit him better.

His mother was about to proceed to what she called "*her* religion," and administer chastisement on the spot, in order to satisfy the Dominie, and show him that, in her house, too, religion and sound morals had the first place. But the schoolmaster thought it better to inform the company what was toward, and thereby bring the culprit to a deeper sense of his delinquencies.

"Your son, Juffrouw Pieterse, belongs to the class of robbers, murderers, and fire-raisers!" . . .

No more than that!

"Gracious goodness! Merciful justice! What next! Oh! my gracious patience! how is it possible? What human beings have to endure!" Something like this—for I will not answer for textual accuracy—was the flood of exclamations which overwhelmed the ten-year-old robber, murderer, and fire-raiser. Poor Wouter!

"I will read you a piece in his own handwriting," said the Dominie, "and any one who, after this, can still doubt the utter depravity of this boy——"

The whole company promised with one voice not to doubt it. The poem, indeed, which Master Pennewip thereupon proceeded to read, **was of a kind** which rendered doubt on that head **very** difficult ; **and I** myself, though I have chosen **Wouter as my hero,** shall not find it easy **to** convince the reader that he was not so bad as would **appear** from his atrocious—

SONG OF THE BRIGAND.

"With my sword—
On my steed—
And my helmet on head,
Ride at **them !** The foeman's skull **cloven in twain,—**
And forward !—"

"Christian souls!" cried the whole company, "is he mad?"

" And forward !—
And never draw rein
Along **the high-road,**
The brigand's abode,—
With a thrust and a blow ;
Drive back the Dragoons—the Viscount's laid low !" . . .

"**Dear** heavens **above** us!" moaned Wouter's mother, "**what in the** world **has this** Viscount done to him?"

" For the spoil "—

" Look at **that now,**—for the spoil !" said Juffrouw Laps, " *I* always say,—they begin with a **Bible,** and then———"

"And the spoil
Is my bride."

" Did ever any one hear the like ?—his bride ! Why, the boy's only just cutting his second set of teeth !"

"And the spoil
Is my bride,
Bought for mine own with the **sword at my side**———"

" With **the sword at his side !!**"

"And the spoil **is** my bride,
Bought for **mine** own with the sword **at my side.**
Like a feather I bear her right into the **hall,**
To the grotto———"

"Gracious patience! what does he want in a grotto?"

> "As swift as the wind
> I ride on with my prey,—
> And I heed not her weeping—her groans are my joy,
> What delight!——"

"Mercy on us! does he call that delight? It makes me go cold all over!"

> "Then again
> Up and down,
> East and west through the land!"

"There he goes again!"

> "Then again
> Up and down,
> East and west through the land,
> Here a villa to raze—there a convent ablaze—
> With rifling of treasure:
> My pleasure!——"

"The devil must be in the boy . . . his pleasure!"

> "And then we are gone!—
> Ride on! ever on,
> New adventures to seek—
> My path it is marked by the steel and the fire—
> On, on, ever on, let me hasten—nor tire,
> My vengeance to wreak!"

"Gracious goodness! what can they have done to him?"

> "For revenge is the task
> He would ask—
> The king of the wood——"

"Is the boy mad? I'll king him!"

> "For revenge is the task
> He would ask—
> The king of the wood—
> Who alone, against all, his sceptre holds good——"

"What sort of a thing is that?"

> "Who alone, against all, his sceptre holds good,
> And his banner of might!—
> Up! Hurrah!
> Who will come to the fight?"

The company shuddered **audibly at this invitation.**

"Up! Hurrah!
Who will come to the fight?
We will spare no creature **that ever was born—**
Now we'll hang all the men——"

"*Lodderyn!** **Trui!** you see I——"

"We'll hang all the men, and the **women**——"

"Lodderyn! lodderyn! lodderyn! **Trui!**"

"And the women **shall mourn,**
For our joy and delight!"

"Our **joy and delight!**" repeated **Pennewip** in a sepulchral voice,—" our joy and delight! ... He ... does ... these ... things ... for ... his ... delight!".

The whole company was near swooning. Stoffel's **pipe** had gone out. But Wouter had a sort of passive strength in his nature; and when his mother had thrashed him enough to **secure** her own **return to** consciousness, he lay down, not altogether discontented, in his corner of the back room, and soon fell asleep, **to dream of Fancy.**

MULTATULI.
(*Ideen.*)

---

* "*L'eau de reine,*" *i.e.*, "eau de **la reine de** Hongrie," known in England as "Hungary water," a fashionable perfume and restorative when eau de Cologne as **yet** was not. Dutch ladies used to take it to church with them instead of smelling-salts. Juffrouw Pieterse's version of the word is pronounced as spelt, the *y* being long like that in the English **word *my.***

GOING INTO BUSINESS.

The plan of "going into business" was quite attractive to Wouter. Perhaps because he did not quite know what it meant. He asked his brother Stoffel about it.

"Well — don't you understand *that?* 'In business' means the same thing as — as being a merchant."

"But what shall I have to sell? And how shall I know what people want?"

"Oh, you must not imagine that you will have to go about with a peddler's pack, and ring at people's front doors to know if they want to buy anything. You're a stupid; you never will understand anything. 'In business,' you see, means — it means——"

Stoffel began to stammer. He was not the first to stumble over a definition — and will not be the last. But there are few who, in such a case, have an ally at home to help them out.

"How can you always talk such nonsense, Wouter?" cried his mother. "There's Stoffel, now, explaining everything to you so clearly, and there you are again making out you don't understand. Who in the world ever told you that you would have to go about the street with a pack on your back, like an oilman or a *mersan de la perreplu?* * Is that what I have brought you up for, and made you take the highest place in the school? You are an ungrateful child. What is the good of your knowing so much, and being able to make such fine letters, with curls and flourishes to them, if you must insult your own mother?"

Readers who care anything for justice, will find it strange,

---

* Intended for "marchand de parapluies." The words in the above form were the refrain of a favourite Amsterdam street song some seventy years since.

and perhaps unfair, that Wouter should have been overwhelmed with this flood of reproach. Unfair? Certainly! But—strange? Why, no! I solemnly affirm my accuracy in depicting a certain manner of carrying on a controversy, of which Juffrouw Pieterse was unquestionably mistress.

But now, supposing Wouter had, in all humility, remarked that he had given no occasion for the above sermon? Well, in that case he would have been overwhelmed with a second lecture on the far-reaching and infamous wickedness of being in the right, which, indeed, under certain circumstances, *is* a fault—and a bad one. MULTATULI.

(*Ideen.*)

TWO PARABLES.

A PROFESSOR of Ichthyology was delivering his lecture. The students were listening—well, pretty attentively as students go—not to mention students of *Ichthyology.*

"The carp, gentlemen, the carp——"

Then followed some facts about the carp.

"Now the carp, gentlemen, as I was saying——"

At that moment a carp came swimming into the lecture-room. How the beast did it, considering how dry it was there, does not concern us. The poor students had suffered from drought for ever so long,—and, after all, a carp is no better than a student.

"There he is himself!" they cried, with one voice.

So they left the professor in the lurch with his lecture on the carp, and went to look at the carp for themselves. Now I think this quite right and natural on the part of the students. But I wish we could do the same, and try to look at men—and women too—for ourselves, instead of listening to somebody's dicta about Man! MULTATULI.

(*Ideen.*)

"AM I NOT JUST LIKE PLATO?"

THERSITES AND PLATO.

PLATO once had a bad cold—so bad that it was evident to every one. Thersites imitated his way of coughing, and said:

"Am I not just like Plato?"

However, this was not the worst—any man is free to ask a question. The worst of it was that thousands upon thousands of people immediately replied, "Just so. Hurrah for Thersites, the new philosopher!"

The man founded a school on the spot. And, therefore: *Cave, caveto, caveto, cavete, cavetote, caveunto!*

MULTATULI.
(*Ideen.*)

EGOTISM.

"You talk a great deal about yourself," say many who never get talked about, either by themselves or other people. "This is against the tone of good society."

"I advise you to seek better society than mine."

"You talk a great deal about yourself——"

"Yes. Would you prefer me to speak of you, . . . or your cat, . . . or your dog, . . . or your ass?"

Do you wish that? Well, content yourself, I have often done so, but you did not know it at the time, because you are always confusing yourself with your neighbour's donkey. Your neighbour has also been complaining; he says that I have been all the time talking about *your* donkeys. Compensation! The donkeys themselves have never complained, the good, dumb beasts.

"You talk a great deal about yourself——"

"Yes. I want to be honest."

"You talk a great deal about yourself——"

"Yes. I am my own latest love. I had loved long, and often, and ardently, before *that* love was born. But now that it does exist, . . . and is the last . . ."

"You talk a great deal about yourself——"

"Yes. If it wearies you, what hinders your exchanging me for the *Aglaia?* What hinders your becoming a subscriber to 'The Life, Fortunes, and Business of the Kappelman Family'—in one vol., cloth gilt?"

"You talk a great deal about yourself——"

"Quite so. When you do what Havelaar did, and the rich young man in Matthew xix. did *not* do, I will talk about you."
MULTATULI.
(*Ideen.*)

THE STORY OF CHRESOS.

CHRESOS lived in Bœotia. By profession he was mayor of a little village, whose name I do not know, neither can I tell you how he had strayed into Bœotia, since his family belonged to Athens—nay, I think he was even related to Alcibiades, who was a Frenchman born too soon. Chresos was a good sort of man, and lived contentedly. He looked after his village as well as he could, and amused himself, in his spare hours, by playing on the lute; but he only did this at home, and never annoyed any one with his music.

And, behold, there came robbers, who ill-treated the inhabitants of the village over which Chresos had authority. He laid aside his lute, and tried to drive the robbers away; but he was told that he ought not to have done this, because the robbers were under the protection of the magistrates in the capital.

Chresos did not believe this, because it seemed to him too bad to be credible. He continued to resist the robbers, and, their force being too great for him, he sent a messenger to Thebes, to ask for help.

Instead of help, he received for answer, that he was an unworthy mayor, and entirely incompetent to fill any office in Bœotia. He did not attempt to deny this. After having advised his villagers to have patience, he left the place with his wife and children, taking nothing with him but his lute. His house was occupied by a new mayor, who, it may be supposed, was less unworthy, in the opinion of the Theban magistrates, and who, also, seemed to be on very good terms with the very robbers whom the stupid Chresos had wanted to exterminate. At any rate, there were no more complaints of violence, although the robbers still remained in the neighbourhood.

With difficulty, Chresos obtained access to the Areopagus, and related what had happened to him. He pointed to his family, who were perishing of want—through a misunderstanding on the part of the magistrates; for he still thought that the whole matter arose out of a misunderstanding. I have already told you that he was not really a Bœotian by birth. This was why he held such mistaken opinions.

But the Areopagus took no notice. Chresos asked his wife to have patience, which was not necessary, and consoled himself by playing the lute. He was no great musician, but there is something peculiar in the playing of a father who sees his family starving; this was why they listened to him, not because Chresos played well. There was something that tickled coarse ears. There were many coarse ears in Bœotia.

When they said, "Well played, Chresos; go on," his hand fell limply down, and the tears stood in his eyes at the thought that this undesired praise was the price of his children's hunger.

Yet he played from time to time, because he could do no other. And his family bore their hunger patiently.

Again and again he appealed to the Areopagus. At last he received the following answer:—

"The Court of Areopagus, &c., having heard the complaints of the ex-mayor Chresos as to the outrages in the village of ——, &c.

"HE PLAYED FROM TIME TO TIME."

"Having likewise heard his request for a decision between him and the Theban magistrates, &c.

"**And** whereas the said Chresos declares that he **and his** family are in a position of great distress, in consequence of a misunderstanding which induced the said magistrates **to** take the side of the robbers who plundered the village,

"And whereas, moreover, many witnesses declare that they have heard the said Chresos playing on the lute,

"In pursuance of, &c., &c.,

"The sentence **of** the Court is, that the **said Chresos** continue playing on the lute, and pay all **costs**."

The Areopagus **had been** bribed,—and its name was HOLLAND. MULTATULI.
(*Minnebrieven.*)

THE FAIRY TALE THAT FANCY *TOLD* WOUTER.

FANCY'S FAIRY TALE.

WOUTER had **found out** that he was a prince. His princedom **lay in the region of the moon** . . . no, much farther off than that.

This is **how he came to it** :—

Long before the beginning of this story,—yes, very, **very** long ago, there **was a Queen of Spirits,** just as in *Hans Heiling.* Her name was A—OO.

She did not live in a cave, as did the one in *Hans,* but held her court far above the clouds, which **is** more airy, and also more fitting for a queen.

She wore a necklace of stars, and a sun **was set** in her signet-ring.

When she went out, the nebulæ flew **up** like dust, and she scattered the firmaments **with a stroke of** her fan.

"HER NAME WAS A-OO."

Her children played with planets **for marbles, and complained** that they were so **hard to find when** they rolled **away** among the furniture. This made Prince Upsilon— the queen's little **son—very cross, and he kept asking for** some other kind of toys.

The queen had a box full of Sirii given him, but in a little while these too were lost. But that was Upsilon's own fault. **He** ought to have taken better care of his playthings. People did what they could to content him. But whatever was given him, he kept calling for something else —**something more** and bigger. This was a fault in the little prince's character.

His mother, who, as Queen of Spirits, **was** a very sensible woman, understood that it would be **a good thing for the** youngster to get accustomed to *doing without* for a little. So she said that Upsilon **was to be** left without any playthings at all.

This was done. They took away everything from him, —even the comet with which he and **his little** sister Omicron were playing at battledore and shuttlecock.

Prince Upsilon was of a passionate temper, and so **far** forgot himself as to say something very disrespectful about his mother.

Princess Omicron, too, led astray by his example (for nothing is more ruinous than bad examples), angrily threw her battledore at the Universe. Which was not nice in a little girl.

Now **in** the kingdom of Spirits there was a law that whoever lost sight of the respect due to the Queen, or threw anything **at** the Universe, should be punished for the same by a temporary loss of all rank and dignity.

Prince Upsilon became a grain of sand.

After having behaved well for a couple of thousand years, he received the joyful tidings that he was promoted to the **rank of a tuft** of moss.

In this capacity he kept his duty in mind, and did everything that a good moss-tuft ought to do. And on a certain morning he awoke as a polype.

This happened about the time when human beings first began to prepare their food by means of fire.

He built one or two continents, and in about two thousand years' time he was rewarded for his zeal by being changed into a shrimp.

In this position, also, no one had the slightest reason to complain of his conduct, and in due course he was transferred to the class of sea-serpents.

He amused himself, innocently enough, by playing at hide-and-seek with the sailors, but did no one any harm; and some time afterwards he received four feet and the rank of mastodon, with the privilege of disporting himself on shore.

With philosophic calm he adapted himself to his new circumstances, and occupied himself with geological observations. A few million ages later. . . .

When I speak of ages, it must be borne in mind that all this time taken together was only a short quarter of an hour in the land of Spirits, . . . or rather that it was absolutely nothing. For *time* was invented for the convenience of mankind, as we give spelling-books to children. For Spirits, *then, now,* and *in the future* is exactly the same thing. They comprehend *yesterday, to-day,* and *to-morrow* in one glance, —just as we read a word without spelling. What *was* and *shall be, is.*

The Egyptians and Phœnicians knew this very well, but we seem to have forgotten it.

A few million years later, then, he rose to the rank of an elephant; and, a spirit-minute or so after that,—that is ten years, I mean human years this time—before the beginning of my story, he was transferred to the class of human beings.

What he had done amiss, as an elephant, I do not know.

But, FANCY had said, if he did not want to be put back another step, instead of being shortly restored to his rank as a prince of Spirits, he must look to his ways as a human being; not make any more verses about brigands, or sell any more Bibles; and then, why, perhaps it might come to pass.

Alas, he would have to put up with Juffrouw Pieterse's not wearing a train. "That," said Fancy, "is so, and can't be helped."

Fancy appeared to be a sort of maid-of-honour of Wouter's mother, who came to visit him in his banishment, so as to cheer him up a bit, and tell him to take courage, for the temporary punishment that had fallen to his lot did not mean that people had ceased to love him.

She promised to come and see him from time to time.

"But," Wouter had asked, "how is my little sister?"

"Your sister has been punished too—you know the law. But she is a dear child. She is submitting to it patiently, and promises to do better in the future. In the beginning she was a bubble of air, and conducted herself irreproachably as such. Then she became a moonbeam, and in this capacity also no one had any fault to find with her. She shone so that it was a pleasure to see her, and your mother had need of all her strength of mind to keep from granting her a respite. So she was soon promoted to be a perfume, and filled the Universe to such a degree that she gave us a headache. This happened about the time when you were beginning to eat grass. Then she became a butterfly. But your mother found that this was not a suitable position for a girl, and therefore soon changed her into a constellation —see, there she is—below us."

Wouter looked for Omicron, but could not find her.

It often happens that we miss something because it is too big.

"See," said Fancy, "there—to the right—no—rather

farther off—there—there—the Pole Star. That's her left eye. You can't see the right, because she is stooping after Orion, her doll. She is holding him on her lap and playing with him."

Wonter now saw her clearly, and cried "Omicron! Omicron!"

"No, no," said the maid-of-honour, "that won't do, prince. The queen expressly directed that your confinement was to be on the cellular system. It is only as a great favour that you two are shut up within the same universe. When your brothers spoilt the Milky Way some time ago by letting floods loose over it, they were put very much farther apart."

Wouter was greatly grieved at this. He would so have liked to kiss all those stars, with the doll in their lap, which were his little sister.

"Oh! Fancy," he cried, "do let me be with Omicron!"

Fancy said neither yes nor no. There was something in her manner as if she were thinking over the possibility of bringing a very difficult matter to pass.

But Wouter, taking courage from her hesitation, repeated his prayer:

"Oh! let me be with my little sister. I don't mind if I have to eat grass again, or build continents. I will do my very best at it, if I may only be with Omicron!"

It seems as though Fancy were afraid to promise what might be out of her power, and, at the same time, that it pained her not to be able to give the promise.

"I will ask," she whispered; "and now . . ."

Wouter rubbed his eyes . . . he was standing on the little bridge over the canal.

MULTATULI.
(Ideen.)

HALF-AN-HOUR AT THE HAIR-DRESSER'S.

FARCE.

I.

FOURNICHON, *the hair-dresser, discovered in his shop,* **busy** *finishing a lady's chignon.*

Fournichon. **There** ought to be a **machine invented to** make our work easier, . . . **say, some simple arrangement in which you throw in a handful of hair on one side and take out a** *perruque perfectionnée* on **the other.** I shall certainly bring up my son as **a** mechanician, **and entrust him** with the invention of this indispensable machine. Let me see, whose turn is it now? Ah! Mevrouw Priddeau,—*a chignon à la sauvage,* of at least three kilos? . . . *Mille tonnerres!* I am quite out **of** black hair! Hi! Pierre!

[*He sends his assistants* **to purchase the necessary** *supplies; almost immediately* **after his shop is hastily** *entered by two students, Charles* **and** *John, who* **drop** *into chairs, as though completely* **exhausted.**]

Fournichon (*rising*). How can I serve you, gentlemen?

Charles (*gasping*). A glass of water, if you please.

[*Fournichon supplies them both, and goes on.*] **How you** startled me, gentlemen! to rush in breathlessly like **that!** Yet it's not the season for mad dogs!

Charles. If it had only been a mad dog!

Fournichon. Surely no tiger has broken loose from the Zoological Gardens?

John. If it had only been a tiger!

Fournichon. Come, come, I shall **not make** myself uneasy. You have been up to some mischief, haven't you? You were pursued by the police, and you saw no other refuge but the hospitable establishment of *M. Fournichon, Coiffeur des Deux Sexes.* Now, am I not right?

FOURNICHON, THE HAIR-DRESSER.

Charles. Yes, that's it,—the contemptible wretch . . . the scoundrel ! . . . The same low cad who got me in for three weeks' solitary last year. Far worse than the maddest dog, or the most savage tiger !

John. The fellow never **will** learn to understand that **a couple of rix-dollars are** worth far more than his so-called official honour, which involves him **in** the constant risk **of** incurring a thrashing.

Fournichon. But what has happened, after all **?** Surely, gentlemen, you did not come running here **in such haste to** tell me that you got into quod last year?

Charles. What has happened? **Nothing, strictly speaking** . . . but a whole lot *may* **happen.**

John. And that must be **prevented,—and that is why we** have come to seek comfort, **counsel, and** help from **the hospitable Fournichon.**

Charles. I'll tell you **all about it. We were just coming** quietly and comfortably from lecture together, **when we** passed a baker's shop, when the servant-girl was just washing the windows. John took it into his head that we might lend a hand, and I seized a pail of water, intending to throw the contents at the window, when the pail itself slipped from my hands, and flew right through **the plate-glass window into** the middle of the currant-buns and cakes ! Unhappily, the aforesaid incorruptible policeman just happened to be in the neighbourhood, **so that he caught us** red-handed, and **we had** to make good use of our legs to escape being locked up at once.

John. You will understand that we did not intend any mischief,—it was a harmless joke, which turned out badly.

Fournichon. Of course. And not only so, **but** there was provocation on the baker's part. If he had chosen another time of day **to** have his windows cleaned, it could not possibly have turned out so. In any case, there are plenty of extenuating circumstances, and **I don't** understand why you gentlemen should have such a violent objection to a day or two under lock and key. That happens often enough, and young gentlemen don't usually think so much of it.

John. That is true, but to-day is an extraordinary occasion. We were going to the fancy-dress ball to-night, and should be very sorry to miss it. So you see us in a fearful scrape, with a gendarme at our heels, and you must help us. [*A ring at the bell.*] What's that?

Fournichon. I don't know; we shall see in a minute. [*Steps are heard coming up the stairs.*]

Charles. John, get out of sight. [*They hide.*]

Pierre (*entering*). Sir, Vrouw Krullemie has just sold her hair this morning for seventy-five cents.

[*The students come out again.*]

John. Bother your Krullemie! Say, Fournichon, if your visitors are in the habit of dropping in unannounced after this fashion, we are not altogether safe here.

Fournichon. Well, look here, gentlemen, you suggested an idea yourselves. Your costumes for the ball must be quite ready by this time; why don't you disguise yourselves in them?

Charles. A fine lark! In the first place they are not here . . .

John. That would matter less, for we might send for them, but we could scarcely show ourselves in the streets in them.

Fournichon. How so?

John. Well, I was going to appear as the Avenger of Innocence.

Charles. And I as the Four Seasons.

Fournichon. You are right, that would never do; but I have another proposal to make. I too intend going to the ball, and have had costumes made for myself and one of my friends, which will no doubt suit you better. You can have those, and give us yours.

John. All right, if they are better suited to the purpose than ours.

Fournichon. Oh! just perfect! You shall see. [*Opens two*

HALF-AN-HOUR AT THE HAIR-DRESSER'S. 129

chests in the foreground, and takes out costumes. These should be so made as to be put on, on the stage, without much trouble.] We were going as an old lady and her granddaughter. The dresses are very simple, and I think they will do admirably.

"I AM QUITE LOST IN THIS CAP."

Charles. Done! I accept that. Now, quick! before any one has time to surprise us.

John. Say, Charles, will you be the grandmother?

Charles. All right, and you the girl.

Fournichon. Don't make any mistakes; the crinoline belongs to this skirt.

Charles. I am quite lost in this cap.

Fournichon. You must have a wig on first.

John. Just look here, Fournichon, this dress isn't long enough.

Fournichon. Why, of course, you're only in short skirts as yet.

John. Ah! is that it?

Charles. John, don't I look charming?

John. Quite enchanting! If you were my grandmother, I should certainly fall in love with you.

Charles. Where's my wig?

Fournichon. Here are plenty, just choose one for yourself.

John. These curls are what will suit me. [*Puts on the wig, and a round straw hat on the top of it.*]

Charles. This grey one will just do for me. [*Puts it on, and then the cap.*] Now, I'm ready! Sapristi! How hot it is. There's the bell.

John. Good gracious, now we've got it!

Fournichon. Quiet now; sit down before it's too late.

Charles. What's the good of that? our voices will betray us.

Fournichon. You must not talk. Just you trust to me, and it will be all right.

II.

CHARLES *and* JOHN *seated at a table, with their backs to the other actors. Enter* BOM DE SAC, *the police agent, fuming and swearing.*

Bom de Sac. When I was with the First regiment, and was three times wounded in two battles. . . . Ah! good-morning, Mr Hairdresser . . . three times wounded,—it would never have happened to me to let two scoundrels escape. Never!

Fournichon. What's your pleasure, Mr—Mr——

Bom de Sac. Bom de Sac, if you please—with the Third regiment—in four battles, five wounds.

HALF-AN-HOUR AT THE HAIR-DRESSER'S.

Fournichon. **Does M. Bom de** Sac **want his** hair cut?

Bom de Sac. Many **thanks, I** always **do** that myself. I learnt that with **the** Fourth . . . when **I was six** times wounded in five **battles.** But, sir, that **is not** the point at present. I was **just** going **to** say that **this** morning two **scoundrels——**

Fournichon. Scoundrels?

Bom de **Sac.** Scoundrels, **or students, whichever you like to** call them.

Fournichon. Well, and what **did** they do?

Bom de Sac. Just imagine, **sir.** I was at the **baker's, and the** maid **was** standing on a ladder outside **cleaning the** window, when **two** good-for-nothing vagabonds **came up,** took up a **pail of** water, and threw it **at** the girl, and **the** girl fell right through the **window** in among the currant-buns!

Fournichon. Not killed, **I hope.**

Bom **de** Sac. No, the **buns had** broken **her fall. But I** was out of the house in **a flash, and** after the fellows. *Sacré nom de guerre!* if I could still run **as** I could **when** I was in the Fifth . . . and wounded seven times **in six** battles . . . they would **never have escaped me!** But they are here!

Fournichon. **Have a** glass?

Bom **de Sac.** If you please. [*Drinks.*] **Thank you. I am** told they came **into** this house, and if so, **they'll have to** come out, sir!

Fournichon. Here! How is it possible? You are quite free to search the **room if you** like. These ladies are my grandmother and my cousin.

Bom de **Sac** (*seeing them for the first time, salutes*). Ah! *Honneur* **aux** *dames,* as we used to say in the Sixth. I hope you won't mind, ladies.

Fournichon. You **need not** give yourself the trouble of speaking to them. **The** old lady is **stone** deaf, and won't understand a word, and she watches over her granddaughter

"SACRE NOM DE GUERRE!"

so carefully that she cannot bear to see **a gentleman speak** to the girl, because she cannot hear what he is saying.

Bom de Sac. Well, where in the thunder can they have got **to?** I was quite certain of finding them here.

Fournichon. And I am quite certain you will do no such thing. [*Looks out of window.*]

Bom de Sac. But—*nom de nom !*—how **is** it possible?

Fournichon. Just look here, Monsieur Bom de Sac, could these be the gentlemen that have just passed laughing? Both of them have white hats.

Bom de Sac (*rushing to the window*). **Where?**

Fournichon. Ah! what a pity! they have just this moment gone round the corner towards the Botermarkt.

Bom de Sac. White hats, you say? The devil!—that must be they, and they shan't escape me this time. [*Exit.*] **It's** not for nothing that I had ten wounds in nine battles when serving with the Eighth.

Charles. Bad luck to the fellow! he has **made it warm for us!**

John. If it had lasted any longer, I am sure I should have made some remarks on my own account. If some one else comes, we really must find some other place, for I really can't sit still so long in these blessed **skirts.**

Charles. Shall we stand up then?

John. Why not. [*Jumps on one of the chests.*] Look here, I'll bet **you** anything you like I can stand half-an-hour like this without moving. Don't I look like a waxwork figure of summer?

Charles. **The** devil you **are!** [*Gets on the other chest.*] And I winter, to match.

Fournichon. Splendid, gentlemen, it couldn't be finer Just stand still like that. [*A ring at the bell.*]

Charles (*getting down*). Preserve us!—now we're in for it.

John. No, Charles, stick to your post.

Charles. I can't possibly stand still all that time.

Fournichon. It won't be necessary. Just stand in any easy attitude, and you can change your position quietly from time to time, without our tiresome visitor becoming aware of it.

Charles. Well, I'll see what I can do. [*Climbs up again.*]

Fournichon. Hush! he's coming!

Enter MEIJER.

Meijer. Good-day, Monsieur Fournichon. Good-day, ladies. (*To Fournichon.*) Why are you laughing?

Fournichon. At your taking those waxworks for ladies. Ha! ha! ha!

Meijer. Waxworks, you say! How astonishingly life-like! It's true, though, it would be a queer position for living beings to stand in.

Fournichon. Well done, are they not? It is an allegorical representation of winter and summer.

Meijer. Very pretty, very pretty indeed! You hairdressers have always something curious on hand.

Fournichon. That's to say, sir, they are not my property. They have been sent to me to look after the *coiffures*, and they are to go to London,—to Madame Tousseau's museum.

Meijer. Oh, indeed!—indeed! Well, art has made great strides.

Fournichon. Great strides, sir! You're quite right there. Just feel now—elastic as india-rubber—quite like a human being.

Meijer. Wonderful! wonderful! But I am in a hurry—can you shave me?

Fournichon. Certainly, sir, sit down! [*Gives him a chair between John and Charles, but rather more towards the back of the shop. Goes on shaving him, and talking at the same time.*] Your barber, sir, does not know his business. Your skin and complexion are quite spoilt.

[*John changes his position.*]

Meijer (*starting up*). Good heavens!

Fournichon. No need to be uneasy, sir; there is nothing really dangerous.

Meijer. No, that's not what I was thinking of,—but that doll of yours—the summer one—is moving!

Fournichon. Oh! that is nothing surprising—perhaps I stepped on the floor rather heavily. You must know these figures are full of steel springs inside, and the slightest vibration makes them move. Just look now!

[*Stamps on the floor. John and Charles immediately change their positions.*]

Meijer. Ah! thank you for your explanation. I really never should have understood it.

[*Sits down again, and Fournichon goes on shaving him till he has finished. Meijer rises.*]

Meijer. Thanks. Can you give me change?

Fournichon. I'll go and get it.

[***Exit.*** *Meijer goes to look at the waxworks.*]

Meijer. They *are* curious, though! I have often seen wax-works before, but never so graceful, so lifelike as these. Whenever any one stamps on the floor, they move. [*Stamps —John and Charles again change their attitudes.*] Just look at that! how pretty! Once more! Sublime! And that's the way they keep on! [*Stamps again, and continues to do so, faster and faster—John and Charles changing their position with every stamp; but at length they begin to grow tired of it —they jump down from their pedestals, seize Meijer, and hold him fast, saying,* "You rascal! this is too much of a good thing!" *They strike him, and push him out at the door— losing their wigs in the struggle—after which they burst out laughing, and drop exhausted into their chairs. Enter F.*]

Fournichon. Gentlemen! what have you been up to now? Such an infernal row I never heard before! You'll wake all the babies in the neighbourhood.

Charles (*laughing*). Oh! the conceited blockhead!

John. The worshipper of waxwork groups!

Fournichon. Well—where is he? What have you done with him?

Charles. We have put him out at the door as quietly and deliberately as possible.

Fournichon. Well—and why?

John. Because he bored us too much. He was so delighted with the mechanism of the figures, that we might have kept on dancing till to-morrow morning if we had not put an end to the business ourselves.

Fournichon. And what about your coiffures?

Charles. Why, that's true! What can have become of them!

Fournichon. Oh! good heavens! here they are, lying on the ground like any old rubbish! [*Picks them up, along with the hat and cap.*] Just look!—they are not worth a cent now!

John. Oh! just put the things away—we don't want them any more,—and if they're spoilt, we'll pay for them.

Fournichon. In that case, sir, it doesn't matter. [*Lays everything on a table. The bell rings.*] Hé! who's that now?

Charles. It doesn't matter to me who it is. Any one may come who likes—I'm not going to act in this farce any longer.

Fournichon (*looks through the door*). Look out, gentlemen —it's the agent—Bom de Sac!

John and Charles (*springing up*). That fellow! No! that will never do! [*They sit down at the table, as before, and put on their headdresses, but without seeing that they have taken the wrong ones, John putting on the grey wig and cap,—Charles, the curls and round straw hat. Bom de Sac heard speaking outside the door :*]—No, sacré nom de nom! Mijnheer Meyer has lent me a hand. What are people thinking of? It was not for nothing I was wounded eleven times in ten battles, with the 9th Regiment. They are here—I'm certain of that! [*Enters.*]

Fournichon. Search as **much as you like, sir, but** remember, if you please, that, in the presence of ladies . . .

Bom de Sac. Of course, of course! I always said, "**Honneur aux dames**." [*Looks at the ladies and salutes, then* **takes** *a step backward in amazement.*] Sacré nom de guerre!

Fournichon. What's the matter?

Bom de Sac. Have I come to my age—not to speak of twelve wounds in eleven battles—to let myself be fooled like this?

Fournichon. I don't understand you.

Bom de Sac. No, perhaps not. But I understand how **it is** possible for these ladies to have changed heads at a moment's notice. Look here! [*He takes off the wigs.*] The young lady is getting grey, **and the** grandmother **is** going backwards to her childhood. Come with **me**, now, gentlemen—I arrest you both!

Fournichon. Your own fault, gentlemen. **I wash my hands** of the whole business.

Charles. We have a word to say to that, John.

John. Certainly.

Bom de Sac. Gentlemen, conspiracies or plots in which more than one person are concerned are forbidden by law. Will you come with me, or not?

Charles. I suppose we shall have to.

John. Do you want us to come with you as we are?

Bom de Sac. Just as you like, gentlemen. I arrest you, and that is all my share in the business. The rest does not concern me.

Charles (*whispers to John, then continues aloud*). Just listen, Monsieur Bom de Sac,—though we find it very unpleasant to have fallen into your hands, we are not children, and we are quite capable of understanding that there **is** nothing for it but to give in. But just let us change our clothes first— we'll give you our word of honour not to go out of the door without letting you know.

Bom de Sac. Very good! We have been young, too, you see. Just go on, gentlemen. If you give me your word, that is enough. [*While he goes on talking to Fournichon, John and Charles take off their costumes and tie Bom de Sac's coat-tails to the table.*] Yes, Mr Hairdresser, when I was with the 11th, and had been wounded thirteen times in twelve battles, then I thought to myself,—it's quite enough, Bom de Sac, you have done quite enough for your country; you're growing old—and a soldier may be too old. I was then brigadier, and understood that it was getting time for me to make room for another. So I came home to my old mother . . . I married a young wife . . .

Charles. . . . and received, in thirteen battles . . .

Bom de Sac. Ah!—are you ready, gentlemen?

John. At your service, my worthy sergeant of police! We are quite ready, and now warn you that we are about to leave. [*Charles and John go out by the door at the back of the stage, arm in arm, saying, as they go*]—Bon soir.

Bom de Sac. Wait—I'm coming with you! [*Tries to go, but finds himself fastened to the table.*] Bad luck to them! are they going to give me the slip after all?

Fournichon. I see a good chance of it. Look here, Monsieur Bom de Sac, you have, in far too many battles received more than too many wounds to be anything like a match for these young fellows. They have been sharper than you,—so you'll have to acknowledge yourself beaten, and e'en let them alone. By the time you get outside the door they will be far beyond your reach.

Bom de Sac. You're right enough there, so I shall keep the whole matter to myself, and wish them a pleasant evening.

Anon.

IN THE LITTLE REPUBLIC.

It was in the smallest Republic of our Continent — Altenet—rich in mines of zinc. It lies, like a tiny wedge, between the great German empire, the small kingdom of Holland, and the still smaller one of Belgium.

Seldom has a stranger set foot here; few know the district even by name; only a single encyclopædia makes mention of it; the atlases have forgotten it,—nay, it has even been forgotten by the political world.

When the separation between Belgium and Holland took place in 1830, the representatives of the various powers could not come to any agreement over this little piece of ground. It was therefore resolved to declare it "neutral territory," till a later Congress should find a better solution to the problem.

The old schoolmaster of the neighbouring village of Oppenaken always asserted that the learned politicians assembled at the aforesaid Congress had been too drunk to know what they were doing. If his listeners looked at him incredulously, or began to laugh, he would indignantly ask, "Don't you believe me? Then I'll prove it!" And then he would fetch an atlas, open it at the map of the Netherlands, and, following with his finger the boundary of our provinces of Limburg and Brabant, continue—"Just look at this line here how it goes—first to the left, then to the right—here crooked, then slanting—then again forward for a bit, then backwards—one minute straight, and then again with a great bend—isn't it just like the line a tipsy man would take in walking?"

In the year 1866 another European Congress took place; but it seemed as though the gentlemen taking part in it had not recovered from the effects of the drinking bout attributed to them by the Oppenaken schoolmaster, for this time Altenet was forgotten—forgotten for good and all.

Thus the Altenetters lived on, independent of all foreign domination. The miners continued to extract zinc from the

"TOO DRUNK TO KNOW WHAT THEY WERE DOING."

ground, and pile it up in the great waggons which transported it to other countries; the peasant ploughed his field and reaped his grain; the wind might be heard sighing in the clumps of trees on the hill-tops, the brook rushing and murmuring between the rocks, and the lark singing high in air—and what could you want more?

The government of the little Republic was entirely in the hands of the burgomaster, Willem Drikus Bloemstein, a broad-shouldered man of portly presence, red-haired and red-bearded, fully conscious of his own importance, and loyally supported in all his works and ways by the elect of Altenet, who were associated with him as Councillors.

It was quite an earthly Paradise—a little Eden full of peace and happiness! Here was no such thing as strife or hatred, for parties had no existence, and life offered no opportunity for insult or injury on political grounds. The taxes were not high, and there was no standing army, so that no one thought it necessary to hold meetings in order to discuss the advantages and disadvantages of compulsory service. The only measure taken for the defence of the country was the weekly drill of the rural rifle corps; and though no one was forced to take his place in its ranks, yet every right-minded man of Altenet felt it his duty to place himself under the orders of General Bauer—on working days an energetic mine-superintendent.

Suddenly this happy state of things was disturbed.

A tiresome man—a German politician—had discovered the above-mentioned negligence on the part of the statesmen of Europe, and pointed out to the Government of his country that here was an opportunity for gratifying its well-known love of annexation. The high and mighty Reichstag took the hint, and resolved to proceed to a speedy settlement of the still unsolved question of the division of Altenet.

A storm of indignation swept through the whole Republic. The head of the State, honest Bloemstein, immediately summoned all the members of the Council, in order to consult as to ways and means of averting the threatened misfortune, and the summons was obeyed by every one.

They were all assembled. Klessens, the rich brewer;

young Holzert, an ugly little man, whose bow legs were a continual challenge to any poodle who had learned to jump through a hoop, but whose shrewdness and clear insight into things were praised by every one; the just-mentioned Bauer, the commander of the rifle corps; Marbaise, the landlord of the "Lump of Zinc"; and Conrads, the wealthy farmer.

"What's got to be done?" was the question addressed by Bloemstein to the notables of Altenet.

"It seems to me we ought to write the Prussian a civil letter, telling him not to trouble his head about us," was the opinion delivered by Klessens, after coughing and clearing his throat for some time.

"You stupid fellow!" replied Bauer, pulling in an impressive manner at his thick moustache, "do you think the insolent dog of a Prussian will care anything for a civil letter? No, my boy, you don't know him yet; *au contraire*, we ought to show him we're not afraid."

"Why, then! there will be war!" was timidly interjected by Conrads.

"Very well then! there *will* be war!" The rest nodded assent.

"But that will surely be a great-to-do,—couldn't we wait at least till the crops are in?"

"We won't wait a moment! I shall march with the Rifles to-morrow, right along the Prussian border, and then the miserable wretches can see that we're not afraid of them!" and Bauer banged the table with his fists.

"That's not nearly enough," suggested Marbaise; "the custom-house officers might forget to write to the Emperor about it, and as long as he doesn't know it, it all goes for nothing."

"We ought to write to him ourselves, and not civilly,—no, indeed!—but as impudently as we can; and you must sign the letter, Bloemstein, just as if you were a king yourself, and put under it 'Wullem the First, President of the Republic of Altenet.'"

"BAUER BANGED THE TABLE WITH HIS FISTS."

"Wullem, Wullem! why, there are so many Wullems," was the opinion of the man addressed; "the Dutch one is called so, and the Prussian too. 'Wullem!'—it's so common."

"But you have another name, haven't you?" asked another Councillor.

"Yes, of course,—Drikus."

"Very well, then,—Drikus the First. What do you think of that?"

"Well, well," muttered Klessens. "'Drikus the First, President of the Republic of Altenet'; it doesn't sound bad, not bad at all."

"Wouldn't it be still better to say, 'President of the *Independent* Republic'?" added the warlike Bauer.

"We might do that," was the general verdict.

"But then we ought to be called Ministers," suggested Conrads.

"Of course!" chorussed the rest.

"In that case, I suppose I shall be Minister of War?" asked Bauer.

"Certainly."

"And I of Agriculture?" asked Conrads.

"Very good, too."

"Marbaise for Finance."

"And whom shall we have for Home Affairs?"

"It seems to me that wouldn't be a bad thing for you, tailor," put in Bloemstein, addressing Councillor Holzert.

"I have no objection," replied the latter; "but I'd just like to say something too."

"Councillor Holzert will now address the meeting."

A sudden silence fell on the assembly; all were straining their ears to hear what thoughts had arisen in the tailor's shrewd brain. Speaking slowly, and emphasising every word, he began,—

"We must have stamps made—big stamps, with your

head on them, Bloemstein; and then we'll **send a letter, with a stamp like that on it, you understand, not to the** Emperor of Prussia, but to Bismarck, because, after all, he's the fellow that does everything; and you must write in that letter, just to rile him, that we are going to let all **the priests** and Jesuits he has driven out come **freely into our country."**

"But **only on** condition **that** they brew **no** beer," interrupted the brewer, Klessens.

The tailor made believe **not to** have heard **this** interested remark, **and ended his speech** with the question, "What do you think of *that* idea?"

"**Bravo, bravo!**" **cried all**; and "You're a sharp lad; you're a clever fellow," added the chairman of the meeting, as he passed his **hand** complacently over **the head whose** portrait was shortly to **be sent to the Chancellor of the** German Empire.

"We haven't done yet," continued Holzert; "we have still to find out how we're going to put your head on the stamps,—with a beard, with **a moustache only, or without** anything at all."

"Why, you do think of everything, tailor!" **observed** Marbaise.

Bauer declared that there **could** be no two opinions on the point—"With **a** moustache, that's quite military," and, as he spoke, he twisted **the ends of** his own.

"But I don't **think it would look very** well—a red moustache," objected Marbaise.

"Why, what **does that** matter? **You** can't see it in the picture," returned **Conrads.** "Bismarck has a white one."

"I don't quite know whether you're right," began Holzert again; "just **look** at Napoleon,—I mean the great Napoleon, —he's got nothing, no beard and no moustache, and yet he sent the Prussians to the right-about, time and again; but what do you think about it yourself, Bloemstein?"

"Well, what am I to say to you? A beard is not respectable, and I shall have mine shaved off; then we can see if the moustache alone looks well; and if that is not the case, I'll have that taken off too."

All thought this an excellent idea.

"Don't get shaved here, though. You'd better have that done at Aix-la-Chapelle, and then you can get yourself taken at the same time for the stamps."

"Among the Prussians? Never! as long as I live. I'll never help them to earn a cent," thundered Bloemstein.

"In Maastricht, then," suggested another.

"All right. I'll have it done on Monday. Has any one anything more to say to the meeting?"

They looked at each other, but no one broke the silence.

"No one's got nothing, then?"

"Just wait a minute," cried Conrads. "You ought to have a crown, Bloemstein."

"A crown?—that's expensive."

"Nonsense; have one made of brass, and well polished up, then it will shine just as if it were gold."

"Then we ought to have Ministers' uniforms. I'll make them as cheap and as quickly as possible," said the tailor-Minister; "and then I'll make a long cloak for you, Bloemstein."

"If the gentlemen will allow, I've something more to say," said Marbaise.

"It's Marbaise's turn to speak."

"We ought to forbid all Altenet girls marrying Prussians."

"What about my Marieke, who's courting with the Prussian doctor?" was Bloemstein's terrified reply. "What a set-out my daughter will make—and, above all, my wife, when I tell them that."

"Then you must just say that our country doesn't permit it," and the whole assembly nodded in token of assent.

"Oh, Lord!" groaned the unlucky President; "it's the hardest thing you could ask me to do."

"Our country! the Republic! the Independent Republic!" cried the others, wagging their heads hither and thither, shrugging up their shoulders, and holding out their hands with all their fingers extended in air.

Here the weighty deliberations came to an end; and

"BOTH WALKED ON IN SILENCE."

thereupon the President and his Ministers slowly proceeded homewards.

Holzert escorted the newly appointed ruler to his dwelling. For a considerable time both walked on in silence. At last the tailor spoke:

"Bloemstein," he began, "if your Marieke is not to marry the Prussian doctor, . . . in that case . . . I'd like to have her. I always had a liking for the girl; but I couldn't say anything; . . . but now I'm Minister of the Interior, . . . that sounds fine, eh? . . . that's something. . . . I think perhaps it might do."

"Why, my good fellow, I've nothing against you. You always were a clever chap, and you've shown it again with those stamps. It would be a good enough idea; . . . but —Marieke! and then my wife!"

"But, after all, you're the master. Why, you're the king of everything in the place! You must put on a bold face, and stand firm!"

"Very well, lad, I'll try."

With wrathful strides, his head well thrown back, and his hand resting on the front of his ample waistcoat, Bloemstein entered his own house.

Marieke sprang to meet him, embraced him cordially, and then said, "Father, I've just had a letter from Heinrich, he's coming to dinner with us to-morrow."

"I'm very sorry, child; but this marriage with the Prussian doctor can't come to anything. I've another husband for you. You're to marry my Minister of the Interior."

"Whom do you say I am to marry?"

"My Minister of the Interior."

"Who's that?"

"Mr Holzert."

"The crooked tailor! what a joke! I didn't know you could be so funny, father!"

"It's no joke; it's quite serious, Marieke!" and he recounted all that had taken place at the meeting.

Marieke, however, was not convinced. "I won't have him!" she cried, and stamped her little foot on the ground; —"and if you say I must, I'll never marry at all!—there! . . . I'll go and tell mother about it!"

Bloemstein did not await the arrival of his better half. Under pretext of urgent business, the ruler of all Altenet, except his own house, hastily escaped up the street, and did not return home till late in the evening.

On the following day—it was Sunday—all Altenet was clean turned upside down.

Bauer had summoned all his riflemen, as soon as high mass was over, and they assembled in full uniform at the tavern kept by the Minister of Finance.

In a vigorous and pithy speech,—which he had been thinking over all night,—he explained to his troops the danger which threatened the country.

His manly language carried his audience with him. The shout, "We'll conquer or die!" raised by the Minister of War, was loudly echoed by every one; and in order still further to raise their courage, they all added, "Another drop all round!" which was poured out by the Minister of Finance in his shirt-sleeves, and with fingers trembling with emotion.

"And now," yelled Bauer, "we're going to make a military march along the Prussian frontier, and then all that *canaille* can see that we're not afraid of them. Marbaise— you with the drum, your eldest boy with the accordeon, and the other with the trumpet in front,—you three are the band. Then you, Ummels, with the flag; and you, Gradus, with the bird; and then we, the people!"

However, it was a considerable time before all of them had left the tavern and taken up their positions.

They were a peculiar-looking troop, of about a hundred and twenty men; mostly broad-shouldered fellows, though not tall—a kind of build common to most miners. They wore all possible costumes, of all sorts of colours; check trousers and black coats—blue blouses, long, short, new, or half-worn;—suits of cloth, wool or linen—here and there a hero marching in *sabots*. The majority were armed with

"CAUSED THEM TO GO THROUGH ALL POSSIBLE MANŒUVRES."

old-fashioned bell-mouthed blunderbusses; some, the tallest of the lot, were provided with double-barrelled fowling-pieces, which at once branded them as poachers.

All, however, had the same head-covering—a green cap, with yellow braid,—and all had wooden pipes in their mouths. The flag matched the caps—white and yellowish green. The place next to the flag was occupied by the silver bird, hung round with all the gold and silver medals worn by the Altenetters in shooting competitions.

"Look out!" **cried** Bauer, who, in token of his exalted position was hung round with a string of small silver plates of different shapes and sizes, and who, besides, showed his superior dignity by smoking, not a pipe like the rest, but a cigar of immense length and thickness, which had cost him two cents and a half.

All placed themselves in position.

"Right-about-face, and along the **cinder path to the** Prussian frontier. Band, advance!"

They advanced, with drum beating and accordeon chirping. Just in full view of the German officials, who had come out to ascertain the cause of the approaching noise, Bauer called a halt. Then he caused them to go through all possible manœuvres, shoulder arms, port arms,—but not "present" —*that* he would never do "for those pig-dogs of Prussians."

These evolutions did not appear to command **any particular** admiration on the part **of the** Germans; pitying smiles were seen to pass **over their** countenances, and when at the command "Right-about-face!" half the company turned to the left, so that the soldiers of Altenet stood facing each other, they burst into a roar of laughter, which so aroused the wrath of Klaos Drehmans (who had spent some years at Sittard), that he stepped out of the ranks, and snorted defiance at the principal custom-house clerk as follows:—

"You! do you know what *you* are? you're a regular

nuisance!" while another member of the Altenet militia yelled at the top of his voice, quite at a loss for a worse epithet, "Oh! thou accursed Prussian of a Prussian!"

It was truly a triumphal march when the Republican army returned from this glorious campaign; the inhabitants uttered loud cries of joy, alternating with abuse of the cowardly Prussian lot.

Bloemstein stood, proudly defiant, in the full consciousness of his presidential dignity, on the "stoop" of his house. And when the standard-bearer had waved his flag three times over his head in the President's honour, and then tossed it on high, the President smiled very genially, and waved back a salute with his hand, blowing thick clouds of smoke the while from his long German pipe, a proceeding which elicited thundering "hurrahs" from assembled Altenet.

The only Altenetters who had not been able to witness this sublime spectacle were Bloemstein's wife and daughter; they had walked out to meet Dr Olthausen coming from Aix-la-Chapelle, and fell in with him near the village of Vaals.

After the usual salutations, Marieke related to her betrothed all the changes which had taken place in the government of Altenet, and also her father's resolution to marry her to the Minister of the Interior. At this part of the story the mother clenched her fists, her eyes flashed fire, and she said, threateningly, "Just let the fellow come into our house, and I'll make him repent his Affairs of the Interior."

To the great surprise of both ladies, Olthausen did not appear to be angry; on the contrary, he began to laugh loudly, and seemed especially diverted by the story of the postage-stamps.

"We'll have a regular good joke out of that," he said, still laughing; "but I won't come to dinner with you to-day."

"Are you afraid of Bloemstein?" asked the mother. "Because you needn't be; I shall be at dinner too."

"No, I'm not afraid of him—only of laughing more than I ought."

"Never mind that; laugh at him as he deserves, and we'll laugh too, won't we, Marieke?"

"*Nein, liebes Madamchen*," returned the doctor, "it will be better if I don't come—we'll have some dinner here."

He went with the two women into the nearest eating-house in the village and ordered dinner, also two sheets of

"JUST LET THE FELLOW COME INTO OUR HOUSE."

paper and an envelope. While the ladies were dining, he wrote a letter on one sheet, slowly and carefully, with beautiful round letters, then dashed off another more hastily, and enclosed both in one envelope, which he stamped and addressed to "Herrn Oscar Olthausen, Rechtsanwalt, Berlin." He then directed Marieke to wait till her father was about to send away the letters with the new Altenet stamps. "Then you must keep back the one addressed to Bismarck, and post this in place of it; and then I assure you that everything will come right, without you or your mother getting into any trouble with the old gentleman."

They remained chatting for some little time longer, and then Dr Olthausen took his leave and returned to Aix-la-Chapelle.

Early on the following day Drikus the First set out for Limburg's metropolis. Arrived there, he turned his steps towards the barber's shop. A young shopman came to meet him, and politely relieved him of his coat and hat.

"See here, lad," began Bloemstein, "did you ever shave a president?"

"Why, yes, sir; only yesterday the President of the Congregation of the Sacred Heart."

"No, I don't mean one like that; I mean a great president."

"Oh, the one of the great club?"

"No—greater still."

"The President of the Tribunal, then?"

"No; greater still—a president of a republic!"

"Of a republic, you say? No, I never shaved one—never in my life!"

"Do you know what he looks like?"

"Why, yes—like a gentleman."

"Very good, my boy; I see you understand. Now, that's the way you've got to shave me—for I'm one."

"You a president of a republic? Ha! ha! ha!"

"What are you laughing at, boy?"

"Because you're trying to make a fool of me."

"Indeed and I'm not. I'm Drikus the First, President of the Independent Republic of Altenet."

The lad laughed no longer; he looked round in alarm, convinced that he had a madman in the room with him.

"Shave my beard off!" commanded Bloemstein.

"Very well, Mr . . . President."

"*A la bonne heure*, my lad! I like that—you know how to behave."

"SEE HERE, LAD, DID YOU EVER SHAVE A PRESIDENT?"

As speedily as possible the wish of this strange customer was gratified.

"Now just wait a bit, my boy. I must see how the moustache looks by itself," and the ruler of the republic placed himself before the mirror.

He remained for some time lost in admiration, then began to turn the points of his moustache first up and then down.

"What do you think of it, lad? Is it good enough for a president of a republic?"

"I don't know."

"Hold your tongue, then, can't you?"

"Very good, Mr . . . President . . . as you please."

Suddenly honest Bloemstein turned round and fairly snorted at the poor youth. "Just shave this side off," he blustered, pointing to the right half of his countenance.

The youthful Figaro hastened to comply, having heard that a madman must not be contradicted or he may become violent. His request having been complied with, the President rose in order to admire himself in the mirror. He covered first one and then the other half of his face with one hand, in order to convince himself which style was most becoming to the presidential dignity.

The attractions of the clean-shaven half at length prevailed, and the last remaining hair was removed.

"What have you got to get?" asked Bloemstein, when this was done.

"Ten centimes . . . Mr President."

"There are two groschen for you."

"I have to give you two centimes change."

"Never mind that—you may keep them. A president of a republic has nothing mean about him."

And with a proud and stately demeanour he departed in the direction of the photographer's. Scarcely had he left the barber's, when the boy hastened to the police-office, to relate how he had just been shaving a fellow who must certainly have just escaped from the lunatic asylum, for he had told him quite seriously that he was the president of a republic. A policeman started immediately with the terrified barber's boy to search the streets of Maastricht for the lunatic.

It was, however, in vain. Bloemstein had already entered the studio of a neighbouring photographer, muttering, "I shall have to explain myself differently here. It seems as though these Maastricht people had never heard of the president of a republic."

When the photographer appeared, he accordingly delivered himself as follows: "I want my photograph taken, but it must be properly done, for I am a king."

"Very good, sir. Shall I give you a gun, then, or do you prefer a bow?"

"A gun!—a bow! What for?"

"Why, I've photographed a whole number of kings, and they——"

"Ah! you know how to do it then?"

"Of course I do."

"What kings have you taken?"

"Why, only yesterday the Gronsveld one, and a few days ago one from Neer-Itteren."

"How—what—kings of Gronsveld and Neer-Itteren?"

"Yes, of course—those of the archery competition."

"You confounded idiot!—did I get shaved for that? Do I look like a king of the archery competition? Why, I am king of a country—of a republic—an independent republic! Do you understand now?"

"Oh heavens!" cried the artist to himself, "the fellow is certainly touched in the upper storey, and I shall have to look out, or he'll knock the whole shop to pieces." He made his visitor a low bow, and said,—

"Very pleased, sir, to be honoured with your custom. May I ask your Majesty to take a seat. . . . How would you like your portrait, full-length, or bust only?"

"Nothing but the bust; it's for the stamps of the country, do you understand?"

"Certainly, certainly, sir, and will you kindly look through this thing?"

"Very good, but remember that I want it to look respectable—do you hear? . . . And just wait a bit—I must see if my hair is all right;" and he hastened to the looking-

"NOW YOU CAN GO AHEAD."

glass, moistened his palms, smoothed his head with them, and took his place, with a last self-satisfied look at his own image.

"Now you can go ahead."

The photographer placed himself in front of his apparatus,

and declared, a moment later, that the picture was a splendid success, notwithstanding the fact that it was impossible to pronounce on that point with any degree of certainty, since he had not the courage to go into the dark room and leave his eccentric customer alone.

"When will they be finished?" asked Bloemstein.

"Oh! as soon as your Majesty likes to have them."

"Can I have them next week? All right then, just send them to Drikus the First, King of the Independent Republic of Altenet."

"I'll do so without fail, your Majesty."

"If they turn out well, I'll come back and bring my wife the queen, and my daughter the princess; and I'll give you leave to hang out a fine gilt signboard with your own name on it, and after that 'Photographer to the King of the Republic of Altenet.'"

"I'll do my best, your Majesty."

The photographer too, immediately after his visitor's departure, hastened away to the temple of Justice, with the tidings that a fellow as mad as a hatter, calling himself king of a republic, had just been at his studio. Another gendarme was at once sent in pursuit.

Meanwhile the object of their solicitude had entered the church of St Servaas. It had struck him that, since his august head ought certainly to be adorned with a crown, he might here find a pattern for the same in painting or sculpture. He remained standing a long time before a picture representing the Adoration of the Magi, but none of the three crowns worn by those royal personages suited his fancy. "They haven't got points enough," he muttered, and searched further, but in vain, till at last he came to a statue of the Madonna, which realised his ideal. There was the crown he had always imagined—with points standing straight up all round it.

He delayed not a moment, but hastened out into the street, and entered the first coppersmith's shop he came to.

"Can you make me a crown like Our Lady's in St Servaas's?" he asked.

"Oh! yes, sir. What size do you want it?"

"HIS AUGUST HEAD OUGHT CERTAINLY TO BE ADORNED WITH A CROWN."

"As big as my head; you can take the measure now."

"What for? You don't want to wear it, do you?"

"Of course I do—nothing is more certain."

"Sir, are you mad? or might you happen to be a Freemason?"

"Mad! mad! Mad yourself, fellow!"

"Just wait a bit, and I'll show you which of us is mad!" and before the poor president could assume a defensive attitude, the smith had seized him and thrown him into the street.

This roused Bloemstein's wrath, and his objurgations speedily collected a crowd in the street.

"There he is!" a voice cried suddenly, echoed by "Now you've got him!" from another quarter, as the barber's boy and the photographer appeared on the scene, escorted by a policeman apiece. In the twinkling of an eye the two officials had mastered the furious president, and in spite of his vigorous resistance, and his protestation that, as President of Altenet, his person was inviolable, the unhappy man was lugged off to the little dark hole known to the population of Maastricht as "the larder."

"What is your name?" was the first question asked him by the police commissioner.

"You might ask it a little more civilly," was the reply.

The commissioner immediately complied with this request.

"Will you be so kind as to tell me whom I have the honour of speaking to?"

"That's the proper way to speak, and now I shall answer you. I am Wullem Drikus Bloemstein, President of the Independent Republic of Altenet."

"And where do you live?"

"Well, I should have thought you had no need to ask. At Altenet, the capital of the Republic of Altenet."

"Thank you."

One of the inspectors was immediately despatched to Altenet to make inquiries on the spot as to the personality of the prisoner.

The officer returned the same day, with the tidings that

"THERE HE IS!"

all Altenet was one great lunatic asylum; that every human being he had met and spoken to there was even madder than the one who had been caught; everything he had seen and heard was sheer nonsense and delirium, and so he had been obliged to return as he came.

Medical aid was summoned, but all in vain; the gentlemen were unable to agree, one asserting that the patient was suffering from *aberratio mentalis*, while another thought things were not so bad as that.

"After all, what business is it of ours?" said one at last. "Send him back to his home, and let them settle it among themselves."

This counsel met with unanimous approbation, and was, in fact, the most practical, and at the same time the easiest, way of disposing of the prisoner.

Bloemstein was furious; and when the gendarmes who escorted him took leave of him at the frontier, he was almost beside himself with rage. He would have liked to take them with him into his dominions, where he was undisputed lord and master; he would then have summoned the commander of the local rifles, and ordered him to shut up the Maastricht officials for a whole day in the cellar below the council chamber. But, alas! fate was against him, he could not gratify his desire for vengeance; but being forced to relieve his feelings in some way, he did so by indignantly shouting after their retreating figures, "You Dutch cheeseheads, you!"

With hasty steps he forthwith sought his chief counsellor, the Minister for Home Affairs, the tailor Holzert. In excited language, and with wild gestures, he related the story of the outrage suffered by him at Maastricht, and asked, in conclusion, "What are we to do?"

The tailor put his hand to his head, and remained for some little time lost in thought.

"What are we to do?" repeated Bloemstein; "we can't let a thing like that pass."

"What are we to do?" replied Holzert, speaking slowly and solemnly. "Why, we must declare war against Holland."

"Declare war against Holland?"

"Yes."

"And what for?"

"For high treason."

"You're right, you're right; we must send for Bauer at once."

"No, not so fast; we must have the stamps first, with your head on them, and then the Hollanders can see whom they have to deal with."

"You're right again, tailor," said Drikus I., flattered not a little by these words.

"Besides that, I haven't finished the ministers' suits yet, and we can do nothing without them; everything has got to be respectable."

"Of course."

During the next few days an unheard-of political commotion prevailed in the usually calm atmosphere of Altenet.

Every evening, when work was over, Bauer's rifles assembled in the Minister of Finance's public-house, in order to exchange ideas as to the coming war with Holland.

Guesses were given as to where the first battle would be fought, and calculations were made as to how soon they would be before the gates of Amsterdam, and how many thousand millions they would make the Dutch pay as war indemnity.

Bloemstein, meanwhile, wrote innumerable letters to all the powers of Europe, to give them notice of his accession. All of them were enclosed in large square envelopes, and laid out in a long row on the table.

"And when once I've stuck on the stamps, with my head on them, why, then, I shall be no end of a fellow, Marieke," he repeatedly remarked to his daughter.

The portraits, however, did not arrive.
After the lapse of a fortnight, Bloemstein's ploughman—

"WROTE INNUMERABLE LETTERS TO ALL THE POWERS OF EUROPE."

for he had no intention of going to Maastricht again himself—was sent to the photographer's, to ask whether the portraits of the President of the Republic of Altenet were not yet ready.

"Do you really want them?—seriously?" inquired the artist.

"I suppose so, seeing as how I had to come here a-purpose."

"Very well, I'll send them next week."

At the appointed time the impatiently awaited packet at last arrived at the house of Altenet's ruler. Something else arrived as well,—the long royal mantle promised by the tailor, richly ornamented with gold fringe.

Bloemstein was quite excited with joy. Without a moment's delay he flung the royal insignia round his shoulders, and then stood before the mirror, admiring his front and back view by turns. He was satisfied—perfectly and entirely satisfied—both with the garment and him who wore it!

"The other fellows must see that too! Thunder! how they'll stare!"

Immediately Bloemstein's man was sent to summon the council, and before long Marbaise, Klessens, Conrads, Bauer, and Holzert entered—all clad in their uniforms, consisting of long coats trimmed with gold lace, knee-breeches, long woollen stockings of a doubtful white, and swords dangling at their sides.

It was quite evident that Holzert had given his whole time and attention to the job, as was, moreover, irrefutably proved by an unexpected incident.

When all were gathered round the big table, loudly uttering their admiration of their ruler's portrait, long Kwoib Hermes suddenly rushed into the room, in his red baize drawers, with the tails of a blue shirt fluttering above them, and shouted aloud—"Thou accursed tailor, where are my trousers? I must go to early mass to-morrow, and I have no trousers!"

"You shall have them to-morrow; to-morrow morning early, Kwoib," replied the indignant tradesman.

"No, I want them to-night. You've promised me them all the week, and I'm going to have those trousers of mine to-night."

"Man, don't make such a scandalous row! Just think where you are—before the ministers of the republican council!"

"The ministers and the council and the whole republic may be stolen, for all I care! I want my trousers, and I'm not going away from here before I get them." And therewith he took a chair, and seated himself among the ministers of the crown.

"Will you get out or not?" asked Bauer, threateningly.

"No; I'm not going before I get my trousers."

Suddenly Bloemstein heard the steps of his wife and daughter, who were coming to see what the noise was. Fearing that they might come in for this unseemly spectacle, he thrust the intruder into the next room, with the words, "There; you'll find some trousers in there; just put them on in the meantime."

Not long after, Hermes appeared in a garment much too short for him, which, however, by way of compensation, was also a great deal too wide.

The assembly was now able to finish its deliberations in peace and quiet. The portraits having been unanimously approved of, No. 2 of the Agenda came up for discussion. This was, "Declaration of war against Holland on the ground of high treason." The debate was lively and confused.

Bauer wanted to summon his men at once, surprise Maastricht the same night, take the garrison prisoners, and march farther into the country.

Conrads, on the other hand, could see no good in such incautious haste. "Let's wait till we get the corn in; then we can bake bread for our men through the war."

"No need of that!" shouted Bauer. "We'll get all the bread we want from the Dutch."

Holzert was inclined to agree with Conrads, but for other reasons. "We must ask for explanations first; that's always the way," he declared. "We ought to give them time to investigate the outrage committed on our president, and make their apologies. Besides that," he added, "till we have stamps of our own we can't declare war."

"That's true, that's true!" cried several voices, "it would never do to declare war on Holland with Prussian stamps."

"Very well, then," raged Bauer, "but you must get them made directly, Bloemstein!"

"I'll promise that," replied the President.

Herewith the solemn session concluded.

A few weeks later the longed-for stamps appeared. They looked neat enough. A striking likeness of Bloemstein was surrounded by a garland of intertwined spades and pickaxes—symbols of labour —and above, in good bold letters, ALTENET.

There were blue, red, and green ones—of one, two, and three groschen respectively.

"Marieke! Marieke!" cried the delighted Bloemstein. "Come here, child; I've something to show you. What do you think of that?"

"Oh, quite beautiful, father!"

"Really, child?"

"And will they be sent to all the kings and emperors— all in the whole world?"

"All in the whole world."

"To Bismarck too?"

"He's going to get one as well; but it won't please him, I assure you, Marieke."

"Now you'll need to send them off at once; may I help you to put the stamps on?"

"Surely, Marieke."

The father and daughter sat down before the table, on which lay the long row of already written letters.

"Here's Bismarck's!" cried the girl suddenly.

"Put double stamps on that," said Bloemstein.

Instead of obeying this order, Marieke contrived to slip the letter into her pocket.

"Shall I take them to the post-office now, father?"

"Yes, do, child—only mind you don't lose any, specially the one to Bismarck."

"You needn't be afraid," and she skipped out of the room to fetch her hat, and perhaps also the letter she had received from her *fiancé*.

It was not long before an answer came from Berlin.

Bloemstein summoned his faithful councillors at once, in order to open the official document in their midst. The ministers hastened to the council-chamber, as fast as their legs could carry them. They took up positions behind their President, and stuck their heads together, trying to see with their own eyes the answer from the German Empire.

With trembling hand Bloemstein opened the missive, and in a voice quivering with emotion, he began to read, in German:—

"*Verehrter Herr* Präsident.

"In reply to your letter, I have received orders from my Emperor to declare war on your Republic, and send off an army of 150,000 men to the frontier, because—

"1. You have caused postage-stamps to be made without permission from the German Government.

"2. It is known to us that you have been taking upon yourself to oppose your daughter's marriage to our loyal subject, Dr Heinrich Olthausen.

"3. You want to force that charming and lovely girl to marry an objectionable, crooked tailor.

"We give you a week to comply with our conditions.

"BISMARCK."

There was a moment's painful silence. There it was, in great fat round letters—"BISMARCK." There was no possible doubt about it.

"The confounded low *Schwerenöther* of a Prussian!" yelled Holzert at last, crimson with passion, and quivering on his little bow-legs. "Declare war, Bloemstein! declare

"DECLARE WAR!"

war!" he went on. "Let them come, the low *canaille!* we'll blow up the mine as soon as they get on top of it, and then there'll be an end of them!" and suddenly turning to the Minister of War, he added, "Bauer, how many men have you?"

"HASTENED TO THE COUNCIL CHAMBER."

"A hundred and twenty-three, counting the band," was the answer.

"That's not one to a thousand," suggested Conrads; "and besides that, we've got the war with Holland on our hands,—it won't do—it won't do! What do you think yourself, Bauer?"

"What I think? I think you're a coward, Conrads, to talk so—a coward, do you understand? Conquer or die, that's our cry!"

"Yes, but we can't conquer, and dying isn't much good. Holzert won't get his Marieke by it if we do!"

"But in that case the Prussian pig-dog won't have her either!" shouted Holzert, banging the table with his fists.

At this, however, Bloemstein's paternal feelings revolted. His daughter, his pretty Marieke—dead! No, he would rather see her married to the Prussian doctor, for the Prussians were not so bad after all! Nay, they even knew how to appreciate beauty—had not Bismarck himself written that she was a "charming, lovely girl"?

Klessens also was for peace, and so was Marbaise. "Against 150,000 Prussians," said the latter, "and a few thousand Hollanders on top of those, you, Bauer, with your hundred and twenty men——"

"A hundred and twenty-three!" interrupted the commander of the Altenet forces.

"Well, a hundred and twenty-three, if you like—but you can't do anything with them!"

A great deal more talking and shouting took place, and at last the President determined to end the debate by putting the question to the vote.

"War!" yelled Holzert. "Peace!" "Peace!" "Peace!" muttered Conrads, Marbaise, and Klessens, in succession. "War!" thundered Bauer; and "I'm for peace," said the President in conclusion.

Peace was therefore resolved on by a majority of two votes.

Several months **have passed.** The **miners are at work again**; **the farmer is** ploughing his fields; the lark **sings high in air**; the Altenet postage-stamps have **been destroyed**; and Marieke is the happy wife of Dr Olthausen.

No answer was ever received **from** the rest of the kings and emperors,—it is just possible that Marieke may have forgotten to post the letters entrusted to her care.

L. H. J. LAMBERTS HURRELBRINCK.

NEWSPAPER HUMOUR.

"Look here, waiter!" **cried a gentleman in a restaurant,** "here's a hair in my **soup!**"

For all answer and excuse, the waiter removed **his cap,** showing a head as bare and smooth as a billiard ball.

"Yes, I see," resumed the customer, "I see it was **your** last hair; that's all right, it will never happen again!"

"So you've written a play, M. Vermorcken?"

"Yes, my friend, I have that honour."

"And it is quite finished?"

"Yes—no—yes; that is to say, not the play itself, yet— but my speech, that I am to make, when I thank them for calling me out on the stage."

FICTION AT SEA.

It is quiet now on deck. The singing forward has ceased, the watch is set, and the larboard watch, who are to come on at midnight, are below—including the tall corporal of marines, whom we heard just now singing bass. But the little monkey of a boy, who took the tenor part in "O Julia!" belongs to the starboard watch, and now has another occupation on hand.

Seated on a tub turned upside down, close to the foremast, he is reading aloud, by the light of a lantern, out of an "awfully fine" book.

The boy (his name is Jozef) can read "real first-rate"; and from each of the listeners seated round him he is to receive the sum of two cents.

The book which he now has before him, and which is covered with oil-stains, because he has to hold it so close to the lantern,—the book which is so "awfully fine," is entitled "Count Matatskai; or, The Bandit with the Grey Beard: A Story from the Mountains."

Count Matatskai is a youthful nobleman who has fallen in love with a mountain maiden, the beautiful but fierce Krimhelia, daughter of a chamois-hunter. After various meetings on the rocks by moonlight, with a faithful old servitor *incognito* in the background, Krimhelia makes up her mind to accept the Count's love, and fly with him to a distant country, where counts and the daughters of chamois-hunters stand precisely on the same social footing. But now a difficulty occurs, and it is this: Krimhelia has sworn an oath to avenge the death of her father, who has been killed in a fight with the band commanded by the Grey-Bearded Brigand.

This is the point Jozef has reached in the story. Several of his audience have already dropped asleep; but the reader does not notice it—he is too much absorbed in his narrative, —and continues, in his "first-rate" manner, which—heard at a distance—reminds one of nothing so much as of the soft but continuous murmur of a babbling brook—commas and other stops being, in this method, so entirely left in the background, or else occurring in such remarkable places, that a reporter would have been forced to reproduce his text somewhat as follows:—

"Krimhelia looked the Count straight in the face.

"Look at me Count said she do you see this glittering dagger as sure as the moon, hangs yonder in heaven and illuminates my pale features so surely will I thrust this, dagger into the heart of the Bandit, with the Grey Beard first and before I throw myself as your consort into your arms but why so pale Count and why do you tremble so?"

Now Jozef is interrupted by the master-tailor, a thin, little man, of whom it is commonly said on board that he knows a thing or two more than most people.

"Now, I know," says he, in his piping voice.

"What d'ye know?" asks the boatswain, who has little or no opinion of the master-tailor.

"As how the gentleman—the Count, I mean—and the other,—the Bandit with the Grey Beard,—that both of them are one and the same man."

"Well, you calico-spoiler—you know that, do you? Well —I know that too, and all of us know it right enough; but you needn't take another man's share in the reading for all that. Go ahead, boy!"

The master-tailor is looked at with contempt from various quarters, and Jozef pursues his reading with a chapter describing how Count Matatskai comes home in a bad temper.

"The Count threw himself down on a, couch adorned with costly velvet, relieve me of my riding-boots—thus he spoke to the grey-headed old servant Gabario who, brought him a silver goblet with sparkling wine saying, that this was his favourite wine from the great vineyard south of the castle but, the Count made a gesture of refusal with his left hand and said me liketh no wine Gabario avaunt and saddle—my horse!"

This was the end of the chapter, and Jozef took breath.

"It's a capital thing," said the boatswain, "when a man can have the things for the ordering in that way. What comes next, Jozef?"

The boatswain is beginning to feel sleepy, and would therefore like Jozef to tell him the end at once; but this Jozef is by no means inclined to do,—he goes ahead valiantly, and by degrees, though he does not observe it, his whole audience drops asleep. At last, when he has reached the closing scene, there is no one to listen to it but the master-tailor, who can scarcely keep his small grey eyes open.

"Just hear this, now!" says Jozef, who—though he has read the book through twice before—is as enthusiastic over this passage as the first time. "Now you must listen! Now the Count is sitting up alone in the rocks, in a . . . cavern, they call it, . . . and now he is the Bandit with the Grey Beard; and the other robbers are sitting in the back of the cavern round a great big fire, and some of them are lying asleep, and the others are roasting great pieces of meat at the fire, and they're drinking wine with it . . . out of gold cups that they've stolen. . . . But the Bandit with the Grey Beard— . . . *he's* sitting all by himself, you see,—and now Krimhelia comes in—you know—the young lady he thinks so much of."

And Jozef resumes his reading — how Krimhelia approaches, cautiously, with the glittering dagger; how the Grey-Bearded Bandit, looking up, suddenly sees her standing behind him; how Krimhelia seizes him by the beard and drives the dagger into his heart; and how, at the same moment, the long grey beard comes **off in** her hand, and she looks with horror on the "pallid **dying** countenance" of Count Matatskai.

Now follows a dialogue between the dying bandit chief and the "almost fainting" Krimhelia, who is "filled with consternation"; in the course of which the tailor finally closes his eyes unobserved.

Now comes the closing scene; the other robbers come out from behind **the** fire, Krimhelia takes to flight, and climbs to the top of a steep dark rock **on the** edge **of a** "yawning abyss."

As Jozef reads, he bends over his book, leans his head on his hands, and sees the whole thing **taking place before his** eyes. **He** sees Krimhelia standing **on the top of the rock.** The day is breaking **in the east. The robbers are pursuing** her, **and** begin to climb **the rock.** . . .

Jozef reads on,—at **a** passionately **accelerated pace, and with the most singular stops imaginable:—**

"There she stood proudly—like **a queen with her** long, loose **hair** and her shining white face **standing out** sharply against the red sunrise-tinted sky **with** horror—she saw in the unfathomable depth at her feet the bandits approaching. Already the foremost was stretching **out** his hand to seize **her** and she **saw, the** morning-light falling **on** his horrible features **when** suddenly, her **ear** was struck by a sound **of** men's voices singing beneath her **in** the **valley** she listens, **it** is the morning song of her brothers, she **lifts** her hands skywards and looks up to the paling moon **and** the stars 'Iecome'! she cries" (all in **one** word) " . . . and with a HOARSE shriek she flings herself **down into** the abyss at the **same moment** the Bandit Chief **drew his last** breath and the Count Matatskai was no more **THE END.**"

"That's all!" said Jozef. "That's fine, ain't it? . . . Oh! lor! . . . they're all asleep."

Jozef cannot at once get over a slight feeling of indignation against an audience, capable of dropping-off "in the middle of a bit like that,"—but as it is not an isolated experience on his part, he soon makes up his mind to pay no further attention to it. He takes the lantern away, goes forward, and lies down on the deck with the oil-stained book under his head—looking up at the moon right above him, and beginning to see, in the air, all sorts of figures, which gradually acquire a likeness to Count Matatskai and the "young lady he thinks so much of."

A. Werumeus Buning.

NEWSPAPER HUMOUR.

FROM SAD EXPERIENCE.

She—"Do tell me, how do you know the age of a horse you want to buy?"

He—"Nothing easier; you just double the age the dealer gives him."

Professor (*at a clinical lecture*)—"This patient has been suffering from a disease of the hip-joint, so that he still walks lame to an appreciable extent. What would you, sir" (to one of the students), "do in such a case?"

Student—"I think, in that case, I should walk lame too, sir."

NATURAL HISTORY.

Master—"The development and improvement of race has not only shown itself among mankind, but may clearly be

FROM SAD EXPERIENCE.

observed among the lower animals. Who can give me an example of this?"

Janneke Snobs—"I, sir."

M.—"In what sort of animals?"

J. S.—"Among asses, sir."

M.—"How so?"

J. S.—"Why, in Balaam's time, asses were only just beginning to speak, and yesterday I heard M. Snugger say that there are plenty of asses sitting in the Chamber of Deputies."

History.

Master—"In what battle was Gustav Adolf killed?"

Janneke Snobs—"In his last battle, I believe, sir."

Precautions.

Many centuries ago, the gallows stood on the banks of the Scheldt; and once, when two thieves were to be hanged, the rope broke, as the first was being turned off, and let him into the water. He swam across the river, and escaped.

"Look out!" said the second to the executioner, "see that the rope does not break with me—for *I can't swim!*"

A gentleman was buying a newspaper at a kiosk, and wanted change for a frank. "I have no change," said the saleswoman; "you can pay me to-morrow."

"But supposing I am dead by to-morrow?"

"Oh, that can't be any great loss," she replied, innocently.

A servant girl, writing home to her parents, said, "I am sorry I have no money to buy a stamp for this letter; I will put two on the next."

Uilenspiegel.

"A GENTLEMAN WAS BUYING A PAPER AT A KIOSK."

In Court.

Judge—"Is this your signature?"

Witness—"I don't know."

Judge—"Look at it carefully."

Witness—"I can't say for certain."

Judge (impatiently)—"Come, make haste, just write your name."

Witness—"I'm no scholar, sir; I can't write."

Economy.

Father—"I should never have thought that studying would have cost so much money."

Student-Son—"Yes; and if you only knew how little I have studied!"

VAN HONSBŒREN, junior, one evening sat gazing at his father, when the latter had fallen asleep sitting by the stove.

"Father," cried the little fellow, suddenly, "you look just like a lion!"

"A lion!" exclaimed Van Honsbœren, waking up, "why, you've never seen any lions."

"Oh yes, father! on the beach at Blankenberghe."

"You stupid boy, those were not lions, they were donkeys."

"Well, those are what I mean!"

Snugger—"*M. le Juge*, I have been fined for letting my dog go about without a muzzle, and he certainly had one on."

Judge—"The *agent de police* says your dog had no muzzle on."

Snugger—"Indeed, he had one on, sir."

Gendarme—"Yes, but he was not wearing it on his head."

Snugger—" The regulations do not specify *where* a dog is to wear his muzzle—and so, to let the beast get his breath, I tied the muzzle to his tail."

Judge—" Five francs fine. **Next case!**"

Snobs has bought a steam-engine, and **was showing it to** his friend Snugger yesterday.

" How many horse-power is that machine?" **asked** Snugger.

" Horse-power!" exclaimed Snobs, " **don't you see it goes** by steam?"

Nothing is more uncomfortable for a woman who has to keep a secret than to find no one who is curious about it.

The human being who can pass a hoarding marked "Wet Paint," without putting his finger on it to feel if the paint really is wet, possesses strength of will and self-control enough to rule a kingdom.

A lady having run against the freshly painted rail of a bridge, and carried off a considerable quantity of the paint on her dress, the bridge-keeper said to her consolingly,—

" Never mind, ma'am, they're going to paint it again to morrow, **any** way!"

FARMER GERRIT'S VISIT TO AMSTERDAM.

Gerrit Meeuwsen and his son Gijs, living in the depths of the country, in the Betuwe district (the old Batavian Island, between the Rhine and the Waal), have made up their minds—after long deliberation—for an expedition by rail to the Amsterdam kermis. As they have never left home before, preparations are made which suggest an Arctic voyage, and they take a solemn farewell of their friends and relations. The railway station is safely reached, after a drive of many miles; and Gerrit severs the last link, so to speak, by sending back Jan—the farm-man—with the trap.

"G'MORNING," said father and son, at once.

"Good-morning, friends," replied the station clerk, who was seated at a table doing sums.

Meeuwsen took off his great woollen gloves, hauled out his double-cased watch, and said, "Might it be about time for the railway to come?"

"Don't know," answered Gijs, who thought that his father was asking the question of him.

The clerk, a good-natured fellow, understanding that the question was addressed to him, replied, "Oh! I suppose you mean the *train*. Yes, that will be coming by very soon,—perhaps in thirteen, or fourteen, or fifteen minutes. Where do you want to go?"

"To Amsterdam," replied Meeuwsen.

"Amsterdam—third-class?" asked the clerk.

"Third-class, what's that?" returned Gerrit.

"Three classes, you know, my good friend," the clerk explained; "first, second, and third. The first is the dearest, the second middling, and the third the cheapest."

"Then the third won't do for us, nor the second neither," said Gerrit. "I always sit in the first seat at church in our village, for I be churchwarden."*

---

* The official known in a Dutch church as *Kerkmeester* combines in himself functions analogous to those of the English clerk and churchwarden, or the Scottish beadle and precentor.

"First-class?" asked the clerk, in surprise, "but—do you know——"

"Never you mind; I want first-class, do you hear?" said Gerrit.

"Well, it's all the same to me," said the clerk, rising. He went to the place where he kept the tickets, stamped two, and received the rich Betuwers money.

"Gracious! there's the train!" cried the clerk, whose calculation of fifteen minutes had been rather too liberal. "Will you come out, please?"

Gerrit and Gijs, the latter carrying the carpet-bag, rushed out on to the platform, followed by the clerk. The approaching train seemed to the travellers to grow longer the more they looked at it, and, when it stopped, both father and son involuntarily took a step backwards.

Neither Gerrit nor Gijs knew exactly what happened to them next; but when they got back all their senses,—for the wind was blowing freshly in their faces,—they saw themselves in a carriage containing, besides themselves, two other passengers, and which allowed free passage to the wind on all sides.

"Bad weather for the money," grumbled Gerrit.

"Why! come and sit over here," cried one of their fellow-travellers, apparently a Jew, who was sitting on the opposite side of the carriage, with his back to the engine. "Sit here, on the first seat; you will be frozen to death over there."

Gerrit looked at his son, and then both stumbled along the shaking carriage to the other end, and occupied the end seats.

"That's a difference!" said Gijs, whose skin felt like that of a plucked chicken.

"Well, this does shake!" said Meeuwsen. "No!—that third-class is enough to kill one!"

Nathan, who was reading a book, which, as Gerrit could

see, seemed to begin at the end and go backwards, did not speak again. The second travelling-companion had turned up the collar of his thick overcoat and was snoring; and our two gentlemen from Betuwe, having nothing to say to each other, were silent, and thought—what, no one ever will know.

After a few minutes' run, a conductor appeared—whence, neither Gerrit nor Gijs could understand—and asked them, "Where for, gentlemen?"

"*Gentlemen!*" exclaimed Gerrit, with fine scorn, "*that* won't go down with us!"

"Farmers, then!" said the conductor, "where for?"

Meeuwsen thought the fellow had no manners, and said, "I and my son for Amsterdam."

"Show your tickets, please," said the conductor.

Meeuwsen began to search for them. . . . "I'd put them away so carefully," he remarked, while turning out all his pockets.

"Well, never mind," resumed the conductor (he was very cold, and wanted to get back to his warm corner in the closed compartment), "you can show me them presently."

"Very good," replied Gerrit, who began to think the man was not so bad after all.

The conductor disappeared again, in the same mysterious fashion, and Gerrit suddenly remembered that he had put away the tickets inside his watch-case.

At every station, when the whistle of the engine was heard, Gijs was seized with consternation, thinking that a child or some other living creature had been run over. Every time the train stopped, the sons of Batavia prepared to alight, and each time they were politely stopped by Nathan, who told them they might just make their minds easy, for they had not got there yet. Gijs thereupon came to the conclusion that the journey would not be over so soon as the schoolmaster had led them to suppose.

At length, after they had left the last of the intermediate stations behind, the mysterious conductor appeared once more, and asked for the tickets; and Gerrit, who had kept them carefully in his hand, under his woollen glove, produced them, and gave them up.

"First-class!" said the conductor. "Why, man, you've certainly had the best for your money!"

"Hi?" said Meeuwsen, who could not understand what the fellow meant.

"Stupid bumpkins!" muttered the conductor in an undertone, happily inaudible to the Meeuwsens, and left the carriage with a loud "Amsterdam, gentlemen!" The train now stopped for good. Every one got out, and there was such a row that Gerrit and his son could not understand what was going on, and stood staring about them quite dazed.

People, carriages, cabs, omnibuses, trunks, drivers with brandished whips, crying, "This way, sir!—Hotel this!—Hotel that!—just off!" There was such a swarming and confusion that our travellers only regained their full consciousness when they found themselves sitting in an omnibus, packed, knee to knee, like herrings in a barrel,—and, probably, dreaming—at least, so they thought.

"Where to, sir?" asked the conductor of the omnibus, in a green coat trimmed with silver lace, of the person sitting next the door.

"The Dam," was the answer. "Botermarkt," said another passenger. "Rokin, No. 11," said another; and another followed with "The Mint."

"Sir?" said the inquisitive man, addressing Gijs.

"I?" asked Gijs, staring wildly; "to the Fair, isn't it, father?"

All the passengers laughed, except three or four who were in a hurry to get to the Exchange.

"Be'st mad, I think, boy," said Gerrit, grinning. "No, mate," he went on, addressing the conductor, "to a lodging."

"Which hotel?" was then the question. "First, second, third, fourth, fifth class? Rondeel, Doelen, Munt—or do you want to go to the Nes?" *

Whether Gerrit was thinking of the third-class carriage in which he had been sitting with Gijs, and contrasting it with the imaginary first-class where he found a place by the side of Nathan, we do not know; but it is certain that he shivered at the idea of a fifth-class, and had his answer ready at once—

"First class, man! First class!"

"*Vieux Doelen!*" cried the conductor, with a smile and a furtive wink at the passenger next the door.

The omnibus stopped, and Gerrit and Gijs were beckoned to come out. How they ever got through the double row of knees is quite incomprehensible; and twice did the heels of Gijs' heavy boots come unpleasantly in contact with corns, whose proprietors, therefore, unkindly addressed him as "Clumsy lout!" and "Dumb ass!"

"How much is it?" asked Gerrit.

The conductor gave a look round, and then said, under his breath—

"Only ten stivers † each, sir. I can't ask you for more."

Meeuwsen gave him a florin, whereupon he asked whether the gentleman couldn't spare him a trifle for himself!

This question was answered by the good-natured farmer thrusting a *kwartje* ‡ into his hand; and the unscrupulous rascal drove away, laughing in his sleeve.

Gerrit, and Gijs with the carpet-bag on his back, stared for a long time at the fine house, with the gilt letters on the front; and at length ventured to go up the steps, though they could not make up their minds to venture in.

---

* The Nes is a low part of Amsterdam, full of taverns and music-halls of the worst description.

† 20 stivers = 1 florin = 1s. 8d.

‡ 5 stivers.

"What do you want?" politely asked a handsome young gentleman, in a snow-white waistcoat and a beautiful black jacket, who came out of the broad hall and walked up to them.

"Lodgings," answered Gerrit.

"For yourself?" asked the young gentleman, who, seen at close quarters, seemed older than his jacket would have led one to suppose.

"I and my son Gijs," said Gerrit.

"You?" again asked the young gentleman.

"Is that so hard to understand?" asked the farmer. "Are there no lodgings here? Can we get them, or can't we?"

The young gentleman walked away, and stopped to speak to another young gentleman like unto himself, who met him in the corridor. Soon after two more arrived, one of them with a napkin over his arm, and all the four began to laugh immoderately; so that Gerrit began to be tired of waiting, and, approaching the group, said, with some violence, "Now, what is it to be? Are we to get rooms, or are we not?" The young gentlemen continued to giggle, but suddenly stopped, and scattered with surprising rapidity, for a dignified elderly person entered the vestibule, and asked what was the matter here. Whereupon Gerrit expounded to him that he had asked, in a straightforward and downright way, for lodgings; that he did not know what the young gentlemen were up to; that he had come with his son to attend the fair; that he had no mind to be what-you-may-call-ummed and made a fool of by those young gentlemen; and that he asked, once more, Could he, or could he not?

The respectable gentleman took a good look at Gerrit and Gijs—the latter was still outside the door with the carpetbag—for some moments; but the open honest face, and generally prosperous appearance of the farmer, reassured him as to the probability of their being good customers. He then laid his forefinger against his nose, and called out to one of the young gentlemen,—

"No. 71 and 72, Karel. *Allons!*"

Karel came. Gerrit beckoned Gijs to come in. Gijs also came.

"Take the gentleman's luggage," said the proprietor of the hotel to Karel, pointing to the carpet-bag, which Gijs still carried over his shoulder.

"Oh, no! thank you," said Gijs, as the young gentleman Karel went about to relieve him of his load. Karel, however, did not leave go. The proprietor was present; and, in spite of Gijs' asseverations that he was far too kind, he seized the bag and flew up the broad staircase like a jumping rabbit.

"If you will follow, gentlemen," said the proprietor, "the *garçon* will show you your rooms." Gerrit, putting up, for the sake of peace, with the title of gentleman, followed the flying *garçon*, and Gijs followed his father.

"Where are we going to?" cried the stout farmer, to whom climbing of stairs was an unaccustomed exercise.

"To No. 71 and 72," said the *garçon*.

"I don't care what number it is—number thousand, if you like—but I didn't come here to climb up a tower!"

"We shall be there directly," said Karel, still flying on ahead.

"Go on, then!" said Gerrit, taking courage; and on they went again, up stairs and more stairs—there was no end to it.

"Are we not there yet?" sighed Meuwsen, when Gijs had counted the forty-fifth flight of steps, and they had come to an arched doorway.

"This way round!" cried Karel, and flew on, still higher.

"No! that's too much; I give it up!" cried Gerrit, holding fast to the banisters. "It's enough to drive a man crazy! I'll go no farther."

"Only a few more," said Karel persuasively. At last,

when Gijs had counted sixty-three, the two, panting and gasping, reached their goal—Nos. 71 and 72.

"*Ici*," said Karel, throwing open both doors almost at the same moment.

"*Ici* or no *ici*," muttered the farmer, "what I say is that no decent man can be expected to do it!"

"This is your room," said Karel, pointing to No. 72, as he saw that Gijs was about to follow his father into No. 71.

"I?" ejaculated Gijs.

"*S'il vous plaît*," said the waiter, and flinging the carpetbag into No. 71, he left the rooms, stood still in the passage between the two apartments, and looking at father and son by turns, went on, "Any more orders? Will the gentlemen dine at the *table d'hôte*, at half-past four?"

Gijs understood not a single word of this; and Gerrit, who likewise did not grasp the subtleties of the situation, answered shortly, "No," being mortally afraid of having to do any more climbing.

Karel having had enough of this exalted society, uttered no further questions or remarks, slammed both doors, reached the ground floor by sliding down the banisters, and left the father and son, each in his own room, to their respective meditations.

The well-furnished rooms were only divided from one another by a thin wooden partition, and their windows afforded a delightful view, to wit, a red-tiled roof, from which arose a tall black chimney.

Gijs looked round, like a cat in a strange warehouse, and did not think Amsterdam so very beautiful after all.

"Boy! where are you?" shouted Gerrit. "What are we to do now? Just come here!"

"Can I do that, father?" roared Gijs, in a voice that could easily have been heard in the street.

"Of course!" cried Gerrit.

Gijs went on tiptoe to his door, and, speeding as though death were at his heels, out of No. 72 and into No. 71.

"Look here, boy!" said Gerrit, when his son was safely inside, "here we sit, and I'm so hungry that I can't see straight."

"So am I," asseverated Gijs.

"Then you ought to call," said his father, "and we might order something."

Gijs muttered something about "so strange," and "if father were to do it himself,"—but, like a dutiful son, he went to the stairs, and shouted—very much as he was accustomed at home to call the calves to their food—"*Huup! huup! huup!*"

No one came. At last a door opened, and an old gentleman in hat and greatcoat came out, and passed Gijs.

"Oh!" said Gijs, his shyness giving way before his own hunger and his father's orders, "would you be so kind as to order something to eat for us!"

"Pull the bell, you young donkey!" was the polite reply. The donkey departed without a word, and, after some searching, Father Meeuwsen found a rope hanging in No. 71, at which he pulled,—and lo! they heard a bell ring. A minute later Karel was again standing before them.

"You must bring us something to eat," said the farmer, who now began to understand that the young man was a waiter.

"*Déjeuner à la fourchette?*" asked Karel.

"Don't know those things," replied Gerrit. "I've never eaten *desernages*, nor *forzettes* either. Just bring us something, my lad,—I don't much care what, so long as we can get something inside us."

Flop went the door again; and five minutes later there arrived at No. 71 some strange substances of whose nature Gerrit and Gijs had not the remotest idea. They began, however, to try and to taste, and though they could scarcely get the things down their throats, they were messed up so queerly with sweet stuff and spice, they managed to satisfy their appetites somehow.

"I've had enough," said Gerrit at last.

"So have I," sighed Gijs, and they rose from table,—to go to the kermis.

We will not relate in detail how Gerrit and Gijs climbed downstairs again, went out at the front door, and announced that they would come back again in the evening; how they were besieged by beggars, shoeblacks, and Jews selling lottery tickets,—nearly all of whom the good-natured farmer succeeded in satisfying; how they were directed from one part of the town to another, and back again, in order to reach the fair; how and when they got there they found booths, just like those in their own village, but much bigger and finer ones. We will not record how much Gerrit paid for the monster cake which he wished to take home to Griet, and which bore the inscription, in sugar letters, "A Fairing for You;" how Gijs was cheated in the purchase of a cup and saucer for Mijntje; how they, furthermore, bought ginger-bread, almonds, and who knows what besides, so that their pockets stood out like hard lumps, and they were nearly fainting under the weight of them. They visited the circus, but were not edified; and when, finally, the great trick rider "*Meseu* Blanus," after two sudden changes of costume, appeared in flesh-coloured tights, and walked about blowing a trumpet, Gerrit could stand it no longer, and seizing his son by the arm, he shouted, "That beats all! so it does! come, boy, come! come!" and hurried him out. When they had struggled out into the crowd again, Gerrit said that they had had their fill of that sort of thing, and more; and Gijs remarked that it was low. They did not attempt to see any of the other shows, and Gerrit unmercifully dragged Gijs past "The Mirror of Mystery," where, as the man at the door said, "The girl can see her lover, and the young man his girl,—all for a *dubbeltje!* Great American Magic Mirror of Mystery!" Gijs would have liked a peep at his Mijntje, but Gerrit was firm.

Having partaken, by way of refreshment, of hot wafers and punch,—a repast which Gijs liked well enough, but his father considered "sweet, but nothing to stay your stomach on,"—they at last, after many wanderings, found their way back to the hotel. The nimble rabbit, Mr Karel, was again to the fore. In the twinkling of an eye he had lit a candle, and flew up the stairs, requesting the wearied rustics, unaccustomed to the hard walking of the streets, to follow him, *s'il vous plaît.*

Gerrit and Gijs followed—yes! and in time they reached the top, but felt just as if a thousand smiths were hammering away in their bones.

"Do the gentlemen wish *souper?*" asked Karel, who by this time had lit candles in each of the two rooms.

"Eat soup now!" said Gerrit, "get away with you! I'm fair filled up with those wafer-cakes!"

"Put boots outside door—when d'you-want-to-be-called?" asked Karel.

"I'm going away to-morrow morning by the first train," said Gerrit.

"Then you'll want a *vigilante?*"

"Go to the ... woodpile!" cried Gerrit, "with all your foreign talk."

"Good-night, gentlemen!" said Karel.

The doors were shut, and the gentlemen were left alone. Now began a conversation between the two—carried on in genuine rustic growls, and yet as softly as if they were afraid of waking "Mother my wife." A few minutes later Gijs retired, with a new blue wadded night-cap, and a "good-night, dad," to No. 72.

Gerrit had at once blown out the wax candles in No. 71. "That's just sinful waste," he said; and Gijs, on entering No. 72, followed his father's example.

They were not long in undressing by moonlight. Gijs put on the night-cap, and stepped into the soft bed. What a thing that was!—soft as pap! . . . Never knew such a thing before . . . He lay listening . . Every moment he heard something . . . some one walking about . . . groping among the furniture . . . at last speaking. At last, he could stand it no longer—he sat up and stared uneasily about. He thought he could plainly . . . hear . . . something . . . at . . the . . . door. Seemed as if . . . you . . . could . . . see . . . the . . . handle . . . turning . . . The perspiration broke out all over him . . . still he saw it . . . plainly . . . and, when the door was really opened, he uttered a yell, but slowly recovered himself on seeing that it was his father.

"Can't rest on *that* thing," said Gerrit, as he came in, meaning the bed, which he found much too soft. "No, Gijs, I'll just come and lie here on the boards."

"I'll do that too," said Gijs, stepping out of bed, and then he lay down on the floor beside his father—each with a pea-jacket rolled up for a pillow—"good-night! pleasant dreams."

Whether the dreams were, in point of fact, pleasant may be doubted, for they formed a first-class raree-show, composed of bare legs and wafer-cakes, guns and horses, omnibuses, and the climbing of towers, in wild confusion. Certain it is, however, that the Meeuwsens, father and son, when they awoke, stared at one another as if they had been bewitched, and had to think a long time before they could remember where on earth they were.

Well, how did they get home again from the fair?—Gerrit to his Griet, and Gijs to his Mijn.

Very well indeed. Physically they were in sad case, but spiritually all right—which does not always happen on like occasions. The bill which Karel handed to Gerrit before his departure was alike illegible to him and to Gijs. Perhaps no one but the hotel-proprietor and the head-waiter could ever have deciphered it—only the total was clear: 16f. 80—accurately reckoned. Gerrit thought, but said nothing; paid; started, when he was told that a tip was expected of him, over and above the bill, but paid it; and left the Verdoel by the first omnibus, and Amsterdam by the first train.

"That's over!" said Gerrit, sitting safe and sound once more beside his Griet in the kitchen. "Once is well enough—but never again! And I had everything first-class!"

This was true enough: for on the return journey he had managed to get into the right compartment of the train—though, to say the truth, he found it much less comfortable than the other.

And Gijs? Gijs was as blythe as a foal in the meadow, when he found himself at home again. When he told Mijn about the circus, and the young ladies in gilt caps who had sold him wafers, and tried to flirt with him, she turned as red as fire, and said it was scandalous; but the cup and saucer, which, contrary to all expectation, had reached home uninjured, were duly admired by her. And when Gerrit, one fine evening, had some of the neighbours in to help in the pig-killing, and entertained them in the kitchen when work was over, the monster cake was tasted, and Gerrit profited by the opportunity to relate all his adventures. Then said Brother-in-Law Kresel, that such a thing hadn't happened within the memory of man!—and Baas Janssen, that morality was getting into a frightful state!—and the old Teunis farmer concluded, "What does a man want on the ice in his clogs?"

J. J. CREMER.

NO SWORD!

OLD Colonel H—— was standing, during one of the summer months, before the open window, puffing the smoke of his havannah into the air, with the feeling of satisfaction produced by a fine day, while his eyes followed the movements of a young officer, whose elastic figure had already, at some distance, attracted his superior's attention.

Suddenly his face darkened. No one so soon feels his toes trodden on as an old military man.

What was that? Were his eyes dazzled by the sunlight? Or could anything of the sort possibly happen under the eye of the strict commanding officer of the regiment? Had discipline really died out among the younger generation of the army?

No, it was no optical deception. He could see it now, plainly—the lieutenant, passing there, on the other side of the street, with a letter in his hand, had *no* sword on! And it was not nearly four P.M. !

"Lieutenant!" cried the fire-eater, in a momentary ebullition of indignation, from the open window; "if I may ask you—one moment!"

The man addressed immediately turned with a military salute, and hastened to the Colonel's rooms, without the slightest presentiment of the storm about to burst over his head.

He rang the bell, and the Colonel's servant opened the door.

Passing through the hall, he gave a hasty glance at his uniform to see whether it was all right—and then he discovered his misfortune. Horrible! He had, in his haste to post a letter, forgotten to buckle on his sword!

For one moment he hesitated; he was really frightened, and saw, looming up in space, all the evil consequences of his mistake, in the form of all possible reports, with "arrest" at the end of them.

The Colonel would send a note to the commander of division, who would endorse and put it into the hands of the captain—and then the fat would be in the fire with a vengeance! All this passed like a flash of lightning through the unhappy man's head, and he looked helplessly round, as though hoping that some good genius would inspire him with a way of escape in this sore need. What was he to do? He could not keep the cantankerous Colonel waiting,—there was nothing for it except to march valiantly forward into the lion's den. But luck never forsakes a lieutenant!

What is that glittering over there in the umbrella-stand?

The Colonel's sword! . . . He pulls out his purse,—thrusts, with an eloquent gesture, a guilder into the hand of the Colonel's man, and buckles on the sword—all in less time than it takes to tell it.

A moment later he stands—in correct military attitude, his left hand held so as to hide the dragon on his sword-hilt from the eagle eye of his chief—before the old gentleman, who, meanwhile, has been stalking up and down the room, fretting and fuming.

"Sir! I must call your attention to——"

A long pause.

The Colonel's glance travels from the sword to the young officer's blushing face, and back again to the glittering weapon.

Then he shakes his head in utter amazement, but recovers himself speedily, and continues in a low tone:

"What battalion do you belong to?"

"The second, Colonel."

"Just so. I only wanted to ask you if—if—Major Ij . . . has returned from his leave?"

"He is not coming back till to-morrow, sir, if I have understood rightly."

"IN CORRECT MILITARY ATTITUDE."

"Ah!—thank you—it had escaped me—thanks."

The lieutenant saluted respectfully, left the room with the greatest air of self-confidence, hastened down the stairs, unbuckled the Colonel's sword—put it away noiselessly among the sticks and umbrellas, after which he hurried away, keeping as close as he could to the wall till he was out of sight.

As for the Colonel, he simply could not believe his eyes! Then something occurred to him. He called his man.

"Did you let the lieutenant in?"

"Yes, sir."

"Was he wearing a sword when he came in?"

"Yes, sir," answered he, with imperturbable calm.

The Colonel smote his forehead with his open hand.

The lieutenant's guilder was well invested.

"Humoristisch Album."

A STUDENT'S LODGINGS SIXTY YEARS SINCE.

THE burghers of the university town—at least those whose houses, at the beginning of the summer vacation, are adorned with cards bearing the inscription "*Cubicula locanda*"—can, during nine months of the year, be looked on only to a limited extent as masters in their own dwellings. It is the student, or the officer, as the case may be, who is established in the best room, who attracts all the attention of passers by, and the neighbours over the way,—who sits at the window, is seen to go in and out at the front door, carries the key, rules, gives orders, receives his friends and acquaintances, and, in a word, conducts himself as the principal person, while the owner or lessee of the house is banished to a back room or some little subterraneous den in the basement. It is to the best room, then, that we must make our way, though the approach to it is not an attractive one. Our way lies, first, through a narrow passage, where we run the risk of stumbling over a doorstep, evidently placed there with the sole object of teaching children and visitors to be careful of their steps. Then we have to seek a dark and narrow stairway, and, having found it, to ascend it. It receives, by day, only a dim and doubtful light from the basement; by night, it is perfectly dark, and its worn and slippery steps follow one another at such strangely unequal intervals, that one is tempted to think the architect must have been interested in the problem how to pile on one another, in a given space, a given number of irregular parallelograms in the most heterogeneous manner possible. When we have succeeded, after having knocked our heads not more than three or four times against all sorts of fantastically projecting rafters and angles, in reaching what is ironically called the *bel étage*, we find ourselves in front of a door which opens very easily and noiselessly, but can never be closed without five or six violent thrusts or tugs, according as you are inside or out. We once more hit our toes against an unexpected doorstep, and at last enter the first of the two rooms inhabited by *Gerlof Bol, S.S. Theol. cand.*

It is evening; the two sash windows, divided by a narrow space of wall, are hidden behind unpainted shutters, on which, here and there, a square, worm-eaten, or dirt-stained spot shows where a hasp or bolt has been, but is no more. These shutters curve outwards, and threaten every moment to escape from the control of the bars (bent crooked as though with their weight), and fling themselves in the face of the incautious person who should venture too near. The walls are covered with a dirty yellow paper, on which green and blue flowers alternate in diagonal lines. Now and then, where the paper has been torn, another piece of the same pattern has been pasted on upside down, probably for the sake of securing a pleasing variety; while in other cases the damage has not been repaired, and an earlier wall decoration, in orange and black, is apparent in patches. On the wall hang the portraits of Van Der Palm and Borgen * in one frame, the lecture list, fastened up with three pins, and a variety of college notices secured in the same way. Near the door is a tolerably roomy alcove, containing the occupant's chief treasures,—in the first place, his books, which, in so far as they consist of quartos, octavos, and duodecimos, are ranged on three shelves against the wall, while the folios stand on the ground in the company of sundry maps in cases; in the second place, two baskets, one of which is full of burnt-out clay pipes, the other of foul ditto awaiting their burning. Item, a closed card-table, bought cheap at a second-hand dealer's, which can never stand on more than two legs at the same time; while the superficies of the once green baize with which it is covered offers a remarkable assemblage of mathematical figures, such as circles formed by the setting down of wet punch or wine glasses, ellipses or squares arising from the dropping of wax, grease, or ink, or the contact with various objects not previously dusted. Item, an umbrella without a knob, whose whalebone ribs, for the most part, have either repudiated all connection with the covering, or shamelessly protrude through it. Furthermore, a trio of eccentric-looking canes, a couple of broken German pipes, a little tin box, a small writing-desk heaped with *dictata*, MS. notes, and dilapidated books; a large reading desk, holding the *editio princeps* of the States Bible; † and, *last not least*, as the English say, a small basket containing full, and a large one with empty, wine bottles.

---

* Two Leyden theological professors in the early part of this century.

† The "Authorised Version" of Holland, published by order of the States General, and in consequence of a resolution of the Synod of Dort, in 1610. It was completed in 1634.

The said alcove is provided with a double door, and when the latter is closed, peculiar skill, or else a lucky conjuncture of circumstances, is necessary to open it, seeing that the handle usually displays a remarkable degree of obstinacy, and calmly turns round in one's hand unnumbered times without lifting the latch.

As to the other furniture of the room, the following is an accurate inventory:—

1. A small mirror in a polished wooden frame,—the glass consisting of two sections, each of a different colour. If you see yourself in the lower half you have a purple countenance, in the upper a **green one, and in** either case your features are cruelly distorted; in fact, no one ever looked into this mirror, either above or below, who did not instantly look out of it again,—so frightfully ugly does every one find **him** or herself, as the case may be.

2. A mahogany sécretaire, which, though it has lost some of the convolutions of the carved fretwork finishing it off at the top, is still, on the whole, tolerably fit for use, and has no other defects than these, that the lower drawer will not shut, that one of the hinges of the flap is loose,—necessitating great care in opening and closing,—and that one of the feet has long ago declined further service and preferred **a horizontal to an upright position,**—in spite of which, **however, the article** of furniture can be made to stand tolerably steady if propped up against the wall. On the top stands a bunch of paper flowers (the landlady's property), protected by a glass shade, flanked to right and left by plaster busts of Homer and Cicero, **and** surrounded with several tea-cups, bearing in gilt **letters** such touching mottoes as "Many happy returns of the day," "A trifle—but a token of good-will," "Walk on roses," "A token of respect," &c. &c.

3. A white-wood corner cupboard, with a fluted sliding-door, which, **if** you go about to open it quietly, refuses to **move,** whereas if you use force you push the whole cup-

board from its place. Only long experience, added to unwearying patience, will enable any one to bring to light the glasses, plates, and knives, or whatever the contents of the receptacle may be.

4. A tiled stove, whose top is pointed out as a frequent resting-place for glasses by a variety of circular stains. Next the stove stands a wooden tub containing coals, and behind it lie a heap of peats and a few blocks of wood, also a poker and tongs. The latter cannot be handled without pinching the skin of one's forefinger, and the legs slip across each other as soon as one tries to pick up anything with them.

5. An arm-chair, and six chairs with plush seats, showing their stuffing through numerous wounds,—all of them venerable invalids, full of infirmities, and especially weak in the back.

6. A square table, with flaps which can be turned up; its upper surface painted green with white spots, and the edges reddish-brown. In the middle of this table we see a lamp and two black-japanned candlesticks with tallow candles in them; further, a broken pair of snuffers, a wooden tobacco-box, a brazier, and an inkstand with other writing materials; and round it are seated several students, all members of the "rhetorical chamber"* entitled, "The Thirsty Pleiades."

J. VAN LENNEP.
The Vicissitudes of Klaasje Zevenster (1866).

---

* "Rederijkers" (*i.e.*, "rhetorikers") Kamer is the name given to the literary societies which still flourish at the Dutch universities. The name has come down from the fifteenth century, and the most famous societies were those of "In Liefde Bloeiende" and "De Eglantier," further reference to which will be found in the Introduction.

A COLONIAL PRIZE-GIVING.

"ANOTHER day on the rack!" Heer Doornik had said that morning to his wife,—not however in so tragic a manner as the tenor of the ejaculation would seem to indicate, as he was just then busy pulling on a particularly intractable boot.

"Is your speech ready?" asked Mevrouw Doornik, in the act of fastening his necktie for him.

"Yes, my address is prepared," he replied, solemnly.

You must know, reader, that Doornik had been, in his young days, a member of a "rhetorical chamber" at Dinxperlo or Buren, I do not exactly remember which, and had reaped harvests of laurels at various lectures—laurels offered to him along with cups of muddy chocolate and *cadetjes* with cream cheese.

This circumstance had stood in his way all his life. The man, whose manifest destiny was to become a schoolmaster, believed himself a second Mirabeau. He would have liked to become a popular orator, or a member of the Second Chamber, or failing that at least a minister. But his ideals had gone the way of the *cadetjes* and the chocolate, they had vanished into nothingness; the future Mirabeau became, first, a pupil in a training-college, then third, and then second master; and, at last, with much labour, he gained his head-mastership.

"I have at last this consolation, that I am to-day once more placed in a position to show the public what the art of oratory is."

This last sentence was uttered with such an elevation of his voice, that his wife thought it necessary to damp his enthusiasm a little.

"I'm afraid the pine-apple tartlets are burnt," she said, "and the cabinet-pudding, too, is not as it should be."

But her husband did not hear her. In one hand he had a hair-brush and in the other a comb, and with these objects he went through all sorts of evolutions, his eyes fixed on the mirror, and his long figure most eccentrically contorted. His wife left him alone; she was well acquainted with this manœuvre, and twenty years' experience of married life had taught her not to disturb her husband when seized by inspirations.

The Indies are not the place for unappreciated genius; all that they could give the great man (except a good salary and an easy life, which, of course, did not count) was the chairmanship of a few committees, and a place in the church council and other assemblies, which got through more talking than business. Besides this, he was a Freemason, and thus at last he had the satisfaction of being able to speak "in public," taking one week with another, at least once a week.

The day of the school examination was therefore, in his opinion, especially suited to this purpose, and he had not practised so long for nothing. His speech was going to be brilliant, his eloquence indescribable, his gestures and facial expression would do the rest. It was only a pity that Hendriks (the second master) had come to worry him, for, above all things, he needed quiet in those days when he was going to show the public what good speaking is.

At last the proceedings were to begin.

The children sang one or two songs very prettily, and the effect would have been exceedingly good, had not the headmaster been of opinion that his voice—not a bad one, but just now fairly hoarse with nervousness—ought to be heard above all the rest.

Then the examination proper began, and the usual incidents took place. Great exhibitions of dumbness on the part of the girls, fearful embarrassment on that of the boys, extreme exasperation among the masters, suppressed giggling among the ladies of the audience, and unnaturally solemn

"IN ONE HAND A HAIR-BRUSH, IN THE OTHER A COMB."

faces among the members of the school committee, who had evidently made up their minds to remain serious whatever might happen.

In the first class sat eight boys, between the ages of twelve and fifteen. But it soon became apparent that six of the eight were mere lay figures; the questions were addressed to all, but the answers, evidently, expected from Anton van Duijn and William Ochtenraat only.

They represented two distinct types, as they sat there side by side. William had a fresh, rosy face, large blue eyes, and a white forehead, crowned with blonde curls,—he was a prize specimen of a Dutch boy. Anton, with his dark hair and jet-black eyes, clear-cut brown face, and tall slight figure, was a handsome *sinjo*; for he had inherited his looks more from his Creole mother than his Dutch father.

Mevrouw Ochtenraat had spoken truth when she assured Mevrouw van Duijn just now that it gave her much pleasure to see how clever and hard-working Anton was.

To-day, however, it seemed as though Anton did not know so much more than his schoolfellow. Was it the fault of the questions put by the master, who seemed still more agitated than common, and became so amazingly tragic in his simplest movements and gestures that he seemed to be reciting one of Racine's tragedies rather than conducting a school examination?

Or was it the way the master knitted his brows and rolled his eyes, wriggled and writhed and stretched himself, that confused Anton?

Or could it have been the little piece of paper that had just been put into his hand, and on which Heer Hendriks had written in pencil, "Keep cool, don't let them make you lose your head!"—could that have been the reason why Anton every now and then failed to answer a question?

William Ochtenraat, on the other hand, seemed in particularly good spirits that morning. Again and again the master managed to bring him round to one or other of the few subjects in which he was at home. He made him tell the story of Alexander the Great's horse, and of the faithful hound who died on the grave of William the Silent, and, finally, of the turf-boat by means of which Breda was surprised. William's eyes sparkled as he told of Bucephalus; and his mother would have liked to kiss him when he nearly choked over William of Orange's dog; and when he laughed over the discomfiture of the Spaniards, the whole room laughed with him.

Meanwhile, poor Anton became more and more uneasy; he no longer nodded encouragingly to his mother, as he had done at first, but his anxious looks sought Heer Hendriks, who was quite as pale as he.

The arithmetic began. Here dogs, horses, and jokes were alike out of place; the thing, therefore, was to ask the Governor's son as few questions as possible.

"Now I shall be all right!" thought Anton; for this was the subject in which he most excelled. But even now things continued to go wrong; time after time he found he could not answer, and something began to glitter in his eyes which ought to have warned Heer Doornik.

Again the master put a question. And the boy cried, pale with that terrible bluish paleness one only sees where there is coloured blood,—"I can't answer that question, sir; and you know I can't, because it's not on what I've learned."

"But perhaps one of the other boys can,—William, for instance?" asked Hendriks.

"Why, no," cried Willie, "I never heard of it."

Heer Doornik—in spite of his fondness for speeches in general—was far from pleased with this speech; he understood how every one must feel that there was something behind this, and shortly afterwards brought the examination to a somewhat precipitate close by giving his wife the sign to order up the refreshments.

Whoever else may have taken bread and butter, or pineapple tart,—whoever else was regaled with the cabinet-pudding,—neither Anton nor his mother tasted them.

"Don't be uneasy, madam," said the Governor, to the widow, as he called one of the boys to bring her a glass of wine and water, seeing that she trembled in every limb. "Don't be uneasy, Anton is sure to get the prize."

The examination was over, the bread and butter and cakes had disappeared, the scholars having displayed in their extermination a far greater zeal and endurance than in the ordeal of answering questions. Now came the distribution of prizes, and—the Speech!

Many a time had people seen Heer Doornik nervous, and heard him get entangled in his sentences, but the display he made to-day was absolutely unprecedented.

The oration lasted fully a quarter of an hour, and it was not the heat alone which made the ladies look so flushed and uncomfortable.

Some new-comers to the place were seriously alarmed lest the man should break a blood-vessel, or dislocate his left arm,—which came in for the hardest of the work,—or lose his balance in some of his sudden evolutions; the children sat staring at him open-mouthed, the gentlemen nudged one another, the ladies effaced themselves more and more behind their colossal fans. Mevrouw Doornik, alone, sat with her hands folded in her lap, gazing in silent admiration at the man of her choice.

The Widow Van Duijn, too, was listening in the greatest excitement, till she felt he was going beyond her comprehension altogether; and Anton stood, never taking his burning eyes from the master's face, waiting for his sentence.

It came at last, after many a long circuit. Considering this, and weighing that, and giving its due prominence to this circumstance, and noticing why, and not forgetting how the two boys in the first class, who alone had any claim to the prize, had learned what they had learned, and answered as they had answered, he thought he was acting in harmony with the esteemed head of the government, and all the gentlemen and ladies who had honoured the school with their presence, by handing the first prize herewith to the most industrious and highly gifted pupil—William Ochtenraat!

Therewith he handed the boy a handsomely bound book, with a gesture so powerful, so violent a swaying of his whole person, that one was reminded of Samson at the moment when he seized the pillars of the temple.

There was a sudden stillness in the spacious school building. The master looked at the Governor. The latter let his glance rest on William, who, more amazed than delighted, looked first at the glittering volume, and then at the deathly pale boy who sat next him, motionless, with clenched fists and set teeth.

Already Heer Doornik, mopping his face all the time with his handkerchief, was approaching the prize-winner to offer his congratulations,—already there were sounds of sniffling and rustling, caused by ladies and gentlemen rising to congratulate the parents, when Heer Ochtenraat slowly rose in his place, and, with a quiet gesture of his delicate white hand, asked for a hearing.

Once more there was silence as of death.

"William," said the Governor, in his clear, resonant voice, "William, tell me honestly, have you earned that prize?"

One moment the boy hesitated, with a glance at the book.

"No, papa!"

"Well, my boy, give the book to the one who has earned it."

Without stopping to think for one moment, the boy went up to Anton van Duijn, and put the book into his hand.

It needs a good deal to excite an East Indian audience, but when Heer Hendriks, with a pale face, and a suspicious look of moisture about his eyes, made his way forward, wrung Anton's hand, and cried aloud, "Hurrah! three cheers for the Governor," the universal enthusiasm found vent in long and loud cheering. Heer Ochtenraat immediately rose to go; he looked at the head-master coldly and sternly, and passed him without a word.

ANNIE FOORE.

HOW MATHIS KNOUPS TURNED "LIBERAL" AND THEN "CATHOLIC" AGAIN.

EVERY one in Limburg who is not "Catholic" is "liberal" —that is an established fact. There may be a few Protestants here and there; but these are *gueux*, interlopers, mostly from the direction of Hertogenbosch, and therefore Hollanders,* who have accidentally come into the country at one time or another. *Gueux* means one who has fallen away from the Roman Catholic faith, and therefore from Christianity. Also, among other rarities, one finds here and there a few Jews; but they, of course, do not count. A "liberal" is one who is not always and altogether of the same opinion as the parish priest and his *Kapelaan* (curate) —outside church matters, that is to say, for if he were to differ from their reverences on any point of doctrine, he would be no liberal, but a heretic. Also that person is a liberal who, for instance, may, on occasion, give his opinion of a sermon thus,—"Oh! yes, they"—*i.e.*, the clergy—"must find something to talk about, I suppose." Or likewise

---

* There are two provinces of Limburg; one of them being part of Belgium, the other of the Netherlands. In the latter (which is the one meant here) the people are Romanists and call themselves Flemings, not Hollanders.

he who, instead of going regularly to high mass, contents himself, on Sundays and festivals, with a "snap-mass,"—a little, short service; or he who dares to declare, with a smile, that he cannot think how all the fast-days came into existence. There are indeed even a few, but only a few, and those only to be found in towns, who recognise no fast-days at all, entirely godless and irreligious people, who never go to church, and do not even attend confession at Easter. Such people as those are worse than any liberals or heretics,—they are, in one word, *bad*.

Thus, whoever is not a liberal is a Catholic; but there are *Catholics*, and *good Catholics*. A Catholic is any man who faithfully performs his religious duties; who would not, for any money, presume to differ in opinion from the parish priest, and never asks whence that gentleman gets the text of his sermons, or how the church fasts originated. But any one who, in addition to all this, also walks in procession with a lighted torch or leads the prayers as master of the confraternity of St Joseph or St Rochus, who duly informs the villagers whom the priest would like elected into the parish council, who comes to the Holy Communion at least once a month, and, in the tavern, of an evening, can describe all liberals, *gueux*, freemasons, and all such like rabble, in their true colours, that man is a good *Catholic*.

Mathis Knoups, master-carpenter, and landlord of the "Sun" at Haffert, did not belong to this category; he was a Catholic *tout court*. He went to high mass on Sundays, and four times in the year to confession. This, he said, was doing no more than his duty; and, for the rest, he had no time to take any further trouble about the church or religion,—every man must know what he is about, and he had to think of his children. . . . There were plenty of other men to carry torches in the procession,—fast-days had always existed, and did not seem to have made people leaner or less healthy,—and he was willing to take for granted that what M. le Curé said in his sermons was true, provided he were not obliged to listen to them. Also, he was quite ready to vote for Jan, Piet, or Klaas, just as M. le Curé pleased,—he had no quarrel with any of the three, and so it was all the same to him.

This was Knoups' way of reasoning, when the question was discussed by the guests who came to take their evening glass of beer at the "Sun." On such occasions, the surveyor Hommels, well known in the town for a "great liberal," would usually answer, "Yes, yes, you village people let yourselves be finely humbugged and led by the nose!"

"Oh! Lord!" Knoups would then retort, "you have been bitten by that dog too!" And then, with a smile of complete assurance and self-satisfaction, he would add, "One has to keep one's soul clean, you see!" Whereupon the ex-burgomaster Kormann would signify his approval in the words,—

"Very good, Master Knoups! the man who does not need that, is not called on to take any trouble about it!"

"Then don't let him trouble himself with my affairs," answered Knoups.

Master Knoups' inn was about twenty minutes' walk from the little town, at the point where the "grintweg" leading to Haffert branches off from the high road. Among the other advantages of this situation was a toll-gate, which was farmed by Mathis. What Limburg carter would not willingly turn in for a half-pint of beer or a dram, at the place where he has to stop and pay "barrière"? Thus the "Sun" was always full of "coming and going folk."

Knoups let his wife attend to the taproom and the toll-gate; he himself was all day long in his workshop, when not busy on his bit of land. Well, Geutruu (Gertrude) was a handy woman, who helped him to provide for the children, had a pleasant word for every one,—if there was a

"M. LE CURÉ."

cent to be earned anyhow,—but who let no one steal the cheese off her bread.

In the evening there assembled at the "Sun" the "permanent company"—the ex-burgomaster Kormann of Haffert, the surveyor Hommels, Spinwek the baker, and one or two other gentlemen from the town, who would sit playing at cards, sometimes till eleven, and frequently asked the landlord to take a hand.

Besides the field, the carpenter's trade, the toll-gate, and the usual custom of the inn, there was another great annual source of income, the Haffert kermis (fair) at St Rochustide in August, when the burghers with their wives and daughters, and the young men from the city, streamed to the village for three days following. And the man who did not put up at the "Sun" had not been at the Haffert kermis.

If on these occasions Knoups did not, taking one day with another, tap his six casks of beer per day, he had every reason to shake his head, pass his thumb over his forefinger as though he had been counting money, drop his under-lip, and sigh:

"It's bad times with people, . . . they're short of money."

"Knoups," Hommels had sometimes said to him, "you ought to have dance-music at St Rochus. Then you might tap ten casks in a day, or even twelve."

Knoups looked serious, pulled somewhat harder at his pipe, considered for a moment, and replied:

"Thirty casks! . . . it would be a good deal."

Next year, having used up twenty casks in the three days, he said to Geutruu:

"Wife, we must have the dancing next year."

"You know best, I suppose," said Geutruu; "every cask counts. But what will the Pastoor say?"

Whereto Knoups replied:

"Well, every one ought to know what he's about, and I have to think of the children."

HOW KNOUPS TURNED "LIBERAL."

"THEIR EVENING GLASS OF BEER AT THE 'SUN.'"

Next year there was music and dancing at the "Sun," and some forty-two casks of beer were tapped.

Knoups and Geutruu laughed in their sleeves.

All the same, it had been a frightful moment for them, when they sat side by side at early mass, and the Curé had preached against dancing, and hinted at the risks run as regards the next world by those who took part in such amusements. Geutruu did not know where to hide her head for shame, and kept bending lower and lower over her prayer-book. Mathis cast a furious glance at the preacher, but the latter stared at the couple till the whole congregation had turned their eyes in their direction; and Mathis himself at last, fiery red at one moment and deadly pale the next, cast down his eyes and bowed his head.

But now that he and Geutruu were home again, and counting the Brabant and Prussian cents—the groschen, half-francs, and *couranten*—which went to make up the payment for forty-two casks of beer, he exploded with laughter, and said, pointing to the money:

"Geutruu, the Curé may give us another sermon for that."

Well, the people from the town had never troubled their heads about the Curé of Haffert's preaching, and the peasants said, "If the burghers dance, why should we keep away?"

When All Saints' Day came, Mathis and Geutruu went to confession as usual.

"If he speaks about the dancing, we'll say that we don't know yet what we're going to do next year," said Mathis at the church door.

However, it was not so easy to get absolution. The Curé was terribly angry, and the confession lasted more than half-an-hour; however, for this once, his reverence at last showed himself willing to lean to the side of mercy.

"But," he added, "if you let the devil loose in my parish again next year, I can do nothing more for you."

At Christmas, Easter, and Ascensiontide they again went

"THE CURE MAY GIVE US ANOTHER SERMON FOR THAT."

to confession, but on none of these occasions was anything said about dancing.

In the beginning of August, a fortnight before St Roch's Day, Mathis said to his wife:

"Wife, we must have the dancing again."

"You know best," answered Geutruu, as before; "but what will M. le Curé say?"

To which he gave the same answer as last year.

And there was dancing at the "Sun." The Curé preached with all his might, but the townspeople went first and the peasants followed, and no less than forty-five casks of beer were consumed at the "Sun." Such a thing had not happened anywhere in the neighbourhood within the memory of man.

But, alas! for the following All Saints' Day. As soon as the Curé caught sight of Mathis Knoups through the grating of the confessional, he closed the slide in his face. Geutruu received absolution, after many entreaties and arguments, because she could plead that she had warned her husband.

"That's his own business," said Mathis; "every one must know what he is about."

Henceforth Knoups went to confession only once a year —at Easter.

"Once is a man's duty," said he; "but to be turned away four times in the year is only mere waste of time and trouble."

Again the wicket was shut in his face. Hommels, in the tavern parlour that evening, laughed over it, and said:

"Well, M. le Curé keeps you all in order like a flock of sheep."

Knoups smiled, and replied, shortly:

"The stayer wins. We shall see who'll hold out longest."

These strained relations between Knoups and the Curé lasted some four or five years, and then another incident occurred.

Hubertienke, Knoups' eldest girl, was now nine, and went to school at Haffert. The master said that she was one of the cleverest and best-behaved children that had ever come under his care. And now that she went twice a week to M. le Chapelain's "Christian doctrine" class, it was quite likely that next St Rochus' Day she would walk with the other children as a "little bride" in the procession, and carry a little flag, a shepherd's crook, perhaps even a cornucopia, or a great crimson heart with gold flames. The child had talked and dreamed of this possibility for a whole year or so, and Geutruu had had a little white dress and white satin shoes made for her in town, and bought a wreath of May-blossom from the milliner.

But Geutruu and her little daughter had reckoned without their host—that is to say, without the Curé. Two days before St Rochus, his reverence had sent for Vrouw Knoups, and asked her whether Mathis was going to have the dance-music again. Whereupon, embarrassed and confused, she had answered, "I think so, M. le Curé."

"Then Hubertine can't walk in the procession," was the Curé's verdict. "If the father doesn't keep his Easter, the child can't be a 'little bride.'"

Geutruu came home with the tears in her eyes.

"Bad luck to the whole thing!" raged Mathis. "Geutruu, you dress the child properly, and take her to the church. We'll see what the Curé does then."

The wife did as he had said—dressed the child in the white frock, put on the satin shoes, and fastened the wreath into her hair. Then she went with Hubertienke to high mass, and when the procession started Hubertienke took her place with the other children of the "catechising."

Scarcely however had the procession got out of the church, and reached the market-place, when the Curé entered the ranks of the "little brides," took Hubertienke by the hand, and made the child take her place behind the file of

"DRESSED THE CHILD IN THE WHITE FROCK."

school children who did not yet come to "Christian doctrine," and were posted a long way in advance at the head of the procession, in their black or dark blue Sunday frocks.

All this was clearly seen by Mathis Knoups, standing among the crowd of spectators. He rushed up, looking daggers, fetched his child out of the procession, and, grinding his teeth, made his way homewards with Hubertienke.

He could scarcely eat his dinner for the next three days.

When Hommels began touching on the occurrence in the evening, Mathis cried, his lips trembling:

"Fine religion that! As he can't be revenged on me, he wreaks his spite on my child! If that's our religion, I'd rather not have no more religion at all!"

From that day forth the publican-carpenter went neither to church nor to confession, not even at Easter, and was in the eyes of every one "a downright liberal." At the elections, he filled in his voting ticket with his own name. When Hommels abused the Curé, and scoffed at religion, then Knoups laughed till he shook all over. And when the ex-burgomaster Kormann exhorted him to return to the bosom of Holy Church, Mathis would answer:

"*Paja!* the whole business isn't worth a cent!" or, "Mind your own business, and let me attend to mine—every one ought to know what he's about!"

That every one ought to know his own business best, he maintained with equal consistency when Geutruu went with Hubertienke and the other children to church on Sundays. Hommels, indeed, laughed at this curious compromise between man and wife; but Geutruu would reply, when teased on the subject:

"I can't bring up the children like heathen savages, can I?"

The breach between Mathis Knoups and the Church had lasted quite three years, when, one baking day in July, the lightning struck Haffert church, and the whole roof was burnt off.

Knoups looked important and thoughtful, as he remarked:

"I should like to know who's going to put the new roof on?"

"Why, I suppose the Curé will somehow beg the money for it!" said Hommels, who did not exactly see the connection.

The thought of the new roof pursued Mathis night and day. He knew very well how *he* would do it—he had some choice timber lying by that would just do—he trimmed the rafters—he made all sorts of calculations, and was able to tell his guests to a cent that evening how much the new roof ought to cost—not an *oortje** more. But, when talking to his wife alone, he said, half vexed and half sad:

"The Curé is sure to take care to get another builder into Haffert this time!"

A week before St Rochus, Knoups went to the brewer in the town to order the *kermis* beer for the dancing-tent as usual. There was no brewery at Haffert, or Knoups would certainly not have gone outside the village.

"I have nothing but new beer for you, Master Knoups," said the brewer; "you will find there's going to be sharp competition this year."

"How so?" asked Knoups.

"Why, you know, don't you, that Stamel-Joob has rented the piece of land just opposite your house, on the other side of the Haffert road?"

Knoups nodded an affirmative.

"Stammering Joob is going into partnership with Crippled Manes, and they mean to get a big dancing-tent over from Prussia, and set it up there."

The landlord of the "Sun" stared at the brewer with all

---

* Fourth part of a *stuiver*.

his eyes. He was vainly seeking for arguments to combat his own inner conviction that Stammering Joob the never-sober host of the "City of Algiers," and Crippled Manes the recruiting-sergeant, who also did a good business as a kind of broker in procuring substitutes for unwilling conscripts, were two dangerous opponents, and capable of anything.

"Where should they get the money from?" he suddenly exclaimed.

The brewer shrugged his shoulders.

Mathis became lost in thought for some minutes, and at last whispered, looking at his purveyor with flashing eyes,—

"Do you think the Curé of Haffert could be mixed up in this?"

Once more the brewer shrugged his shoulders.

"All that I know," said he, "is that Stammering Joob and Crippled Manes have ordered sixty casks of beer of me."

Mathis ordered only twenty casks for the present, and returned home with a long face.

Two days before St Rochus, three great Prussian freight-waggons, laden with planks and battens and canvas, passed through Haffert, and stopped at the Schei, right opposite the "Sun" inn. A moment after, Crippled Manes was seen hobbling up from another direction, with an old police-cap on his head, and followed by a number of schoolboys and loafers from the town, where the rumour of the arrival of the "foreign dancing-tent" had already spread. A large number of hands went to work at once; timbers were unloaded, posts set up, canvas spread out; and in the middle of all the bustle the lame recruiting-sergeant moved about with his bottle of Hollands, encouraging the workmen, and sometimes garnishing the offered glass with some such facetious remark as, "To the health of M. le Curé of Haffert;" or, "To the health of Mathis Knoups, our neighbour!"

However, Mathis Knoups, who, with compressed lips,

stood on the watch behind the door of his workshop, could not hear what he said.

But all this was nothing to the commotion which was caused on the following day—the Eve of St Rochus—in Haffert and on the Schei, by the arrival of twelve Prussian musicians, in faded light-green coats, sky-blue caps, and all sorts of brass instruments,—one or two of them of such a size that they curled all round the blower like serpents. They marched through Haffert playing all the way, drew up in a line before the dancing-tent, which was decked with flags and pennons, and then entered the town, accompanied by Crippled Manes, who now, armed with a big stick, marched in front, and acted the part of drum-major.

All through the night Mathis could still hear the shrill sound of the clarionet and the booming of the great bass instruments.

No need to ask whether Haffert *kermis* was crowded! Everybody went to dance in the Prussian tent. The brewer had to go over twice a day with fresh supplies; and when Knoups came to complain to him, on the third day, that he had only tapped eight casks, it was resolved to cart eight casks away from the "Sun" to the tent over the way.

"Of course," laughed Manes, "neighbours ought to help each other!"

When, two days later, the three heavily-laden waggons had rumbled off over the Prussian frontier, and Stammering Joob and Crippled Manes were marching away to the town, arm in arm, and not very sober, the latter turned back and shouted:

"Good-bye, Master Knoups! next year we'll be neighbours again, for a time!"

"Low riff-raff, that come to steal the bread out of a man's mouth!" said Knoups—who had heard it this time—to Geutruu. "Well, *that* article's spoilt for good and all; I shall have to put all my strength into my own trade!"

The following week, a notice, posted up on the Haffert Raadhuis, announced to all and sundry that tenders for the new roofing of the church were to be sent in to the authorities by that day fortnight.

"It's no good *my* sending in a paper," thought Mathis; "the Curé and the burgomaster are all in the same boat, and the Curé will take good care I don't get the contract."

It may be supposed, therefore, that he looked amazed when Geutruu, returning from the town one rainy afternoon, stood still, right in front of him, and said:

"Now I'm going to tell you something! You'll have to send in your paper for the church roof!"

"I!—for the roof!" cried Mathis.

"You, for the roof!" repeated Geutruu. "Just listen now. I had just got outside the gate when it began to rain. I was going to turn my skirt up over my head, when somebody came running after me, and called out, 'Vrouw Knoups! Vrouw Knoups!' I turned round, and who should it be but M. le Curé's sister, Joffer Marianneke. 'Come along under my umbrella,' says she, 'and I'll walk home with you!' I said, 'Too much honour, Joffer Marianneke,' and 'Thank you, Joffer Marianneke,'—but it was no use, I had to come along under her umbrella. And then she told me that M. le Curé quite expects you to send in your paper for the contract, and that it grieves him so much that there should be a black sheep in the congregation; and she is coming next week to drink coffee with us. And what do you say now?"

Knoups listened, astonished, and at the same time excited.

"H'm!" he said then, ". . . we must just think over that . . . one ought to know what one is about!"

It was a very busy day for Geutruu, when Mam'selle Marianne, the Curé's sister, came to coffee. She had baked special cakes—*vlaai* and *krintemik*; and, when her guest had arrived, she went herself to fetch Mathis out of his workshop. Mathis laid aside his apron, wiped his forehead with it, and followed his wife indoors.

"*Serviteur*, Joffer Marianneke," said he, accomplishing with some difficulty an awkward kind of bow.

"I've just looked in to see how you are getting on, Master Knoups," said the Curé's sister, taking a bite at her slice of currant-loaf.

"Very kind, I'm sure, Joffer Marianneke! and I wish you a good appetite!" replied Knoups.

"To-morrow M. le Curé is going round with the alms-bag, Master Knoups, for the new roof to the church. Are you going to give something too?"

"H'm, h'm! If M. le Curé does not pass my door, we'll see what we shall do, Joffer Marianneke!"

Next day came M. le Curé with the alms-bag.

"Master Knoups, I am going to *all* our parishioners." He emphasised the "all." "Will you contribute something towards the new roof for the church?"

Now that Knoups was standing before his enemy, it seemed as though something boiled up in him,—as though he would have to say something quite different from what he had thought out beforehand,—and yet there was such a tightness at his throat that he could not bring out a word.

He kept his eyes fixed on the priest, made one or two great efforts to swallow the lump in his throat, and at length burst out, clinching his fist convulsively:

"M. le Curé, why did you revenge yourself on my child for the grudge you had against me?"

And at the last words he struck his clinched hand against his chest.

"*Chut! chut!* Master Knoups," said the Curé, with a deprecating wave of the hand; "I have duties to fulfil, —and, after all, you had been warned."

"If you had said publicly, in the pulpit, Master Knoups

is a heretic,—if you had turned me out of your church, some Sunday, in the middle of high mass, I could forgive it; but . . . my child . . ."

"Come, come, Knoups, don't go dragging drowned cows out of the ditch,—think of the new church roof. You're a carpenter, and if I meant ill towards you I would not have come to you with the alms-bag."

These words soothed Knoups somewhat. He silently offered the Curé a chair, and sat down opposite him. Then he put his hand under his blue blouse into his jacket pocket, took out a paper, unfolded it, and laid it before the priest.

"M. le Curé," he said, "here is my tender for the contract. If the work is given to me, I will deduct twenty gulden from the sum, as my contribution to the roof."

"And then, Knoups, and then?" asked the Curé, in a tone of serious admonition.

"How do you mean, M. le Curé?"

"Are you going to have the dancing again?"

"M. le Curé," answered Knoups, "I am quite willing to live in peace and friendship with every one; but I ought to be allowed to earn a few stivers when I want them."

"And do you think, Knoups, that this dancing business is all profit? Do you know that people of position are shy of your house for that very reason? Why do the professors from St Aloysius' College, and all their students,—and the Christian Brothers, and all their schoolboys—why do they always pass the 'Sun' by? You have a good head for reckoning, I've often heard, Master Knoups. Did you ever figure out what it would come to in a year if two hundred young fellows were to come every week, or say every fortnight, to have a glass of beer?"

Knoups' whole face shone with excitement.

"Why, one could lay out a skittle-ground with that!" he cried.

"Well, are you going to repent of your ways, and come to church again, Knoups?"

"Would you give me absolution if I did?"

"If you had no more dancing—why, there would be no further reason for refusing it."

Knoups sat still, and thought for a little. Then he took his broad carpenter's pencil, wrote on the paper, "*less twenty gulden for the roof*," and said:

. "We'll see, M. le Curé, we'll see. And, after all, I'm not the worst."

The same evening, in the "Sun," Hommels was talking about the elections.

"Pooh!" cried he, "convictions! I hate the sound of the word. Money is all they care about, or the honour of sitting in the council and having their say in everything! . . . There you have the burgomaster Driemans; he has been liberal three times, and clerical three times, and every time he got in! . . . and the *rentier*, Lankmans, formerly president of a dramatic society, who ate meat on Fridays, chosen as a defender of the Faith! . . . and our deputy, Judge Stechelmans, who formerly, when he was a school inspector, cursed and swore when he found a crucifix hanging in a school, he too is a pillar of the Church! And the priests know all that very well, but what do they care? such men are of use to them, and that's enough! . . . *Sufficit*, you know!"

"So, so," said Knoups, in a naively satirical tone, half shutting his eyes, "is that what they mean by politics,—a question of money?"

Knoups sent in his tender for the contract for the new church roof. There was indeed an offer made at a lower figure by a builder in the town, but the Curé and the burgomaster said that Knoups had the best timber on hand—even though it had been bought with the proceeds of the dancing, as Knoups said—and gave the contract to him. Knoups turned his dancing-floor into a skittle-ground, went to confession on All Saints' Day, and got his absolution all right.

Since that time Mathis Knoups has become a Catholic again. Hommels does not frequent the "Sun" now.

"One can't put one's foot down there without tumbling over a professor from the College, or one of the Christian Brothers' boys," he said. And when he makes his appearance, now and then, to tease Mathis, and asks, "How do you feel now, Mathis, as a New Catholic?" Mathis answers:

"Yes, you may laugh, Mynheer Hommels, but just wait till you come to die—then you'll be frightened too. . . . And one must look after one's soul,—isn't it so, Geutruu?"*

EMILE SEIPGENS.

---

* This story appears to have several morals, the reader being left free to choose the one most in accordance with his own views. The author himself is strictly impartial. Perhaps the most obvious is, that it is not good to match your wits against those of the Roman Catholic clergy, unless you have capital to back your opposition, and not always even then. M. Seipgens does not obtrude his own views, and we are not quite sure whether the conclusion is meant to be serious and edifying, or whether there is an underlying *pointe d'ironie*. The story gives a lively picture of life and manners in the Limburg district, that picturesque and little known region which, though part of Holland, is in some respects so un-Dutch. The language spoken there is less like Dutch proper than some broad and harsh dialect of German, such as they speak about Cologne. After some hesitation between the two, we have given this sketch of Seipgens' in preference to "Kobus Mulders' Vote," —which also turns on politics and clerical influence, and is, in some respects, more characteristic; but the crisis—when Mulders and his family are cut off by the flood—comes too near tragedy for such a book as this.

NEWSPAPER HUMOUR.

Otherwise Engaged.

Police-Magistrate—"What insolence! to break into a house, in a busy street, in the middle of the day!"

Thief—"I was already engaged for the evening."

Wedded Love.

Jan—"Oh, Julie! how pleased I am to see you!"

Julie—"Is that true, Jan?"

Jan—"Yes, my little wife, my——"

Julie—"If we were out at sea, and I were to fall overboard, what would you do?"

Jan—First, I should see what time it was; then I should inform the captain that there was some one overboard, and ask whether the vessel could be stopped. When it was stopped, I would have a boat let down, and row back to the place where you had fallen into the water. It would be quite easy to find, because I should have noticed the time at which we were there, the rate we were going at, and the direction the ship was taking. If you were still floating, it would be all right; if you had sunk, we should have to wait till bubbles——"

Julie—"Oh! you heartless scoundrel! You murderer! I'll never go anywhere with you!"

(And then she went to her mother and told her that Jan was a fellow of uncommon sense and shrewdness, who could not fail to make his fortune, &c. &c.) *Tybaert de Kater.*

Professor (at Medical lecture)—"What would you do, if you found the condition of the patient in this case had become worse?"

Student—"I should thank Heaven I was not in his skin."

"OTHERWISE ENGAGED."

On the Steam-Tram.

"Hallo!—Conductor!"

"What is it, sir?"

"Why is the tram stopping here? There is no station—I can only see one house."

"Oh, we're stopping because Farmer Verschueren's wife wants to come to town."

"I wish she'd make haste, then!"

"Yes—but she wants to take a dozen eggs to market, and she has only eleven. The hen is on the nest, and as soon as she has laid the egg we are going on." *Tybaert.*

A LAWYER had had his photograph taken. He was wearing his morning coat, and had his hands in the pockets.

"Is it not a good likeness?" asked the photographer, showing it to one of his friends.

"Speaking—as far as the face is concerned; but, for the rest, there is something wrong about it."

"What is that?"

"A lawyer never puts his hands in *his own* pockets."

At the Chemistry Class.

"What is found in salt-water besides the chloride of iodine we have just been speaking of?"

Youngest Pupil—"Herrings, sir."

Overheard in the Street.

"Good morning, William. Why! how changed you are!"

"Don't be offended—but my name is not William!"

"Well, now!—he has changed even his very name!"

"BONIFACIUS," said Madame Snobs, "the way you are taking to drink is disgraceful! You didn't come home till nearly morning, and now you want to go out again before dinner-time! You ought to be ashamed of yourself. If I

was a man like that, I would drop into the ground for shame!"

"You are quite right, wife," said Snobs; "just give me the key of the cellar."

Snobs was for some time Justice of the Peace at Bommerskonten, and is now Mayor of that village. The first time he celebrated a marriage there, he asked the bride—

"Do you take Kobe Kullemans, who is standing beside you, for your husband?"

"Yes, sir," replied the bride.

"Prisoner at the bar," continued Snobs, "what have you to say in your defence?"

Snobs—"What clever answers that fellow Snugger can give, to be sure, when one asks him anything!"

Madame Snobs—"Why—I have never noticed that."

Snobs—"Indeed it is so. Yesterday I asked him if he would lend me twenty francs. He did not say either yes or no, but he asked me if I thought he was mad."

PRACTICAL.

"John," said the lady of the house to the new man-servant, who had several times startled her by falling into the room like a bombshell, "when you come in, you must knock first, and wait till you hear some one say, 'Come in.'"

When the lady and her husband are seated at dinner, John comes up to the door, opens it just wide enough to put his head through, draws back, shuts the door, and knocks.

"Come in!" cries the mistress, in amazement. "Didn't you understand me? You were to knock, and then wait till I said, 'Come in,'—instead of that, you peep round the door first. What do you mean by it?"

"Why, I had to see if there was any one in the room to tell me to come in!"

Uilenspiegel.

Jewish Courtship.

Rachel—"But, Moses lad, you say you are so fond of me—would you really go through the fire for me?"

Moses—"Of course, Rachel, darling—that is to say, if I was well insured."

JEWISH COURTSHIP.

Mother Spons—"What do I see, Mother Snaps!—you look quite well to-day, and yet I was told you could not get out of your bed."

Mother Snaps—"Well—and no more I can,—for as soon as ever I get up, that husband of mine will carry it straight to the pawnbroker's!"

"WHO wrote the Psalms?" asked Pater Dodd, somewhat sharply, of his class. All were silent, and the good priest repeated the question.

"It was not I, sir," responded Janneke Snobs, beginning to cry.

"I ask you who wrote them!" repeated the priest.

"Yes, sir," said Janneke, heroically, at last, "I did it, but I'll never do it again, as long as I live!"

AT SCHOOL.

THE master is explaining the arithmetical operation of subtraction:—

"Now, Jantje, if your mother gives you five slices of bread and butter, and you eat two, how many will you have left?"

"Mother never gives me so many, sir."

"Well, then, if you have five marbles in your pocket, and take out two, how many will there be left in it?"

"None at all, sir,—there's a hole in my pocket."

A.—"Our business is so extensive that we have to keep a man on purpose to thrash the apprentices, and he's at it all day."

B.—"That's nothing to ours! Our establishment is so immense that we have to keep St Bernard dogs in the corridors to look for the customers who lose themselves there!"

A MAN who had repeatedly called on a nobleman to obtain payment of a debt, was refused access by the well-drilled footman, in the words, "The Baron does not receive to-day."

"That is all the same to me," replied the creditor; "I don't care,—as long as he will *give*."

At a Restaurant.

Snugger (who has been waiting over an hour for his beef-steak)—"Look here, waiter, are you the same that put this plate on the table?"

Waiter—"Yes, sir."

Snugger—"Heavens! you've grown out of all knowledge since then!"

A Pleasant Trade.

A SMALL boy goes howling along the street. Our friend Snobs accosts him with, "What is the matter, my little man?"

Boy howls.

"Where do you live?"

Boy howls still.

"What is your father's name?"

More howling.

"What is your mother's name?"

Still more.

"What does your father do?"

"Beats mother. Ow! ow! ow!"

Disconsolate.

Kind-hearted Farmer's Wife—Pietje, my boy, what's the matter?"

Pietje (*howling*)—"Can't eat any more apples."

"Well, put them in your pockets, can't you?"

"Oh! oh! oh! My pockets are full! Oh! oh! oh! oh!"

Judge—"But why in the world did you go so far to steal wine, when you might easily have got it in your master's cellar?"

Prisoner—"I knew my master's wine too well to steal even one bottle of it."

Allemansvriend

Judge (to convicted thief)—"You seem to understand your business."

Prisoner—"Yes, my lord, and if you could steal as well as I, you wouldn't care to sit on the bench any longer."

Vlaamsche Illustratie

In the Confessional.

Boy—"Rev. Father, I have stolen twenty-five yards of stuff from farmer Klaas."

Priest—"Oh! that is very bad."

Boy—"Yes; mother said it was bad, when she saw it, but still she thought it would do to make sacks of."

Allemansvriend.

NEVER estimate a man's value according to the silk umbrella he carries; he has probably left a cotton one somewhere in place of it.

WE are all ready to set up as moral physicians, and each of us can give his advice; but a University diploma is necessary before you can cure a child of the stomach-ache.

MANY a man who says that he works like a barge-horse, is probably thinking of the time when the barge-horse is standing in the stall eating oats.

A WORD is enough for the wise. This is probably the reason why an advocate has to plead for half a day before a jury.

KOBE SNULLEMANS was about to be married, but he had only two francs, and the priest asked a fee of twenty.

"Oh! your reverence!" said Kobe, "just marry me a little then, as much as you can for two francs!"

Tybaert.

Janneke Snobs—"Mamma, how do the niggers on the Congo know when it is Sunday? they have no clean shirts to put on."

Conductor (to his clerk)—"Did you give the hundred francs to the chairman of the Board of Works?"

Clerk—"Yes, sir."

Con.—"What sort of a face did he make?"

Clerk—"He looked very much offended."

Con.—"Didn't he say anything?"

Clerk—"Yes, sir."

Con.—"What did he say?"

Clerk—"That you and I ought to go to jail!"

Con.—"And what did he do then?"

Clerk—"He took the money."

Uilenspiegel.

Unnecessary.

Kapblok, the butcher's man, is running, knife in hand, after Snugger's dog, who has stolen a piece of meat out of his shop.

Snugger—" Kapblok, where are you running to with that knife?"

Kapblok—" Don't you see the beast has got hold of a piece of the best beef?"

Snugger—" Is that all? Just put your knife back again; he never cuts his meat, he can worry it down well enough without that."

"KAPBLOK, THE BUTCHER'S MAN."

Janneke Snobs (on his grandfather's birthday)—"Grandfather dear, I have come to wish you many happy returns of the day, and I hope you may live a long time this year!"

Tybaert.

In the Carnival.

"Well, Krelis, are you going to put on a mask?"

A Voice—"If he would just wash himself for once, and put on a clean collar, no one would know him."

A Heart-Felt Petition.

When Mané was still a minister, he was tolerably well known as a henpecked man. In church, on one occasion, he closed his extempore prayer with the following words:—"And now, O Lord! we pray for the wives of preachers. Some people think they are angels, but Thou, who knowest the hearts, art well aware that . . ."

History does not record what took place between Mané and his wife when he returned home that day.

Inspecting General (to Private)—"Are you satisfied with your rations?"

Private—"Yes, sir."

General—"How about the meat? Does every one get served alike? or does one get much and another little?"

Private—"No, sir; we all get very little."

Sentry—"My good woman, what do you want with the pillar-box? You've been standing there half-an-hour at least."

Old Woman—"Well, I don't mind if I tell you, sir. I put a letter in, and I'm waiting for the answer."

Tall Barrister—"Not so fast, my friend. You know I could easily put you in my pocket."

Short Ditto—"If my learned brother were to do so, he would have more law in his pocket than in his head."

"Professor, I have come to express my gratitude. All that I know, I owe to you."

Professor—"Come, come, friend, don't mention it. *Such a trifle* is really not worth remembering."

"INSPECTOR GENERAL: 'ARE YOU SATISFIED WITH YOUR RATIONS?'"

At the Hatter's.

"WHAT! you say this hat is thirty florins?"

"Yes, sir; real Panama."

"But I don't see any holes in the top."

"Holes, sir?"

"Of course; the man who is ass enough to pay as much as that will want holes to let his ears through."

Lawyer—"My friend, you are an ass!"

Witness—"Do you mean, sir, that I am your friend because I am an ass? or that I am an ass because I am your friend?"

Waiter—"Why, sir, there was a gentleman here last week painting this very place."

Painter (absently)—"Yes. Was he an artist?"

Waiter—"An artist? No, sir; he was a *very respectable man*."

The Uncle (from whom one has expectations)—"My dearest boy, I have thought over the matter for some time, but I really cannot give you the sum you want. I never depart from my principles, and one of them is, not to undress before I go to bed."

Nephew (constrainedly)—"Very sorry, very sorry, indeed . . . . (With an effusive grasp of the hand.) Good-night, uncle! GOOD-NIGHT!"

On a River Steamer.

Gentleman (first-class)—"Captain, I say! this is an unpardonable want of delicacy. Can't you direct this cursed smoke towards the *second-class passengers?*"

The Next Regiment.

Country Lass—" Soldier, may I give you this pound of tobacco to take to my cousin Jan? He's in the 3rd, and I see you're in the 2nd; so you're just next to him."

Soldier—" With pleasure, lass; give it here. I'll see that he don't have anything to pay for carriage." (He rides away, in a state of total indifference to Cousin Jan, and all that concerns him. Jan's cousin goes home, happy in the thought that he is going to get his tobacco so cheaply.)

Very Select.

" Do tell me, Baron, is there not a very clever surgeon living in the village near your castle?"

" I am told so, madam, but . . . you understand . . . a country practitioner like that . . . I cannot put any confidence in him. . . . I only have him sent for when one of the servants is ill."

Shopkeeper (catching boy with both hands in the till)—" You young scoundrel, what do you want there?"

Boy—" I . . . I . . . I'm looking for my cap."

Shopkeeper—" It's on your head all the time, gallows-bird."

Boy—" On my head? Oh, no! you're out there. That's not my cap; that's one I borrowed till I could find my own."

An Incorruptible Official.

Suitor (from the country)—" Sir, here is a bit of a ham, home-cured, just to thank you for——"

Official—" What? Idiot! rascal! Do you think a sworn civil servant is going to let himself be bribed? Hand over the ham at once! Hand it over, I say! And now out with you! There's the door! Out you go! March!"

Silent reflections of a member of the dangerous classes.—"It's mighty queer; this makes five times I've been had up for stealing, and each time they've let me off... Hanged if I understand it; but it does seem as if they meant me to go on!"

College Porter—"Yes, sir; our late colleague was one who always discharged the duties of his office with the greatest zeal. And now he is dead, and has not left a cent to pay for his funeral. We have therefore resolved to get up a subscription; and I have taken the liberty of coming to you, thinking you would contribute something towards so worthy an object. We still want ten guilders."

Student (in a voice trembling with emotion)—"Ten guilders... I am deeply touched... instead of ten I'll give you a hundred; but do please bury a few more college porters with the money."

On Parade.

Short Subaltern (to tall recruit)—"Fellow, how dare you have the impudence to look down on me like that? Come, stand up straight—eyes right—look straight before you."

Recruit—"Good-bye, sir!"

Short S.—"Are you mad, you scoundrel?"

Recruit—No, sir; but if I am to keep looking straight in front of me, sir, I'd better say good-bye, sir, please sir, for I'll never see you again in my life, sir!"

Tenant—"Gracious goodness! You have raised the rent again... and what for?"

Landlord—"What for?—you want to know what for? Why, for one thing, there's the new clock-tower and clock right in front of your window. Do you think I intend to make you a present of that?"

Mistress (giving out provisions for the kitchen)—"Don't you want any butter, Mie?"

Maid—"No, thank you, Mevrouw. I belong to the Temperance Society, and must not take anything *strong*."

1st Soldier (in the country)—"What are those things in the field over there?"

2nd Soldier—"Those are traps to catch moles."

1st S.—"That's just one of your larks again! Just as though the moles would be fools enough to go and get caught in that little spot of ground, when there are acres of fields all round."

2nd S.—"Well, how is it that, when the town is so big and the cell at the police-station so small, you're always in it?"

A Double Misfortune.

"Do you not think it a deeply significant fact, Henri," said the poet to his friend, "that I was born on the same day on which Goethe died?"

Henri—"Both events are cruel misfortunes to literature."

Mrs A.'s housemaid has come round with a message:—

"Mistress's compliments, and she would like to know if you will come to spend to-morrow evening?"

Mrs B.—"Very pleased, I am sure . . . Are there more people coming?"

Housemaid—"I have them here on a list."

Mrs B.—"Let me see . . . Why, there are at least thirty names here!"

Housemaid—"Yes, but most of them know that the children have the chicken-pox, and mistress was reckoning on that!"

At the Solicitor's.

"Good-morning, sir! May I ask you to advise me what compensation is due when another person's dog does damage in any one's house?"

"Certainly, sir. The injured party is entitled to two guilders compensation."

"May I ask you for that sum, then? It is your dog that I have to complain of."

"Ah! Then it is your property that my dog has damaged? Nothing can be fairer than that I should pay you the legal compensation. Here are twenty cents."

"Twenty cents!"

"Yes. As thus:—

Your claim is	fl. 2 0
My fee, for advice	1 80
Balance due to you	0 20."

A Slight Mistake.

A man, who thought himself a scientist, gave a public lecture on electricity. The hall was at first tolerably well filled, but the audience were not long in finding out with whom they had to do, and began to go out one by one. At last only one man remained, who listened with the greatest attention, and thus encouraged the lecturer to continue. At the end of half-an-hour he interrupted himself, and said politely—

"I beg your pardon, sir, but I hope I am not trespassing on your kindness? I shall have finished in ten minutes."

"Ten minutes! You can go on for another hour—or all night, if you like—so long as you don't forget that you engaged me by the hour!"

The unhappy man perceived too late that it was the cabman who had driven him down to the lecture-hall.

Horseman (passing window of farmhouse)—"I say, you **stupid** lout, **I** want **to** know why you are always laughing **when I ride** past?"

Peasant—"Why, **sir, it is because you** always happen **to** ride past when I am laughing."

A.—"How are you, old fellow? Have you heard who has got that situation in the Home Office that you **were** trying for?"

B.—"Some ass or other, I suppose, who doesn't in the least deserve it!"

A.—"Of that *you* should be the best judge; you are the **lucky man!"**

THE CANDIDATE.

It is now full two years since Dominie Groshaus departed this life. For forty years the worthy man had tended his flock at Harder, without a thought of laying aside his staff, and quite resolved to edify his congregation for another ten years or so. But Death was not of the same opinion as the deaf old gentleman. One fine morning he came along, and gently took the staff out of the shepherd's hand.

"*Le roi est mort, vive le roi,*" now came true at Harder. Scarcely had the grave closed over Dominie Groshaus, when they began to think of choosing a new pastor. This time it must be a liberal; that was plain as a pikestaff. The Harder people wished to show that they could advance with the times. But where to find him—that was the question. The stipend was not large, and the number of "advanced" candidates exceedingly small,—a bitter disappointment for the Harder parishioners, for your farmer knows no greater enjoyment than in listening to the trial sermons of a "whole regiment" of candidates. As matters stood, however, there was nothing for it but to cut their coat according to their cloth, and six probationers were accordingly invited to display their gifts. The Harder people were not fortunate; for, behold, the last of the six had already arrived, and been quartered at the schoolmaster's, and they had not yet found the right man! It will be understood that they were waiting the last trial sermon in a state of great excitement. No one's heart, however, beat so high as Mr Slop's, for the last candidate pleased the schoolmaster uncommonly well—yes, uncommonly. He had enjoyed a most delightful evening in the young fellow's company. The conversation went as if on wheels. Tantalising prospectives of **instructive conversations,** profitable exchange **of** thought—of society such as **he** had often **vainly longed** for—opened themselves to the master's **mental** vision. Therefore it was his most ardent wish that **this** candidate should succeed. **He** was just considering what he could do to promote his success, when the probationer suddenly put a question to him point-blank.

"Can you tell me, sir, the reason why my friend Burgers did not give satisfaction here?"

"Oh! well—what can I say to you?—the man **was** the victim of a stupid joke. His hair is, as I suppose you are aware, . . ."

"Red—yes, fiery red," sighed the probationer, with **a faint** smile. "Yes—that hair of his!"

"Well," pursued **the** schoolmaster, **"on** the day **Mr** Burgers was preaching here, **Jaap** Stricker, a farmer, who is known **as the worst** joker in the village, happened to be sitting in the pew just behind the elders. When the young **man,** who was certainly doing his best, rather raised his voice at the end of his sermon, and at the same time threw his arms out quickly, Jaap Stricker bent over to the burgomaster, and whispered to him, 'The fire is bursting out.' That joke, sir, was the *coup de grâce.*"

"*Il n'y a pire que le ridicule,*" thought the probationer, "even among these farmers." And suddenly — **as the** schoolmaster drew the little stove towards him in order to light his pipe—there rose up before him the image of Hein Burgers, the rejected, as he used to sit at students' gatherings, with his honest, jovial face, crowned—alas! with **locks** of too brilliant a colour. He saw once more the gloomy **Van** Overveen pretending, with his melancholy smile, to light his cigar at Hein Burgers' flaming head; he heard one and the other call out, on finding that his pipe had gone out, "Just pass Hein this way, will you?" . . .

"I was just saying," the schoolmaster continued, carefully putting the cover on his pipe, after a vigorous pull or two,—" I was saying that was the finishing touch. For even if Mr Burgers' hair had been black instead of red, the man's chance was gone. In the first place, he forgot, when he entered the church, to salute the elders—ahem!—just nod to them, you know!"

"Aha!" said the candidate, making a mental note of the fact.

"And, besides that, there was something in his sermon the burgomaster did not like."

Here the schoolmaster's lips opened, and the pipe slid into the corner of his mouth. His eyes wandered over the ceiling, while he exhibited that vibration of the diaphragm which, according to Darwin, is the symptom of suppressed mirth.

"Pah!" . . . he continued, after a pause, emitting a thick cloud of smoke, under shelter of which his face came back into its normal condition. "You must know that there occurred in his sermon an allusion to Galileo. This was what offended the burgomaster."

"Galileo!" exclaimed the probationer, springing from his seat. "Galileo! what earthly objection can the burgomaster have to Galileo?"

"Much more than you think," returned Mr Slop, with a solemn countenance, but laughter in his eyes. "Much more than you can conjecture. Our burgomaster has, along with many good qualities, a weakness—a prejudice—what shall I call it? The fact is, that he does not believe that the earth turns round . . ."

The shout of laughter emitted by his hearer reduced the schoolmaster to silence.

The two men looked at each other. The master laughed too—the probationer's mirth was infectious—but not so loud. And while the young man continued to give free rein to his emotions, Slop quietly groaned to himself.

"Could a man have done a more unlucky thing?" he went on at last. "Why need he have dragged in Galileo at all? As soon as I heard the name, I thought to myself, 'There goes your chance, my dear young gentleman!' And if he had confined himself to mentioning the name, no harm would have been done; but he did worse—he called Galileo's opponents narrow-minded people! And at last, as if to complete the disaster, he uttered it as his settled conviction that there was no one among his hearers who believed in the stability of the earth. Then I could see that it was all up with him, for the burgomaster flushed up, red as fire. Moreover, he nodded twice, and looked at the preacher with angry defiance."

"Stop, sir! stop!" cried the candidate, holding his sides. "But surely, then, your burgomaster — what's the man's name?—Gorter—surely this Gorter is an original of the first water?"

"He is indeed. Let us only hope that Galileo has not brought the whole modern movement into discredit with him. I sadly fear that such is the case. At any rate, sir, you are warned. If he enters on the subject to-morrow—as he is almost certain to do—keep a good look-out, and mind you don't fall into the snare."

On the following morning the church was as full as it could hold. The candidate gave particular satisfaction. His delivery was more than satisfactory; his voice was as clear as a bell. Such was the verdict of the parishioners. Very well content, and with a great air of mystery, the elders received the preacher at the end of the service. For when the farmer has once made his choice, he takes good care not to give the slightest hint of it—sly diplomat that he is! The candidate was to dine at Burgomaster Gorter's. Aaltje, the good-natured, bashful, kindly wife of that dignitary, had prepared ribs of pork. With heartfelt satisfaction did the couple take note of the young man's hearty appetite. He did not require any pressing, and played as good a knife and fork as if he had been at home. This pleased the burgomaster well. A good appetite is usually the sign of good health. Who would buy an unhealthy cow? And what person in his senses would wish to possess an unhealthy minister?

At the end of the repast, a walk in the orchard was proposed. The burgomaster, pipe in mouth, stumped along in his wooden shoes, solemn and dignified—a sphinx in a peaked cap—beside his guest, and took him to see the pigs. Then they slowly returned to the house, the farmer still preserving an air of tremendous mystery.

At last Mijnheer Gorter broke the ominous silence.

"I was very well pleased with your discourse this morning," he said.

"Were you, sir? I'm glad to hear that."

"They want a modern man in this place. Well—I'm modern, too!" The burgomaster's chin moved backwards into his black silk neckcloth, while a smile of grim self-satisfaction played about his lips. "I'm modern, and progressive too," he went on. "But there is one thing I can't get over. I don't believe that the earth turns round. No one can make a fool of me about that. Every morning when I go out into the fields, I see it with my own eyes lying perfectly still. Now that has nothing to do with modern thought,—that turning round, I suppose,—has it?"

"Oh!" replied the candidate, fairly driven into a corner, "it certainly does have a little to do with it; but, after all, it's not the principal point. One may be a good and honest and religious man, and yet be of opinion—I mean, believe —that the earth stands still. St Paul, for example——"

"'There you are!" roared the burgomaster, bringing his hand vigorously down on his companion's shoulder in the fulness of his satisfaction.

And thus, through his well-timed consideration of the burgomaster's hobby, the sixth candidate was elected to the parish of Harder.

T. H. HOOIJER.
(*De Gids*, 1881.)

E P I G R A M S.

(SNELDICHTEN.)

Tys was a painter—a doctor then he became,
And said to his friends, who murmured at the **same**,
"My faults as a painter, sure, **every** one could **see**,
But now **my** errors are underground, the better 'tis for me."

TROP DE ZÈLE.

HANS boasts he skated from Cologne
In one day to the Hague. "In one,"
His man confirms him, "true as you stand **here**—
But 'twas the longest day of all the year!"

'TWAS asked, Which was the longest day?
My farmer friend, who would not stay
Till I had searched the calendar aright,
Said, "Why, sir, 'tis the one that has the shortest night."

DIRCK once was given to language most profane;
I strove to turn him from his evil ways in vain.
After long years I was successful. How?
With this one word: "'Tis **not** the mode in Paris now."

TO A PREACHER.

YE preach so long, good sir, that we the opening have forgot,
And therefore when ye reach the end, we understand it not.

Pete ran against me in the street one day,
Nor moved aside: "He would not yield the way
To every fool." "I can—and do!" said I—
Stepped from the path, and let the fool pass by.

Old Father Jan did chide his son because he sleeping lay,
Instead of getting up to work at dawning of the day,
And told him how a certain boor, at daybreak in the field,
Had found his fallow ground a pot of gold did yield.
"Yes, father," said young Jack, "'twas early, it may be,
But sure the man that lost the gold was earlier than he!"

Jan will take where'er he can,
Out of purse and out of sack,
Out of cupboard, chest or pack,
Out of kettle, pot, and pan,—
Jan's a very *taking* man.

Clothes and Men.

The tailor's shop for highest praise, say I,
With royal courts doth vie;
Best skill boast which of these two can?
There the man makes the clothes; here the clothes
    make the man.

Dirck went out once to buy a hat, 'tis known,
And sought to pay for it with words alone.
"Nay," said the mercer, "I'll not come to that,
To meet *you* and uncover to *my hat!*"

How can a miller be a thief?
Methinks the thing were past belief;
What use for gold or gear can find
The man who lives upon the wind?

Prudent Ignorance.

Peter knows nought, and will know nought;
    I know the reason why:
    He fears distress and injury,
And has not the old saw **forgot**—
*What a man knows not **hurts** him not.*

The Courtship of Jan and Griet.

"Well, is it ne'er to be?" said Jan;
    " I've faithfully **done all** I can:
I've served **you** as a friend," quo' he,
    "So long **in all** humility,
And serve you still!" "'Tis true," said she,
"And yet you will not serve for me!"

A knight, a doctor, a new nobleman,
A **duke, a count,** to make of **any man,**
Is **no great art, and** this **can princes do.**
Would Heaven grant us but **some princes,** who
Could by authority of ring and seal,
With men of sense provide the commonweal!

"My parents," Andrew said, "**were** drowned **at sea,**
Therefore **no** vessel, ship, or boat, for me!"
"**My father** and my mother," Adrian said,
"**Died** in their beds: shall **I not** go to bed?"

Twelve **men to try a** crime is British use:—
A thief was asked **his jury for to** choose.
"The **twelve** apostles—honest men **they** be."
Then **said a man**: "But those we shall not see
Before the day of judgment." "Gentlemen,
I'll gladly wait the trial until then."

Once poor, and kind of heart, thou'rt rich and greedy, Jan!
The touchstone proves the gold, the gold doth prove the
    man.   Constantijn Huygens, 1596-1687.

I MET a kinsman of mine but now,
And asked him where he lived, and how?
"Like any prince," so said my friend,
"I have enough to eat and drink, and debts without an end."

"I MET A KINSMAN OF MINE."

SAID Jan, twice wedded to a scolding wife,
 'Church-going's the great pleasure of my life;
'Tis strange and sweet to see a man, O rare!
Keep full five hundred women quiet there!"

THE VILLAGE ON *THE FRONTIER.**

CHARACTERS.

MARIA (*Maid*).
MICHIEL (*Man-servant*).
NICOLAAS (*Landlord and Burgomaster*).
LIEUTENANT EDELING.
VAN WERVE, } (*Refugees*).
CLARA (*his daughter*) }

CAPTAIN D'EGLANTIERS.
LIEUTENANT TAELINCK.
SERGEANT PLUCKX.
CORPORAL NESTIERS.
PRIVATE PASSEREAU.

ACT I.

A Village Inn. Evening. MICHIEL *asleep in a chair.*

Maria (*the maid—behind the scenes*). Michiel, where are you? [*Entering.*] He is lazy enough for a member of the Brussels Committee. Michiel, get up!

Michiel (*awaking*). Well, what's up now?

Maria. Wake up, at any rate! Isn't it perfectly scandalous to lie there, at seven o'clock in the evening, snoring like an ox?

Michiel. Does that hurt any one?

Maria. Is there no work to do then?

Michiel. That won't amount to much. Travellers won't give us any trouble, it's not worth their while to cross the frontier just now; and the farmers have their money under lock and key, and not a cent about them to take a dram with.

Maria. Is there nothing else for you to do? Couldn't you take your rifle, in your spare time, and drill a little? Everybody is drilling just now; there isn't a child but can load at twelve different rates. And you, of all others, ought to be ready to give an account of yourself when the rebels come

---

* The scene of this play is laid on what is now the frontier between Holland and Belgium,—the time is 1830,—when the southern provinces of the Kingdom of Holland revolted. The Liberal (French) party allied itself with the Clerical Ultramontanes against the Government, and the news of the Paris Revolution precipitated the outbreak of a riot at Brussels (August 25), which soon spread over the country.

to pay us a visit. People on the frontier, if no others, ought to be always in readiness.

(*Sings*) "Only with vigilance, powder, and ball,
　　In time of need, one can live at all
　　　Upon the Belgian border."

Michiel. Well! you've got hold of that sentiment by the wrong end. Let me tell you the right way of it.

" He who would live in a border place
Must always exhibit a double face.
Let the Dutch army come—we'll fly
Old Holland's colours right merrily;
Let the Brabanters march this way,
And the Belgian flag goes up to-day,
　　And so in varying order.
Not by courage or powder and ball,
By cunning alone we can live at all
　　Upon the Belgian border!"

Maria. Do you know that you deserve to be hanged, with such infamous principles as that?

Michiel. Why, it's just to escape hanging that I want to put them into practice, as our schoolmaster says.

Maria. Our schoolmaster used to say you were an ignorant ass; but I see that at any rate you have remembered something.

Michiel. He shall be sorry, one of these days, for having spoken of me in that way. But, never mind that, I have a good idea.

Maria. A fine one, I expect!

Michiel. Just listen. We cannot help it if one party or the other wants to annex us; so we must try and keep friends with both, and make each of them believe we are on their side. Now, I've asked the house-painter for a couple of pots of paint: there they are. You say I never carry anything out; now you shall just see.

Maria. Well—and then?

Michiel. Why, you **see, the** Orange **flag is still on the church tower?**

Maria. **Yes ;** and if you dare to touch it, **I'll** scratch your eyes out!

Michiel. My idea was to paint it with the Brabant colours on the side towards Brabant. If the Dutch come from the north—very good! they see the Orange flag. If the Brabanters come from the south—very good too! they'll see their own colours.

Maria. Well, that's a nice invention!

Michiel. Isn't it? I think they ought to give **me a prize** out of the village treasury; for in this way I am **saving every** one from embarrassment.

Maria. But you've forgotten one thing!

Michiel. Forgotten! What's that?

Maria. When the wind changes, the Brabanters will see **Orange, and the Dutch** the Brabant colours ; **and then,** perhaps, both of them will bombard the village, **and you in** it—which would not be the worst loss of all.

Michiel. That's true; I never thought of that. **But, after** all, is there no contrivance to prevent that? **With a rope,** for instance?

Maria. You're a nice politician! It doesn't do to **forget** that the wind may change. So leave politics alone for **the** future, or I'll tell the master what sort of fellow you **are.**

Michiel. Would you go and tell tales, just because I have **a** little more sense than the master? He will get us all into trouble before he's done, because he can't give and take.

Maria. **Then both** of you taken together ought **to make** a man after your own heart. If you ask any of the poor people hereabouts, they will tell you whether or not he knows how to give; and if you were in his place, you would certainly do nothing but take.

Michiel. Yes; having is having, but getting's the trick!

Much good has the master done himself, with all his giving away. Then you have the King; what numbers of people he has helped out of his own pocket-money! And what has he gained by it? Nothing! They are breaking his window-panes with his own three-guilder pieces!

Maria. Would you follow the example of such ungrateful wretches?

Michiel. Just now the question is, What pays best? And if we are ever to be man and wife, it will surely be necessary to scrape a little money together first, if we want to live like decent people.

Maria. We man and wife! You may make your mind easy on that point!

Michiel. It's not to be? Very good—you'll change your mind some day, and come asking me on your bare knees to make you my wife,—some day when I'm a great lord, just like the man with the whale,* who is now a general among the Brabanters.

Maria. If being a fool and a scoundrel is enough to give a man high rank among the rebels, you will have plenty of chances; but I won't talk to you any more.

Michiel. Have you anything more to say? Because, if not, I'll go to sleep again.

Maria. Nothing but this, that for the present, not being a general as yet, you might go to Peter Kluisken's and fetch the pig that the master has bought.

Michiel. A nice little job! To tramp all that way at this time of night, and in the direction of the Belgian sentinels, too. Well, just you look out; if I meet them, I bring them here—upon my word I will.   [*Exit.*

Maria (*alone*). The scoundrel! He is quite capable of doing it. And *he* expects to marry me? Not if I know it.

---

* This is an allusion to one Kissels, who had been getting his living by exhibiting a whale's skeleton at Amsterdam, and joined the Belgian side on the outbreak of the war.

Enter NICOLAAS, *the landlord, with a newspaper in his hand.*

Maria. Well, sir, what's the news?

Nicolaas. Good news, my girl. A division of our brave North Netherlanders is marching this way; perhaps they may even pass through this village.

Maria. That would be a pleasure. I wish some of them would stay here, then the brigands, who yesterday were only a few miles from this place, would never dare to show themselves.

Nicolaas. I think they will keep pretty quiet for the future.

Maria. Are there any more news in the paper, sir?

Nicolaas. H'm! h'm! not so fast, child. [*Glances over the paper.*] They do not seem to have made up their minds yet at Brussels whom they are going to have at the head of the Government.

Maria. I can quite believe that; and I don't think there are many men very eager to undertake the management of such a confused state of affairs.

Nicolaas. They may seek long enough, the ungrateful hounds, before they find another ruler under whom they will be as happy as they were under our good old King.

Maria. Any news besides, sir?

Nicolaas. Do let me read in peace. . . . H'm! yes; they are complaining of scarcity in all the Belgian towns.

Maria. Of course they are. They may hate the Dutch, but they'll find they can't get on without Dutch money. What other news is there?

Nicolaas. The Powers have resolved to keep to the non-intervention system.

Maria. Non-intervention! what's that? It must be a fine thing whatever it is; every one is talking about it.

Nicolaas. Well, how can I best explain it? It means . . . not to meddle with other people's affairs. For instance, if your neighbour comes and asks you to help him because his house is on fire, and you tell him to put it out himself, for it's no affair of yours,—that's non-intervention. But listen ... I hear the sound of horses' hoofs. Who can it be?

A voice outside. Does the burgomaster live here?

Nicolaas. Coming!

"JUST COME IN, LIEUTENANT."

Maria (looking out). Lancers! lancers!

Enter EDELING, *with two lancers.*

Edeling. I want to speak to the burgomaster. Does he live here?

Nicolaas. Just come in, Lieutenant. Come in, gentlemen, I am very glad to see you. What will your honour take? Maria, run to the cellar, there's a good girl, and bring up a bottle of the best. [*Exit Maria.*

Edeling. Not for me, thanks; I don't want anything. My time is short, and so are my orders.

Nicolaas. I won't listen to a word before the gentlemen have had some refreshment.

Enter MARIA *with wine;* NICOLAAS *opens bottle.*

Edeling. I do not care for useless compliments. I am commissioned to buy some cattle here, and bring them at once to headquarters. How many head can you let me have, and at what price, to be paid in cash at once?

Nicolaas. We will see. (*To Maria.*) Is Michiel back yet?

Maria. He is only just gone out.

Nicolaas. Then you will have to do the errand. Run at once to Peter Slof and Cornelis de Ruyter, and ask them to come here at once. I want to see them about a cattle contract. Well, what are you dawdling for?

Maria. Because—because—— [*Looks at the lancers.*] I'm so glad! [*Runs out.*]

Nicolaas (*offering wine*). Come, just one glass!

Edeling. If you insist. (*Suspiciously.*) Are you not going to drink too, Burgomaster? (*Drinks.*) What's to pay?

Nicolaas. Who's talking about payment? Haven't I even a glass of wine to spare for our brave defenders?

Edeling. Well, but you're an innkeeper. Take these two guilders and put them in your pocket, for it's against orders for us to get anything on credit.

Nicolaas. And I say I won't have the money. I can be obstinate enough, too, when I once begin. Take it, and give it to the Government as a voluntary subscription on my part. You don't trust me, Lieutenant, and that grieves me to the heart. I see I shall have to put on my Sunday coat; perhaps that will give you more confidence. [*Fetches a coat, with a medal on it, and puts it on. The lancers salute.*] Now, do I look like a man who would betray you? I won that at Waterloo.

Edeling. Forgive me for suspecting you; but so many of

your class, especially on the frontier, have turned out traitors, that suspicion has become a disagreeable duty. What is the general feeling in this village?

Nicolaas. Not what it ought to be. I fear that, if the rebels were to arrive, there are those, here and there, who would join them. It seems as though people were struck with blindness; they want change at any price. They have let themselves be persuaded that they will have no taxes to pay under the Brabant Government. That's the worst of the people here; they are stupid, they don't reason.

Edeling. They don't know any better, I suppose. Do you think your friends will be here soon?

Nicolaas. Presently, I hope. Your honour seems to be in a hurry. Is it far to headquarters?

Edeling. A couple of hours. We are to march again at day-break to-morrow. I am sorry we are not going farther, for I fear we shall not meet any of the enemy. I would willingly have paid them a visit.

Nicolaas. You are very eager for fighting.

Edeling. Particularly so; for, besides my wish to do my duty by my king and country, I have a private account to settle with the gentlemen from the south. They are keeping my bride a prisoner.

Nicolaas. Your bride! I thought women, at least, would have been respected.

Edeling. Her father is a well-known soldier; when the first disturbances broke out in the place where he was in command, he gave orders to fire on the rebels. They never forgave him, and when he had the misfortune to fall into their hands they kept him in prison—his daughter refusing to leave him.

Enter MARIA.

Maria. Here come Peter Slof and Cornelis de Ruyter.

Nicolaas. Very good! Shall we go to meet them, and look at their beasts together?

Edeling. Willingly. **Thank you for doing** the errand (*to Maria.*), and here is something to remember the Lieutenant **by.** [*Gives her money, and exit with Nicolaas.*]

Maria (alone). A guilder! Well, I'll keep that as a remembrance. A nice man that lieutenant! One can see he comes from Holland. But who are these strangers coming in so timidly?

Enter VAN WERVE *and* CLARA.

Van Werve. Can we get a night's lodging here?

Maria. Please don't take it ill of **me, I must ask first** where your honour comes from? **We** can't take any **one in** for the night without first knowing who it is we are sheltering.

Van Werve. I will answer your question to the Burgomaster. Where does he live? and **can I** speak to him?

Maria. He lives here. The Burgomaster and the landlord are the same person. The master will be home directly.

Clara. Will you please tell us what province we are in?

Maria. In North Brabant, Mejuffrouw.

Clara. Thank Heaven! then you are **safe, father!**

Maria. Safe! Then you are refugees?

Van Werve. Clara!

Clara. I was imprudent, father—forgive me. **But I could** not control my joy at finding myself once more in our own country, after all that we have gone through.

Van Werve. I am not yet sure that we are **safe here.**

Clara. If we had anything to fear here, I feel sure, from **this girl's honest face,** that she would not betray us.

Maria. **I** betray you! I'd sooner die **a** thousand times over. **But** come and sit down—you seem tired.

Clara. It is true, we have been walking for a long time, and I begin to feel it.

Van Werve. My dear child, what a difficult and anxious journey you have exposed yourself to, to save your father. (*To Maria.*) Yes, my good girl, I have been in prison,—my daughter has succeeded in saving me, and it is to her courage and devotion I owe it that we have been able to pass the enemy's outposts and reach this village.

Maria. It's lucky you just happened to come to-day. A few Dutch soldiers arrived not long ago, who will be quite ready to escort you to a safe place, if you prefer not to stay here any longer.

Van Werve. My comrades! Oh, where are they? Take me to them.

Maria. I will call them,—or—wait—I think I hear them coming.

Enter EDELING.

Maria. What, alone, Lieutenant? Where are the rest?

Edeling. They have gone on with the oxen. I found I had left my cloak here. But whom do I see?

Van Werve. The voice seems familiar.

Clara (*hastens to him*). Edeling!

Edeling. Clara!—Mijnheer van Werve! . . .

Van Werve. So you've enlisted, Edeling? Well done, my boy! That is what I should have expected of a true-born Dutchman like yourself!

Edeling. Your words remind me that I am no longer my own master. I am expected every minute at the camp.

Clara. Cannot we go with you?

Edeling. I have only my horse; but perhaps there is a conveyance of some sort to be had in the village.

Maria. Oh! three if you like. I will go at once to order one.

Van Werve. Stop a moment, girl. I—alas!—I have no money to pay for a conveyance.

Edeling. Here is my purse—but I really must go.

Van Werve (*putting back the purse*). I must not accept it. I can never return it. I possess nothing now.

Edeling. Nothing?

Van Werve. Not a cent. The little ready money we had

with us we have been obliged to spend on the road; **and this** morning I had the misfortune, to leave behind——

Edeling. Well?

Van Werve. My portmanteau, **with** my whole fortune in it, at the village where we stopped for the night.

Maria. Well, portmanteau or no portmanteau, you will have to drive, and I'm going to fetch the carriage. [*Exit.*

Van Werve. It **was no** carelessness on our part; the pursuers were at our heels—we had no time to save anything but ourselves.

Edeling. And isn't **it** enough for me to see you **safe, sir,** you and my Clara? Is not everything I have yours? Take my purse. As soon as you can get a vehicle, follow **me as** quickly as you can, for I must not delay one moment longer.

Enter MARIA, *hastily.*

Maria. Save yourselves, for Heaven's sake! save yourselves! they're coming!

Omnes. Who? What? [*A noise outside.*]

Maria. The brigands! Don't you hear them? **They're** shouting, "*Vive de liberteyt!*"

Edeling (*draws his pistols*). The first who dares——

Maria (*seizes him by the arm*). Are you mad? What is the good of your pistols against a whole band? Quick! **out** at the back **door.** (*To Van Werve and Clara.*) And **you**— into this room! I'll come back to you in a minute.

Edeling. But if——

Maria (*pushes him out at a side door*). No buts! make haste!
[*Exit Edeling.*

Van Werve. Can't we follow him?

Maria. Certainly not. He is a young fellow, and can take care of himself. Three of you would arouse suspicion, and perhaps lead to mischief if he tried to defend you. Just come in here. [*Opens the door of a room on one side.*]

Clara. We leave our fate in your hands.
[*Exeunt Van Werve and Clara.*

Enter MICHIEL, *bringing with him a number of Belgian volunteers, among whom Captain D'Eglantiers, Lieutenant Taelinck, Sergeant Pluckx, Corporal Nestiers, and Private Passereau. They speak the broad Flemish or South Netherlands dialect, largely interspersed with French words. On entering, all of them, including Michiel, sing, to the air of* "*La Dame Blanche*"—

> Victory ! Victory !
> The enemy's away !
> Who conquers through sheer bravery
> But Old Brabant and liberty ?
> Victory ! Victory !
> Glory and loot to-day !

Maria. Well, they do look like lunatics ; and there's that villain of a Michiel with them.

D'Eglantiers (*wiping his sword*). The victory is ours, comrades ! Our courage has repulsed the enemy, and maintained the glory of our name. Lieutenant Taelinck, see that none of the Hollanders escape who are hidden away here, do you hear?

Taelinck. I have seen to that, Captain. All the exits are well guarded.

Maria (*aside*). The poor quarter-master ! how will he escape?

Michiel. What will the gentlemen please to take ? Everything in the house is at your service.

Maria. Just listen to the contemptible rascal ?

D'Eglantiers (*to Michiel*). You're a fine fellow ! Just let the lass fetch a *litre* of wine from the cellar.

Michiel. Do you hear ? Fetch wine for the gentlemen.

Maria (*treading on his toes as she goes out*). You villainous traitor !

D'Eglantiers (*to Michiel*). Do you live in the house?

Michiel. I live here, Captain. (*Aside.*) I need not tell him in what capacity.

D'Eglantiers. You are a brave *citoyen!* Without you, **we** should never have found the way to this village so soon. I think I might make you Burgomaster.

Michiel. Indeed you couldn't do better, Captain. I will at once give orders to have the Brabant flag hoisted.

[*He is about to leave the room.*]

D'Eglantiers. There's no need of that. It's *obscur* out of doors, and one can't very well distinguish the colours. But I'll tell you what **to do. Go at once and fetch the notables of the** village, and tell them to come here to-morrow with the first *lumière* to hold a meeting of the council. **Corporal** Nestiers, go along **with** the Burgomaster, **and whoever does** not come with you at once, *de bonne volonté*, you must bring him **by force**; for liberty **must** triumph.

Michiel (*aside*). **Michiel,** Burgomaster !

D'Eglantiers (*sits down*). I shall make **my** headquarters here provisionally. Let's see—what has **to be done** now? . . .

Enter MARIA, *bringing wine. All sit down and* **drink.**

D'Eglantiers. Ahem !—reports . . . **but who is to write** them ? Lieutenant Taelinck, can you write ?

Taelinck. No, Captain.

D'Eglantiers. Why **are you a** lieutenant then **?**

Taelinck. **But you can't do it** either, Captain—or read, **for** that matter.

D'Eglantiers. Silence ! **I'm** a captain to give orders, **not** to write. Sergeant Pluckx, can you write ?

Pluckx. Not I—but there's Private Passereau, he knows how.

Passereau. Plait-il ?

D'Eglantiers. I'm asking if you **can write.**

Passereau. Verdikke !* eh ?

---

* A Flemish expletive.

D'Eglantiers. If you can write—don't you understand?

Passereau. Je n'entends pas—verdikke!

Pluckx. Verdikke is the only word of Flemish that Passereau knows.

D'Eglantiers. So he can't write Flemish. (*To Maria.*) Can you write, my girl?

Maria. At your service, Captain.

D'Eglantiers. That's curious! Sit down here, then, and write as I dictate.

Maria (*sits down at the table—aside*). What an idea! ... Yes, I think it will do!

D'Eglantiers. Write: Report ...

Enter NICOLAAS, NESTIERS, *and two others.*

Nestiers. Captain, here is a fellow who has been rebelling against us.

D'Eglantiers. Well—what has he been doing?

Nestiers. He forcibly resisted our entrance into an *écurie* in which there was a lancer's horse standing.

D'Eglantiers. And where was the lancer who sat on the horse?

Nestiers. He is nowhere to be found.

D'Eglantiers. Well—just look through the whole village till you find him. [*Exeunt Nestiers and others.*

D'Eglantiers (*to Nicolaas*). Who are you?

Nicolaas. I am the Burgomaster.

D'Eglantiers. The ex-burgomaster! I have put another burgomaster in your place—do you understand? But if you will make your *soumission* to the Committee, then, perhaps ...

Nicolaas. Never!

D'Eglantiers. What!—do you know that I can have you *fusillé?*

Nicolaas. So you may, if you like!

D'Eglantiers. What do you say? Stop where you are—I

shall have a word to speak with you presently—do you understand? (*To Maria.*) Write!

Nicolaas. **What!** Maria, are you giving this scoundrel any help?

Maria. Why not? The gentleman was in such trouble because he could not find any one able to write.

D'Eglantiers. Where did I leave off dictating?
(*Sings*)   Write with care—or you'll regret!
Maria.   Captain, not a word I've written—
                You have told me nothing yet!
D'Eglantiers. Write: Our army, fear-compelling,
                Took six hamlets in **a day.**
Nicolaas.   Since they saw no **en'my—surely**
                No great **wonder anyway.**
D'Eglantiers. Of the foe **full seven hundred**
                Fell before our conquering force!
Nicolaas.   **Numbers** which, if rightly sifted,
                Come to just one lancer's horse!
D'Eglantiers. Out of all my valiant heroes
                Only one has fall'n—the **which—**
Nicolaas.   As **I've** just had information,
                Fell dead drunk into a ditch.
D'Eglantiers. Good!—you now may cease your labours!
                So!—a **neat** despatch you see,
                Accurate and interesting,
                As they always ought to be.
Nicolaas.   Such as all despatches be!

D'Eglantiers. Well—now let us just look at it. H'm that's written very cleverly. Now for the proclamation. Another sheet of paper! Write: Proclamation! Have you **written that** sentence?

Maria. Yes—what next?

D'Eglantiers. We, Captain d'Eglantiers and Lieutenant Taelinck,—to all who are about to **read** these presents—salutation!

Maria (writing). To all who are *able* to read these presents . . .

D'Eglantiers. About to read, I said! Fellow-citizens! we are bringing you *la liberté*. We have risked our life-blood to procure it for you: we also hope that you will show yourselves *reconnaissants* . . . Hey! now what do you say to such a sentence as that? That's what I call eloquence!

Maria. Undoubtedly! That is very neatly said, Captain.

D'Eglantiers. I see you're a girl of taste and intelligence. Go on—and that you are to give us . . . give us . . . everything that is necessary. Well, that's short and to the point, isn't it?

Maria. A very fine style, and any one can understand what is meant at the very first reading.

D'Eglantiers (gratified). Can't they just?

Maria. Now you're going to sign both papers, aren't you, Captain?

D'Eglantiers. Yes; I'll put a little cross to them—that's my mark. Lieutenant Taelinck, are you going to sign them too?

Taelinck (half asleep). Yes, yes. [*They sign.*]

D'Eglantiers. Now the report must be enclosed in an envelope, and sent to the General, and the proclamation will be posted up to-morrow.

[*Maria hastily hides the signed paper in her dress, and folds another, which she hands to D'Eglantiers.*]

Maria. Here you are, Captain. (*Aside.*) I have it all right.

D'Eglantiers (hands the paper to Private Passereau). Get on your horse at once, and take this paper to the General.

Passereau. Verdikke! Dans la nuit——

D'Eglantiers. Go at once! [*Exit Passereau.*] Well, that's finished. Now I'll go and get an hour or two's sleep. You'll call me, my good girl, when the council is assembled, won't you?

Maria. Yes; and in the meantime I will go and post up the proclamation.

D'Eglantiers (*takes it hastily from her, and puts it into his pocket*). No; I must first read it out, or have it read, to the council. Now, where is my bedroom?

[*He is about to go into Van Werve's room.*]

Maria (*quickly*). No, not there. The left-hand door, sir.

[*Points to a door on the opposite side.*]

Nicolaas (*aside*). I don't understand it. Why does she want to put that fellow into my bedroom? (*Aloud.*) Maria, are you mad! the other room is——

Maria (*interrupting him quickly*). Just suited to a prisoner.

D'Eglantiers (*pointing to Nicolaas*). Then he must be put in there.

Nicolaas. But——

Maria (*quickly, aside to Nicolaas*). Leave it to me!

D'Eglantiers. Good-night! (*Turning to the Volunteers.*) If Nestiers comes with the portmanteau, tell him to bring it into my room. Do you hear?

[*Nicolaas goes into the room in which Van Werve and Clara are hidden, while Maria takes a candle and shows D'Eglantiers into the left-hand bedroom.*]

Taelinck (*crouching over the fire*). B-rrr! it's famously cold!

Pluckx. I believe you! The Government really ought to provide us with better clothing.

Taelinck. That's just the beauty of liberty, that every one has to look out for himself.

Pluckx. And that's just what I mean to do, so soon as that girl comes back.

Edeling (*appears in the doorway and looks in*). These fellows are everywhere! I am caught in a trap.

Pluckx. But just tell us now, Lieutenant, who is supposed to be governing us at the present moment? for every day I hear of a fresh sovereign, who has been recommended to us

Taelinck. Who is governing us? Why, Liberty!

Pluckx. I shan't be sorry to see some change, then; for I haven't yet seen the colour of Liberty's money. I think the lass must be very hard up.

Enter MARIA.

Maria (aside). Is this rabble going to stay here all right?

Pluckx. I say, my girl, look here. Have you got a blanket or rug you could let me have?

Maria. What for?

Pluckx. You'll soon see that—*comprenez?*

Maria. I have; if you will be sure to give it back.

Pluckx. Oh! you shall have it back soon.

Maria (takes a blanket out of a chest). Here is one; but you shall not have it, unless you give me your tunic as a pledge that you will return it.

Pluckx. Come, none of that chatter!

Maria. Gently, gently! You have seen that the Captain lets me write his proclamations for him. Nothing would be easier than for me to put in a word against you, if you don't behave yourselves.

Taelinck. The girl is right, Pluckx.

Pluckx. Well, here's my *sarrau,* then! It's not a bad exchange. [*He gives his tunic to Maria, and cuts three slits in the blanket.*]

Maria. What's that for?

Pluckx. A new-fashioned overcoat for the winter. [*Puts his head and arms through the slits. All laugh except Maria.*]

Maria. Well, as you've spoilt my blanket for me, you shall not have your tunic back either.

Enter NESTIERS.

Nestiers. Come, men, here are your billets; and here (*laying it on the floor*) is the Captain's portmanteau.

Pluckx. You mean the portmanteau that the Captain looted this morning.

Maria and Edeling (*aside*). **Is it possible?**

Taelinck. Well, be quick **and** give **out** your billets. **I'm** going to stay **here.** I suppose there's a second bed in the Captain's room?

Maria. **Surely.**

Taelinck. Allons donc! Right-about march! Place a sentry outside the front door, and see that no one goes **in** or out without permission from the Captain or me.

[*Goes into D'Eglantiers' room with the portmanteau. The others retire. Enter* EDELING, *to whom Maria hands Passereau's tunic, in which he escapes.*]

Act II.

Middle of night. D'EGLANTIERS *alone with the* **portmanteau** *under his arm and a candlestick* **in** *his hand.*

D'Eglantiers. I see they've brought me the portmanteau. Let's seize the golden moment, while old Taelinck lies snoring like an ox, to inspect the contents a bit. [*Breaks the lock, and rummages through the portmanteau, taking out a necktie or some similar article, which he puts on.*] What do I see? This seems to be a handsome capture! And I'll be hanged if these are not Government bonds! *Ma foi!* Now I'm a rich man, and **can let** the service slide with an easy mind! I shall lose nothing by resigning—no one ever got his pay **out** of a Provisional **Government!** However, we must keep a sharp look-out, and **not let** any of my comrades find **out** what has been in here! **All** honest fellows, no doubt, but suffering **from** the same complaint as myself! Where shall I hide the packets? The portmanteau won't lock now; and, besides, several of them have seen it already.

[*Remains standing, with the bonds in his hands. Enter* MARIA.]

Maria. Up already, Captain?

D'Eglantiers (*starts, and tries to hide the papers*). What,— what is it?

Maria (*aside*). That's the portmanteau in question. (*Aloud.*) Nothing, Captain; I came to see if you wanted anything.

D'Eglantiers. Nothing! or,—wait! (*Looking at her attentively. Aside.*) The girl seems trustworthy . . . otherwise . . . yes, I suppose that will be best!

Maria (*aside*). What is he considering with himself?

D'Eglantiers. My good girl, I have here some of the army reports; could you tell me of a safe place, where no one comes poking and prying round, and where I can *cacher* them in safety till my departure?

Maria (*aside*). He's running into the trap of his own accord. (*To D'Eglantiers, pointing to the cupboard.*) Shall I hide them in here, under the house linen? But in that case you must give your men orders not to go about plundering my cupboards.

D'Eglantiers. I'll promise you that, but just open it.

[*Maria opens the cupboard; D'Eglantiers hides the bonds inside it.*]

Maria. I think, Captain, that packet must contain something more than reports and general orders!

D'Eglantiers. No, it really does not, by——

Maria. Well, I'll believe you; so you need not swear about it. But it looked to me rather like bonds. [*Locks the cupboard, and is about to put the key in her pocket, but D'Eglantiers prevents her.*]

D'Eglantiers. Stop! I keep that key, do you hear?

Maria. Do you, sir? they're bonds! Otherwise you would not be so much afraid of losing them!

D'Eglantiers. Yes, if that were true——

Maria. Then you wouldn't be captain of a volunteer company, would you?

D'Eglantiers. No, certainly not!

Maria. No, if you **were only rich, you'd** already **be a** Member of Congress,—perhaps even of the Provisional Government...

D'Eglantiers. Yes; I do really **think,** if I were richer——

Maria. **Not a** doubt about **it!** A man of your talents and your eloquence would certainly have reached a high rank at **Brussels,** but for the want of means.

D'Eglantiers. You're flattering me; but, after all, think of the numbers of conceited fools that have been elected to Congress! They do **nothing but** talk **and mismanage** matters.

Maria. I really **think that** you ought to be there, **sir. It's** quite a mistake your not going! Brussels is the only place fit for you.

D'Eglantiers. I tell you once more, you're a **flatterer ; but** I promise you one thing,—as soon as I've hoisted **the Brabant** flag on the church-tower of this village, I'll go to Brussels and ask for my discharge.

Maria (aside). A pleasant journey to you,—so long as the bonds remain here!

Enter TAELINCK.

Taelinck. You're up early, Captain?

D'Eglantiers. Yes, yes, good-morning! (*Looking sideways at the portmanteau.*) May the devil——

Taelinck. It seems to me you've been looking out for yourself already. **Was** the portmanteau quite empty like that?

D'Eglantiers (*somewhat embarrassed*). Well, there wasn't much in it.

Taelinck. You're not a man **of your** word, Captain! **You** promised that we should share and share alike, **whatever** was in it.

D'Eglantiers. When there is nothing, there's nothing **to** share; **do you hear?**

Taelinck. You might at least have waited to open it till I was there.

D'Eglantiers. Lieutenant, you're becoming insolent; you're forgetting discipline!

Taelinck. I shall let the General know that you keep all the loot to yourself.

D'Eglantiers. There stands the girl,—ask; let her *témoigner* whether there was anything in it but——

Maria. But eight linen shirts, which the Captain gave me to put away in the cupboard. Shall I get them out, Captain?

D'Eglantiers. Yes, yes,—here's the key! (*Aside.*) That's a little jewel of a girl!

> [*Maria opens the cupboard, and takes out a pile of shirts, which she drops on the floor. While the two officers are busy picking them up, she hides the bonds under her apron.*]

Maria. There they are,—eight of them!

Taelinck. That's five for me,—but was there nothing more?

Maria. Nothing. [*She locks the cupboard, and returns the key to D'Eglantiers.*]

D'Eglantiers (*aside to Maria*). If I ever get into the Government, I'll see that you have a pension.

Maria. I should like to ask you something, sir. First, about the landlord,—my master, you know,—the man you took prisoner yesterday, and who is in that room; will you set him free again?

D'Eglantiers. H'm! h'm! a rebel like that? but, since you ask it . . . well, go and fetch him!

Maria. And in the second place, will you let my sister and my uncle, who are sleeping here, go back to their own village undisturbed?

D'Eglantiers. Where do they live?

Maria. Why . . . not very far off.

D'Eglantiers. Well, if they lived at the other end **of** nowhere, I should let them go, since it is you that ask it!

Maria. **Very** good; I'll go at once and tell them. [*Exit.*

D'Eglantiers (*aside*). That's the right sort of girl! she's saved me from all my anxiety.

Taelinck (*aside*). I don't feel anything like easy about that affair of the cupboard!

Enter NICOLAAS.

Nicolaas. Captain, **the maid** tells me you have given orders **for** my release.

D'Eglantiers. Yes; because that girl asked me, I've let you go, but mind what you're about next time. The council is going to assemble here, and you may vote with the rest, because **I** want liberty to flourish.

Enter PLUCKX.

Pluckx. Captain! here's the council; are you ready **for** them?

D'Eglantiers. Yes, yes, let them come; but,—I tell you what,—let ten or a dozen of our men comé in too, so as to maintain full liberty during the discussions; do you hear?

Pluckx. Very good, Captain.

[*Pluckx goes out, and returns with the principal men of the village, headed by Michiel, as Burgomaster, and some Volunteers.*]

Nicolaas (*to Michiel*). What in the devil's name are you doing here? Look alive, and get to the stables!

Michiel. Why, master, are you there? That's lucky. I'll have you for my man-of-all-work, master!

Nicolaas. Why, man, are you gone wrong in your head? or——

Michiel. Not at all! The Captain here has made me Burgomaster of the village;—so you **see, sir,** that things look very bad for you.

D'Eglantiers. Silence! The council is going to be opened, **and every one** is to sit down.

[*The "Notables," with Michiel in their midst, sit down in a circle, while D'Eglantiers takes his place at a table, with Taelinck by his side.*]

D'Eglantiers. The *séance* must be public, as is the proper thing for all liberal governments.

Nicolaas. Of course—so that every one can hear the nonsense that is talked.

D'Eglantiers. Therefore, Pluckx, open the door; but don't let every one in, or the room will be overcrowded, you understand?

Nicolaas. A very wise precaution!

[*The front door and shutters are opened. It is daylight.*]

D'Eglantiers. Citizens! in the name of the Government, I offer you *la liberté, les lumières, et l'ordre légal*. Do you understand that?

The Schoolmaster. It seems to mean the same thing as freedom, enlightenment, and law and order.

Nicolaas (*standing up*). Surely, sir, it is scarcely necessary to give us what we have possessed for a long time already!

D'Eglantiers. Silence! I bring you liberty in all things,—no more coercion,—no more monopoly! Education and trade are free. Is there a school here?

The Schoolmaster. Certainly, sir, the Society for National Education—

D'Eglantiers. Done away with! Abolished! The parents are free from henceforth, and, as a natural consequence, the children also. No more schools; at any rate, none of the National Education Society's!

Nicolaas. That I am quite willing to believe.

D'Eglantiers. Silence! Is there any factory in this *commune*?

Nicolaas. There are six, in which hundreds of people earn their living.

D'Eglantiers. Monopoly must be abolished. Every one ought to be allowed freely to make what he likes. Therefore all the factories must be sacked.

Nicolaas. **The** factories sacked? Is that the freedom you are bringing us? (*Turning to the Notables.*) **And** you are going to **allow** this? (*Confusion in the meeting.*)

D'Eglantiers. Silence! *Volontaires!* the first man that contradicts, you are to shoot through the head. Otherwise free discussion becomes an impossibility.

[*The Volunteers take aim.*]

Michiel (*quaking with terror*). Of course—the Cap—Captain is right. The—(*in confusion*)—the factories must take **his** word for it. What a kind amiable man the Captain **is**! Long live the Captain!

D'Eglantiers. **All** the ready money in the village **must at** once be placed in my hands, in order to clothe my valiant troops.

Nicolaas. They can take care of themselves in that respect. (*Points at Pluckx.*)

D'Eglantiers. All the wine and provisions in the place must be presented to my troops as a voluntary gift.

Nicolaas. Anything else?

D'Eglantiers. All swords, guns, knives, spades, **axes**, pickaxes, ploughshares—in **short**, all iron tools must **be** handed over to me.

Nicolaas. He's not hard to please, *he* isn't.

D'Eglantiers. And the council is to deliberate whether it would **not be well to send in an address** declaring their submission **to the** Government.

Michiel. A very good idea.

Nicolaas. I should like to say a word.

D'Eglantiers. Speak up!

Taelinck. He can't speak. He is only the ex-Burgomaster; he is not entitled to a share in the proceedings.

D'Eglantiers. **Never** mind—let him speak as one not entitled.

Nicolaas. If I may speak without danger, I should like to ask what *is* the Government that we are to submit to? I have already heard some half-dozen sovereigns mentioned; and really I should not be surprised if you had offered the crown to a Chinese mandarin.

D'Eglantiers. Tut! tut! all you've got to do is to submit—it doesn't matter to whom. That's not your business.

Nicolaas. Then I vote against such an absurdity.

The Schoolmaster and others. So do I! so do I!

D'Eglantiers. I shall put you under arrest if you don't vote as I tell you.

Nicolaas. Is that what you understand by liberty?

D'Eglantiers. You are at liberty to talk as much as you like, but you must vote as I wish.

Nicolaas. I thought you were more liberal than that, Captain!

D'Eglantiers. I can't waste time arguing with you. [*Takes the proclamation out of his pocket.*] Here's my manifesto. Let the Burgomaster read it out loud.

Michiel. Silence! Let every one listen! (*Reads.*) "Proclamation,—We, Captain D'Eglantiers——"

D'Eglantiers. That's me, standing here.

Michiel (*reads*). "And Lieutenant Taelinck——"

Taelinck. Here's the man you're reading about, *compère!*

Michiel. "To all that shall read these presents, salutation! salutation!" (*Bows.*)

D'Eglantiers and Taelinck. Salutation!

Michiel (*reads*). "Citizens! a Dutch army, ten thousand strong, is marching on this village!" What's this?

D'Eglantiers. That's not on the paper, you scoundrel!

[*General consternation.*]

Michiel. It *is* there—read for yourself!

D'Eglantiers. Then it's a forged document—*parbleu!*

Pluckx (*examines the paper*). It's signed by you and the Lieutenant, sir.

All. Go on! go on!

Michiel (*reads*). "As I am not in a position, with the forces at my disposal, to withstand so powerful an **enemy, I hope you will not take it ill of me if I beat a retreat**——"

All. **Well, now!**

Michiel (reads). "Within a quarter of an hour!"

Nicolaas. A pleasant journey **to you!**

D'Eglantiers. What sort of **an** infernal thing is this? [*Snatches the paper out of Michiel's hand. Aside to Taelinck.*] Yes, indeed, there's my mark!

Taelinck. And mine, too!

D'Eglantiers. Then the girl has cheated us!

Pluckx. If ten thousand men are marching on us, the best thing we can do is to march off in the other direction.

Nicolaas. **And we will go to meet them.**

Michiel. Yes, we'll escort them in in triumph!

[*All the Notables,* **and the majority of** *the Volunteers, leave the house.*]

D'Eglantiers. What the——! What are you doing! Stay here! It's all a swindle!

Enter MARIA, *with* VAN WERVE *and* CLARA, *disguised as peasants.*

Maria. Captain, here are my sister and my uncle, who——.

D'Eglantiers. Here! you child of Satan! I'll **sister and uncle you!** What sort of a paper is this that you've written? Come, now!

Maria (aside). The fat's in the fire now, and no mistake!

D'Eglantiers. Answer me! what sort of a paper is it?

Maria. Why, sir, haven't you read it?

D'Eglantiers. I've heard it read, and——

Maria. Did you let it go out of your own hands?

D'Eglantiers. Insolent, too? Who's asking questions, you or I?

Maria. A word in confidence, Captain? [*Draws him* **aside.**] Don't you understand?—that was a trick of mine to——

D'Eglantiers. A trick?—a fine trick! I'll——

Maria. Hush! hush! do! I knew that the Dutch troops were coming, and in order to let you know it privately I wrote it down on that paper. I hoped you would read it by yourself, and then act as circumstances might demand.

D'Eglantiers. Well—in that case! But it is strange, though——

Enter PLUCKX.

Pluckx. Captain, it's time for you to show yourself. Half of our men want to leave, and the villagers are beginning to arm!

D'Eglantiers. What the—— [*Breaks off, and looks towards the cupboard.*] I must get hold of my bonds first. Lieutenant Taelinck, go on. I'll follow immediately.

Taelinck (*also looking at the cupboard*). Aren't you coming with us, Captain?

D'Eglantiers. Presently, presently.

[*Taelinck goes out slowly, followed by Pluckx. D'Eglantiers runs to the cupboard, opens it, and searches in vain for the packet.*]

Maria (*aside*). What shall I do now? Wait!—I have it.

[*Hastens out and comes back with Taelinck.*]

Maria (*to Taelinck*). It is just as I told you—the Captain has been hiding gold and jewels in that cupboard.

Taelinck (*comes forward, and taps D'Eglantiers on the shoulder*). Well, Captain, what have you got there, say?

D'Eglantiers (*surprised*). Eh! what?

[*Turns round, and seeing Taelinck, hurriedly closes the cupboard.*]

Taelinck. You've hidden our booty there,—that's quite clear. Open that door again, and look sharp about it.

D'Eglantiers. What's the good?—there's no money in it.

Taelinck. I'll report you!

D'Eglantiers. I won't give you the chance! [*Draws his sword.*]

Taelinck (*defends himself*). You miserable thief.

[*They fight.* **Van** *Werve and Clara are about to take the opportunity of escaping, when Pluckx enters with his men.*]

Pluckx. What! fighting here? Why, the Hollanders are coming!

D'Eglantiers. What! Where? **When?**

[*Shouts of* "*Oranje boven!*"* *outside. Van Werve rushes at Taelinck and disarms him.*]

Van Werve. **Yes**!—"Oranje boven!"

Pluckx. Here **they** come! *Sauve qui peut!*

[*Tries to escape by the front door.*]

D'Eglantiers. Where's the back door?

Maria (*calls after him*). Don't forget your bonds, whatever you **do**!

[*As D'Eglantiers attempts to leave by the back door, Michiel enters, accompanied* **by** *several Soldiers,* **and** *knocks him* **down** *with a pitchfork, while Taelinck* **is** *being held by Van Werve. Edeling, Nicolaas, Soldiers, and Armed Villagers enter by* **the** *front door, and disarm Pluckx and the rest* **of** *the Belgians.*]

Michiel. **Halt**! Captain! you were mistaken after all! "Oranje boven!"

D'Eglantiers. Traitor of a Burgomaster!

Edeling. My Clara!

Michiel. See there! I knew we should catch them.

Nicolaas (*to the Dutch leader, pointing at Michiel*). Captain, you had better secure this rascal! it was he who brought **the** rebels here.

Michiel (*as he is seized by the Dutch*). How! what?—why, I showed you the way myself!

Maria. The pitcher to the well—Michiel!

[*The insurgents and Michiel are led away.*]

---

* "Up with Orange!"—the Dutch national war-cry.

Edeling (seeing Maria). Good-morning, my lass—didn't I come back to see you, as I said I would? (*To the others.*) This is the girl who helped me to escape.

Van Werve. She has served us all.

VAN LENNEP.

PROVERBS.

He who lives with cripples learns to limp.
The best steersman stands ashore.
Self is the man.
He gives an egg to get a chicken.
They are not all princes who ride with the emperor.
He howls with the wolves when he is in the wood, and bleats with the sheep in the field.
A little too late, much too late.
Stand still a while, you lose a mile.
The nearer Rome the worse Christian.
Call no herring before he's in the net.
He who has choice has anxiety.
Don't put too many eggs under one hen.
If fools were silent they'd be wise.
No man dies of threats.
The fowl that cackles most does not lay most eggs.
No mad dog ever ran for seven years.
One can see by the stockings whose leg is broken.
You should hang your cloak towards the wind.
No man ever limped for another's sore foot.
It's ill stealing where the host is a thief.
'Tis ill eating cherries with lords.
When slovenly people turn over a new leaf they polish the bottoms of the saucepans.

What belongs to the ravens * will never drown.

All offices are greasy.†

What the sow does the little **pigs** must pay for.

With much pounding **the** stockfish becomes tender.

No man sees his own hump-back.

'Tis an ill water, said the horse, for he could not swim.

'Tis an ill morsel that chokes one.

Let them pump who are cold, I have my coat on.‡

All that come of cats will go mewing.

Let the plover peck, I have the eggs in my hat.

Though the ape should wear a golden ring, yet he is an ugly thing.

He who has a fine cat should bring **no furrier into his house.**

Lands become sand, sands become land. (*Landen versanden, sanden verlanden.* An epitome of the physical **history** of Holland.)

The greater jurist **the worse** Christian.

When **the gnats** dance **in January the** farmer **comes to** beggary.

Beware of a fair Spaniard **and** a swarthy Englishman.

Better sit still with an owl than fly with a falcon.

The first man in the boat has the choice of oars.

It's the third strand that holds the cable.

Man overboard—an eater the less.

A tired horse would rather see **a** dirty stable than a clean high-road.

A woman's hair pulls worse than the main-topsail.

---

* *I.e.,* **is** born to be hanged. **The site of the gallows is the** *Rabenstein* in old German ballads.

† "Grease" here has the sense of what is figuratively called "palm-oil."

‡ An illustration of comfortable, "Philistine" selfishness. The pumping is supposed to be going on either on board a leaking vessel, or at a break in the dykes.

At Boulogne there are more traps than mice.
White and black* were the making of Venice.

A hundred Dutchmen, a hundred knives.
A hundred Frenchmen, no knives.
A hundred Scots, two hundred knives.†

In Italy—too many feasts, too many chiefs, too many storms.

The Spaniard seems wise, and is not.
The Frenchman seems a fool, and is not.
The Italian seems wise, and is so.
The Portuguese seems a fool, and is so.‡

A husband's mother is the devil on the floor.
A house full of daughters is a cellar full of sour beer.
'Tis easy piping to those who love dancing.
Smoke, bad air, and scolding wives, are what drive men out of the house.

---

* *I.e.*, cotton and pepper.

† This is puzzling at first sight, but apparently is a comparison between the three nations in point of foresight and prudence,—the knife standing for anything needed in case of emergencies. The Hollander is always prepared, the Frenchman never, the Scot makes assurance doubly sure.

‡ Another uncomplimentary proverb has it that the Portuguese apprentice wants to cut out clothes before he knows how to sew.

A DUTCH PODSNAP.

"A GLASS of wine, mamma?"
"No, thank you, papa."
"You, Caroline?"
"No, thank you, papa."
"Frederica?"
"No, thank you, papa."
Ditto, ditto, for Marie, Antoinette, and Hortense.
"Hendriek doesn't take any wine?"
"Oh! no, papa."
"And my Lijsje?"
"Oh! it would be dreadful, papa!"

Mijnheer Van Arlen, having gone through this ceremony, half-filled his glass, filled it up with water, and then carefully corked the bottle, to be put away for to-morrow. In this way it would be made to last ten days, and as a rule it did so; for the above invitation to his wife and seven daughters was renewed every day, and every day regularly declined. However, there were some exceptions to this rule: in the first place, when papa was on a journey. Every year papa had to take a journey for the Minister; it was a mission of mysterious importance, whose destination no one was to know. It always came off quite unexpectedly, immediately after the receipt of his second quarter's salary. On these occasions the bottle, if it still contained any wine, was emptied by the family, and papa's own particular tumbler—a most precious one, of ruby glass, with a flower-pattern, and the initials H. M. engraved on it—put away in the china-cupboard for the space of ten days. For this unexpected, mysterious, and important journey always lasted exactly ten days, during which time the daughters enjoyed the mild joke of calling their mother "Madame Veuve," and were solemnly requested by her not to do it, for, as she said, it was a sort of joke that always sent a cold shudder through her. She preferred being called "little bride," which took place once a year, on her wedding-day, an occasion which formed the second of the exceptions referred to above. On this occasion papa always provided mamma with the surprise of a glass of port at dinner, and all the seven daughters had some too, though in their hearts they would have preferred not taking it, for they detested it—and it always gave one such a colour in the evening!

The third exception—which was only half a one—occurred when papa had a relation or a friend from out of town on a visit, when mamma would take a glass; and then the bottle had to be finished, for wine only turns flat if it is left standing.

To-day, however, was merely an ordinary day. Papa had received no instructions as to his journey, and the wedding anniversary was some time off; though the friend from out of town was expected, and might arrive any week. He was something more than a friend—he was a late brother-in-law; for Mevrouw Van Arlen—Hortense Muggenhout, as denoted by the initials on the tumbler—had had a younger sister, who had married Heer Van Noost Prigson, a most respectable man, as appears from his double-barrelled name, which was never forgotten, either by himself or the Van Arlen family. Mijnheer Van Noost Prigson had lost his wife not long after the birth of his only son.

Uncle Van Noost Prigson had written to-day he would come; but he was a man of business,—of much business,— and he wrote so quickly that three-fourths of each of his letters were illegible. Fortunately, papa was also a man of business, and in his responsible position was brought into contact with so many matters—cipher, among others—that he was able to read the writing of Uncle Van Noost Prigson, at least the greater part of it. This time, however, the most important part of uncle's letter was in figures, and he always made his figures very indistinctly. He said he might possibly come on the **3rd (it** might also have been the 8th), unless it were the 10th—or **(for** the figures might equally well have stood for that) the **21st—while** at the end of the letter he added, with equal distinctness, that it was to be between the 14th and 16th, for which again one might have read the 24th and 26th. Equally uncertain was the duration of his visit; its purpose, indeed, was explained, and this papa thought fit to keep to himself. It must surely be **a** matter of importance, thought the eight ladies, for **the** thought that he—with his vast experience of all sorts of business—should have failed to decipher this **part of the** letter never entered their heads for a moment.

Papa filled **a** most important office,—it was in the year 1846,—and in consequence of one thing or another, perhaps in connection with the mysterious journeys, he had, one 6th **of** December, received a token that the State appreciated his **services.** Since that day, the said token had been inseparable from the black coat, without which no one ever saw Mijnheer Van Arlen. It was quite in harmony with the impressive wrinkle on his forehead, which looked as though Van Arlen had for years been staring upward in a bent position,—in harmony, too, with the compressed lips, which seemed **in** continual fear of letting a State secret escape; while his hair had become quite white, probably from the anxiety occasioned by the weighty matters which occupied his head. The daughters found in papa the type of a handsome man, and at the same time of a thoroughly respectable one; **mamma** adored him with the enthusiasm which every good housewife is bound to feel for her husband, and never spoke of him except as "Mijnheer Van Arlen." Conversely, he always referred to his wife as "*Mevrouw mijne echtgenoote;*" * and

---

* Lit. "Madam my consort."

he preferred to allude to his daughters in numerical order, unwilling to admit the outer world to so great a degree of familiarity as to speak to it of his daughters by their Christian names.

Either the bottle had stood too long on this particular day, or some other cause had spoilt Van Arlen's taste for it; anyhow, he did not finish his glass, and, when dinner was over, fixed a penetrating gaze on the door, and remained silent.

"Are you not well, papa?" asked Caroline.

"Quite well, my child!"

"Difficult business?" asked Mevrouw, sympathetically.

"Oh! all business is difficult, mamma," said Van Arlen, weightily, and stared into nothing more perseveringly than ever.

Mamma sighed, and the daughters looked sadly at papa. Could Uncle Van Noost Prigson's letter be the cause of the trouble?

"Will you have any dessert, papa?"

The dessert was standing ready, as usual, on the small side-table. A box of flat biscuits, a butter-dish, a corner of cheese under a glass cover, and a little dish of fruit, or, if there was none to be had, of preserved ginger. But papa did not care for dessert, and never took any, except when the above-mentioned relation or intimate friend from the country was present; for "a dinner is not complete without dessert."

"No, thank you, my dear? Will you?"

"Oh! you know I never do. Shall we say grace?"

Grace was said, reverent and short, as is befitting in a house where a good tone prevails, and papa folded up his napkin neatly, and laid it beside his plate; whereupon Leida fetched the matches, and gave papa a light, which he accepted with a gracious nod, just as he had done yesterday, and the day before, and all the year round, with the exceptions aforesaid. Then eighteen-year-old Leida gave her papa a light kiss on his forehead, just above the broad wrinkle.

"Why, papa! you must not be so gloomy; just let me kiss the trouble away," said she.

"What tricks next?" asked papa, sportively; and mamma called her a monkey, and all the six sisters thought it such a good thing that Leida was in such spirits, and had such a knack of getting papa into a cheerful humour.

Van Arlen lit his cigar, and went slowly and thoughtfully to his own room, whither he was called by his weighty official cares, and where a mysterious locked portfolio lay ready for him. He turned the key in the lock, sat down in his easy-chair, and went to sleep. He was quite right to lock himself in,—a State secret might so easily have escaped him in his sleep,—nay more, the secret of his after-dinner nap, which was entirely unknown to his household and the outer world, might have leaked out. About half-past seven there was a modest knock at the door; the person knocking waited patiently till all the State secrets should be covered up; and when the door was opened, the table before Van Arlen was strewn with papers. The inkstand, however, remained on the mantelpiece.

But she who entered the room suspected no deception, and was not on the look-out for traces of it. Year after year it had been Mevrouw Van Arlen's habit to bring her husband his "first cup" at this hour, and the ten minutes which he was accustomed to give her served for the discussion of domestic matters. Papa listened attentively to what mamma had spent on milk and on bread, on peas and beans and matches,—nothing is too small for a great man,—and then handed out the exact amount from the secret drawer of his writing-table.

"And then, papa, Caroline and Frederica and Marie ought to have new hats."

"And the three others?"

"They can have the old hats of the three eldest done up with new trimmings."

"And what becomes of *their* old ones?"

"They can use them for every day."

Van Arlen tried to form in his own mind a visible picture of the change; but his habit of considering affairs of State somewhat dimmed and confused his sight in matters of everyday life.

"I do not rightly understand you, my dear. It seems to me that the three eldest might just as well have the hats of the next three, as the next three have the hats of the elder ones passed on to them."

"Caroline, Frederica, and Marie are the eldest."

"Is that a reason, mamma? Let us take, as our fundamental principle, impartiality. Let us act without respect of persons—it is a wise rule, a guarantee for the stability both of a government and a household. Let us give no occasion for jealousy by measuring with two different measures."

"But, papa——"

"Believe me, my dear, parents who show partiality are sowing the seeds of unfriendly feeling, discord, hatred. Let us be wise, and not bow to any antiquated principle of primogeniture. What human experience has found to be fatal in society, must not be introduced into our smaller circle by us, the individual units of society."

"But in that case they might as well all keep their own hats, and trim them up afresh."

"Let it be so."

How mamma was to settle matters with her daughters was her business; the head of the family was concerned solely with the legislative, not with the executive department.

"And Leida must keep her old hat because she has been so untidy; but she will have to have a new ribbon on it."

Van Arlen nodded assent.

They must have been **great men who first** preached impartiality, and abolished the right of primogeniture. Here, in this individual instance, was a saving of three new hats,—what economy would be effected by the application of the system to a whole State!

"And you yourself, mamma?"

"I have been thinking of keeping on the mourning for another **year.** My black dresses are all quite good still."

"And we were so fond of poor Cornelia! **When the** mourning is worn out the dead are forgotten, people say. We must show that it is not the case with us."

"Or that **we have been** careful of our clothes," Van Arlen might have added; but though this inference did not enter his head, **another did.**

"So we shall not go out this year?"

"I'm sorry, for the girls' sakes; but it really is a duty. But, all the same, we must not keep them quite shut up either."

"No, of course not."

Mijnheer and Mevrouw Van Arlen were silent for a little.

"We must not keep them shut up," repeated the mother, thoughtfully. "Do you think it possible **you** might some time be transferred, Van Arlen?"

"Oh, Hortense! don't ask such questions."

"It is not out of curiosity, but in the interest of **our** family. You are in such favourable relations with people in high positions."

"What do you think is the cause of this, mamma?"

"Well, your knowledge, your ability, your great——"

"Do you think that a man possessing such qualities—mind I don't say I possess them—has much chance of being sent away to a distance?"

"No, but—it is hard."

"It may be hard,—but when a man is indispensable—I don't say that I am indispensable—he has to put up with it. The feeling that he is doing his duty conscientiously to the State, ought to have most weight with him,—and it certainly makes things easier."

Van Arlen finished his tea, and handed the empty cup to his wife—the usual sign that the audience was over.

"Another cup?"

"Yes, please—but no sugar."

This condition was as stereotyped as the dessert; papa only took one cup with sugar; the ladies did not care for sugar, except at evening parties, when they took it to prevent mistakes and confusion.

Van Arlen then went to work,—read, signed documents, made a note here, and drew his pen through a sentence there,—and became so absorbed in his work that he never heard Marie come in on tiptoe, to set down the humble domestic cup of tea on the table covered with State documents. At the stroke of half-past nine Van Arlen rose, and once more made his appearance in the family sitting-room, where an old-fashioned card-table had been set out. After working all day, he found that his mind needed some relaxation. His wife and two of the daughters,—who took turns in this, as in other things, were already seated; the cards were dealt, and he had only to begin. They were playing whist for recreation, and not for money—therefore no reckoning was necessary; but the marking was done with laudable accuracy, and every mistake was severely reproved —for the furthering of every one's enjoyment; for enjoyment without seriousness does not deserve the name.

Papa never spoke a word except what was required by the game, and did not like any talking to go on in the room; so that the five daughters who were not playing, sat silent round the big table, each with her needlework, thinking about the hats they were **not to** have, the mourning **that** their mother was to **go on wearing, the ball to which they** were not invited, the opera they never went to, the new fashions other people were going to wear, the novel they were in the middle of, but **which must** not be read aloud **now papa** was in **the** room, the riches they missed, the enjoyment they did not know, the past that was so poor, and the future that did not promise to be richer.

There was a ring at the bell.

All the ladies looked up; even papa laid down **the cards** he was just about to deal.

"Brother Van Noost Prigson!" said Mevrouw, in a tone of some anxiety,—as well she might, for there was no meat in the larder—in fact, nothing in the house but a **small** angle of cheese, and a few ounces of ginger from the uneaten dessert.

Van Arlen said nothing: he was never precipitate, and **in** all circumstances of life preserved his presence of mind.

"What a quiet little ring!" said Frederica.

"Could it be a message from the Minister, papa?"

"Leen has not heard the bell—shall I ring?"

Mevrouw Van Arlen assented, and the sitting-room bell was heard—a quicker and more excited ring than the heavy, respectable front-door bell.

"The bell rang, Leen."

"Yes, ma'am, I'm **here.**"

"No—the front-door bell."

"No, indeed it didn't, ma'am."

"We all heard it."

"Impossible," muttered the maid to herself, as she went to see; "**or** else it must be **some one** who pulled the bell and ran away—and you can't be always on the look-out for that."

All listened in strained expectation. The front door was opened, but no sound of voices came from it; it was closed again, and Leentje was heard shuffling **off** to the kitchen.

"She might come back and say who it was," mamma assented.

Leentje was again sent for.

"Who rang the bell, Leentje?"

"Just as I thought, ma'am,—it was some boy that ran away."

Mijnheer Van Arlen was inwardly very indignant that his family—among whom so good a tone prevailed—should make such an exhibition of themselves in the presence of a servant. Mamma blamed the girls' curiosity, but could not unconditionally accept the theory of the boy,—Leentje had been too long at the front door for that. If it turned out that she had been speaking to a "fellow" there, she would have to leave next day. That sort of thing would not do in a respectable house. The girls likewise declined to believe in the boy—the bell had been rung too quietly. They wanted to go out and look whether anything had been pushed under the door. Then it struck Antoinette that the mysterious ring might be connected with burglary, and this opinion gave rise to some eager whispering, which caused papa to turn a frowning brow, not once, but twice, in the direction of the large table. In an unguarded moment Leida slipped out into the passage, to institute an investigation *in loco*, but neither on nor under the door-mat was there any trace of a paper. All conjectures remained fruitless.

If the little street-boy, with the newly mended kettle on his back, who, merrily whistling his favourite tune, had crossed the quiet street, and pulled the bell, to give his aunt's sister-in-law a run from the kitchen for nothing,—if that small evil-doer had known what a change and excitement he had caused in a respectable family, insomuch that Van Arlen himself, who filled such an important post, had laid aside for a moment the business which occupied him, he would probably have repeated the experiment on the following evening—if only out of pity for the monotonous life of the seven ladies, to whom even the pulling of **the bell** was **an** event.

The night has passed;—the little, sputtering, **flickering** night-light, which burns in Van Arlen's bedroom—for **Van** Arlen does not believe in having no light in the house, **one** never knows what may happen—has consumed all its oil and gone out. The insolent sun, which has no pity **for** faded carpets and curtains, has penetrated everywhere; **and** if one could walk through the Van Arlens' house at this hour, when their high tone is still asleep, one would lose much of the reverence inspired by the important position, the refined manners, and the ceremonious intercourse with each other of its inhabitants.

But at this hour in the morning no one walks through Van Arlen's house except the maid, who, by the terms of her engagement, **is** bound to "do" two **rooms** before breakfast. This involves rising before five, though she does not go to **bed** any earlier for that; she is also supposed to answer the door, go out once in four weeks, **"if** it suits,"—and have neither right nor claim to any extras beyond her wages, which are moderate, and her perquisites, which are *nil*.

To be weighed against all this is the great advantage of living with respectable people, and that is a great deal in these days, Mevrouw **says.** Besides this, Leentje is **a** "whole" orphan, and therefore ought to appreciate the privilege of finding a home with such a family—though it is true that Mevrouw Van Arlen will never engage a servant with any parent or relative living, to save trouble with **their** families.

But **the Van Arlens are far too** respectable to **let us** waste any more time over their servant,—more especially as by this time they are all assembled at breakfast, with the exception of the head of the house, for persons who do much brain-work need more rest than those who only tire their bodies—so Mijnheer says. Mevrouw is seated before the tea-tray—the daughters take cold water. Nothing is wholesomer than cold water. Moreover, butter—at least, much butter—is bad for the health. Bread in large quantities is also unhealthy, and the ladies prove, by the extent of their breakfast, that they quite subscribe to this opinion. The "whole orphan," also, is educated in the same doctrine, but she is allowed to poison herself every morning with coffee— so long as she does not exceed her two ounces a week.

"I don't know how it is, mamma, but that ringing the bell last night does worry me," said Frederica, by way of morning reflection; and the other girls reflected also, and talked it over, and objected, or supported each other, as if there were really an interesting question at stake,—till papa's arrival restored silence. He cast one glance over the paper, which no one was allowed to inspect before him, for fear the news might evaporate, and then put it into his pocket,— for girls have no business with newspapers, and his wife did not care to see it. During the meal he spoke little—he was oppressed by the prospect of all the important affairs awaiting him; and he ate his bread and butter, and drank his tea, with a solemnity which made it difficult to realise that they were only ordinary bread and tea.

Presently he rose. "Oh! papa! you scarcely give yourself time for breakfast!" said his wife, and he did not dispute the proposition. He kissed her and his daughters on the forehead in silence, put on his hat, and went to his office, thoughtful and abstracted, as if bowed down by the weight of his position. He did not even see people who bowed to him; as for miscellaneous human beings, they were not worth his attention.

Suddenly some one stopped him.

"This is lucky! I was just on my way to your house!" cried this person in a loud voice,—so loud that all the bystanders could hear Van Arlen being addressed like an ordinary human being. "Have you been out to a funeral this morning?"

A well-regulated smile hovered for a moment about the official's mouth,—" No, brother."

"You look just like it. How are they all at home?— your youngsters growing up—eh? Nothing particular going on?"

Thus talking, Brother Van Noost Prigson walked along beside Van Arlen, and entered with him—no, actually preceded him—into the door of the building where he exercised his important functions. Preceded him! Van Arlen went down five per cent. in the estimation of his subordinates that day; and when his own messenger, with a low bow, threw open the door of his private office, Van Noost Prigson was again the first to tread the magnificent carpet, on which inferior officials scarcely dared to set foot when expressly summoned by their chief.

"Not much to do—eh?"

"On the contrary, I am very busy to-day."

"Well, well—reading and signing documents, and all that sort of thing—I could do that too."

"I shall have to sign about three hundred and forty separate papers."

"Well—I'd do that in half-an-hour; but if you really are busy, I won't keep you. I'll come and dine with you to-day."

"Very good—and in that case, I'll see——"

"Don't give yourself any trouble. I'll call in and see Hortense myself. You know you needn't make any difference in your ways for me, and I daresay you couldn't very well afford it either."

Van Arlen looked at his brother-in-law as if to ask, "Do you mean to insult me," but his expression changed as he met the glance of the cheery but penetrating eyes. "Living is dear at the Hague," he said.

"The more fool you, then, to stay here—and with seven daughters, too! Just listen, Van Arlen,—I have a plan, but I can't carry it out without your help."

"Let me hear it before I promise."

"My plan is—to make Van Arlen rich ... Where did you get that ridiculous thing?" he suddenly broke off.

"Which?" asked the official—following Prigson's eye, which was directed to his breast.

"Why—that bit of ribbon. I never heard of your getting it. From Santa Claus, I suppose?"

"I don't understand you, Prigson; if you mean my Order, I make it a point of honour to wear it, and I don't like its being made a joke of."

"A joke, my dear fellow? I have the most fervent respect for all orders of knighthood—especially if they are sent home on St Nicholas' Eve ... Come in! Beg pardon—I forgot this was *your* place. Can I stay?"

Van Arlen glanced at the door,—it was only a clerk with documents, and Prigson was suffered to remain while the clerk waited and the official signed.

"This is the sort of thing that goes on all day long."

"Well—it seems to me you earn your money pretty easily. But say, Van ... I suppose no one can hear us talking here?"

"No one."

"Well,—it doesn't matter to me, but I shouldn't like it on your account,—I want some money."

Van Arlen drew the palm of his hand across his forehead, and stared at his brother-in-law without answering.

"I'm so fearfully in debt that I don't want to give the alarm. I should be much obliged if you could let me have those thousand florins I lent you. In a month or two you can have them again, if you want; but I've got to live till then, and I have nothing left."

"It comes at a very inconvenient time, Prigson."

"My dear fellow, I would like nothing better than to give you a receipt for the whole sum in full; for you're a good fellow, and have to struggle so hard, one ought not to make it harder for you. But, just **say now, when** *would* it be convenient?"

Van Arlen thought for **some** minutes.

"At the beginning of next year," he said slowly.

"I wish I could wait so long. I wish I could; but I have an expensive undertaking on hand, which will perhaps by next year put me in a position **to** accommodate you. But, for the moment, I *must* have money; and I dare not try to raise it myself for fear of ruining my credit, which I can't do without just now."

"Come in!" said Van **Arlen**, in answer to **a knock at the door.**

"His Excellency would like to speak to you," said the clerk.

"So those fellows let themselves be called Excellency, do they? I thought that was bad form now-a-days," said Prigson, loud enough to be heard by the clerk. But Van Arlen did not reply, **he was** too **thankful** for the **chance of escape from** his brother-in-law.

"I suppose you'll be gone some time? An Excellency like that has plenty **of** time **for talking;** *he* doesn't work himself to death," said Prigson.

"It may be a couple of hours before I can get away."

"**In that** case I'll say good-bye. By-the-by, is there any place where I can see the papers? Are you a member of the Besogne Club?"

"At the White Club you'll find all the daily papers."

"And **will one** of your cards be enough to admit me?"

"**I haven't a** card here, but——" Van Arlen looked round, and his eye fell on the card of one of his subordinates. "This **will do** just as well."

"*Merci!*" said Prigson, with a just perceptible smile, and left him.

When Van Arlen returned from the Minister's private room, he sent to ask the functionary whose card he had given to Prigson to come to him, and, while waiting, wrote a note to his wife, informing her of that gentleman's arrival.

Before the note had reached its destination, however, the person in question had already appeared on the scene. He had been shown into the *salon*, where, after sending up his name, he paced up and down for about half-an-hour, vainly seeking for diversion in the four framed engravings representing the divisions of the day, typified by English ladies in the large bonnets and short waists of a fashion forty years old. The alabaster clock, with gilt ornaments, was not going—it had not gone for twenty years,—and the vases were as clumsy in form as monstrous in colouring.

"Everything dates from the year twenty," muttered Prigson, after a hasty glance at one article and another, "and these things never break! The whole house and furniture is of the year twenty—the girls too. Is none of them going to appear? Hortense surely doesn't require to make such a toilette."

He pulled the bell. It had given no sound for the last ten years;—but, as it happened, the maid was just passing the door.

"Look here, my girl—you seem smart enough—just run upstairs and tell your mistress I have only ten minutes to spare, and I have to go out of town again directly."

"Thank Heaven!" thought Mevrouw, when the maid came up with the message, "then he won't stay to dinner!" and in another moment she was downstairs, endeavouring, by extra cordiality, to remove the impression which the long waiting must have produced on Prigson.

"I'm sorry, brother, you can't stay to dine with us in a quiet way," she said after a time.

"If you really make a point of it, Hortense, I can alter my plans to suit," answered Prigson; "but you must not let me put you out in any way."

"Oh! not in the least; certainly not. You are always

welcome, and our table is large enough. **And what are you doing just now?**"

"At this **moment I am living on my means, for the last** enterprise came to nothing. But now I really have my eye on something good. You must **try** and persuade Van Arlen to take it up; it is certain to make him rich——"

He was interrupted by "Good-morning, uncle!" in three different voices; and the three eldest Van Arlens **proceeded** to welcome Prigson, who, in entire disregard of the tone **of** the house, embraced them one after the other.

"Always the same," said their mother, smiling, and shaking her finger at him, and the three girls blushed and sat down. Then appeared the two next, to be welcomed in the same way; and presently the two youngest turned up, to be likewise honoured by their **uncle.** All seven **were as neat as if** they had come out **of** bandboxes, **and each had some fancy-**work in her hand.

When the subordinate official whose card Van Arlen had given to Prigson appeared in the former's room as desired, he was received with—

"Oh, Mijnheer Talm, I have just taken the liberty of using your **name."**

"You do me a great honour, sir."

"One of my relations, Herr Van Noost Prigson, **from** London, wished to be introduced to the White Club, and you know I can't go there!"

Mijnheer **Van** Arlen meant that his position was too important to allow of his doing so. The official bowed—he quite understood that.

"I happened to have your card lying here, and I thought you would be willing to do me that service."

"Certainly, very much flattered. Can I be of any further service to your relative? Take him about anywhere? But I don't speak English."

"Oh, he speaks Dutch quite fluently," replied Van Arlen; "if one did not know it already, one would never guess that he came from London. So it might be as well not to mention it."

"Very good, sir."

Mijnheer Talm was about to withdraw, with a low bow.

"By-the-by, Mijnheer Talm, is Department Y in order?"

"I thought there was no hurry about it."

"The Minister has been asking me about it to-day, so I should be glad to have it as soon as possible."

"I can promise to have it ready to-morrow."

There was work enough in Department Y to occupy Talm all day and all the evening, perhaps half the night as well; his meeting Uncle Prigson was scarcely possible under the circumstances.

In any case, there was not much chance of this happening; for when Prigson had left the Van Arlens' house, with a promise to return at dinner-time, he went straight to the White Club, and got himself introduced by a Secretary of Legation; and when Leida went to the confectioner's to double the stock of dessert-ginger, she saw Uncle Van Noost Prigson sitting at the club window! Her heart beat high with so much grandeur.

And Talm's conversation for the next six weeks consisted principally of the English millionaire whom he had introduced at the White Club at his chief's request. He thought it would do him no harm at the next chance of promotion.

We left Van Arlen alone in his private room at the Government office. There are moments in life when one prefers not to be alone, yet has not the courage to break away from solitude; moments when a seemingly impossible resolution must be taken, when one would be thankful if —instead of thinking and acting for one's self—one could blindly follow the dictates of another. All the weight of his important position had never oppressed Van Arlen so much as the idea suggested to **him by his** short interview with Prigson.

Imagine a man who, without knowing a note of music, is handed the score of a symphony and told to read **it.** That was about his state of mind with regard to the question Van Noost Prigson had asked him. He had **not** a thousand guilders in the world—not even a hundred.

He walked up and down his room, staring at one thing and another, but unable to forget that thousand guilders, and the smallness of his salary. If he had a thousand—no, not one, but ten, twenty, a hundred thousand—would he not be a happy man? Then he would really live, as he now only had the appearance of doing;—distinguished society, pretty dresses for his wife and daughters, all pleasant things vainly desired, would be his! Imagination has peculiar force **in** such cases, and Van Arlen's painted this ideal life for him with rough but forcible touches, till he was once more recalled to reality **and** the starting-point of his reverie—the thousand guilders!

Where was he to get them? He *must* have them. Sell his possessions? The furniture **was** worth nothing. The pictures?—who knew if the English engravings might not be rare and valuable? He did not **understand** such things. He had indeed pretended to some knowledge of art, but he had none. If he had only the smallest grain! What would a collector give him for **them?** Two hundred and fifty guilders each? Surely they might be worth that. Perhaps more—perhaps——

Then arrived documents for signature, and Van Arlen signed his name—signed again, and yet again, and imagined that he was endorsing bank-notes. Why was his name not of equal efficacy when written **on a cheque?** He could always pay the amount later on; it was only for the time he wanted it.

Suddenly Van Arlen stood still. "Temporary — only temporary—and if I pay it back, no one will ever ask after it." He opened a locked cash-box; it contained more than enough to help him; it did not belong to him; it had only been left in his care, to give account of when the sum was complete. He stood up, and wiped his forehead, and once more paced up and down.

Who was going to inquire after it? The Minister? He had other things to think of. His colleagues? The affair did not concern them; they did not even know of its existence. His inferiors? They would certainly mind their own business; and if they did not,—after all, he was their chief, and could give them what answer he thought fit. There it lay. He opened the little parcel. Surely no one knew the numbers!

There was a knock at the door. Van Arlen started as if he had committed a crime, yet kept looking at the money that had been entrusted to him. It was in an unsteady voice that he said, "Come in."

"Mijnheer Van Teuten would like to speak to you."

"Van Teuten?—I'm busy—well, one minute, then. Tell him to come in."

The man ushered into the private room wrote a magnificent hand. For the moment that was nothing to the point—yet, after all, it was something, for Van Teuten owed his career to it—"the best hand in the department." He did not write quickly—that was beneath his dignity—but for really beautiful writing no one could come near him.

Van Teuten was visibly disturbed, as he stood facing Van Arlen, who sat leaning over his desk. The cash-box was shut.

"Well, Mr Van Teuten?"

"Mr Van Arlen—I'm come—I hope you'll excuse it. I've come to make a request, on which my future depends."

Van Arlen looked up from his paper, and coughed importantly, fixing his dark eyes on the chief clerk, as though he suspected him of high treason.

"You know perhaps that—that I have absolutely no means of my own, and, with the title of assistant secretary (which I owe to my handwriting)"—here Van Teuten raised his head with a certain pride—"in spite of my handwriting, still only draw the salary of chief clerk."

"Do you want to be promoted, Mr Van Teuten?"

"Promoted—that is to say, sir—not exactly; but, Mr Van Arlen, I can't live! I'm poor, sir, and—if I write a good hand—Heaven forbid, sir, that I should boast of it; but, well, it is hard that one should have one's merits, and be forced to suffer from poverty."

Van Arlen gazed fixedly at the owner of the fine handwriting, and asked him for a definite statement of **what he** wanted—his time was valuable.

"Do excuse me, sir; but I'm nervous—I'm agitated. I shall have to pay my rent on Saturday—three-quarters' rent, sir,—and I've nothing—nothing—not so much as *that!*"

"Very sad for you, Mr Van Teuten, but you know that I can be of no use to you in this matter."

"Nay, Mr Van Arlen, you can. I only want two hundred guilders—nothing more, and then I am saved—saved! And, you see, if I stood alone, sir, I shouldn't care—I should find some way out of it,—but I have a wife and five children. **Oh**, God! Mr Van Arlen, it's **my** last hope. Don't let me go like this!"

Van Teuten pulled out a red pocket-handkerchief, and dried a few tears with it. Van Arlen stared at him, still lost in thought, and forgot the man's request in the comparison he was drawing in his own mind, between this case and his own. At last he asked slowly, "What do **you** want me to do?"

"Lend me two hundred guilders, sir,—that's all that I hope, I entreat, I beg of you——"

"Just listen to me, my good Van Teuten, and don't get excited,—tears are not becoming in a man of your age. We've all got to work for our families, and some men in this world happen to be better off than others—but that's no reason for giving way to passionate grief. As to your request, it's out of my power to grant it. Next time there is any question of increase in salaries, I will do my best to improve your position, but for the moment I cannot help you. If I did, I should have all your colleagues asking me for the same thing to-morrow, and my position will not allow of my coming to the assistance of officials in this way."

Van Teuten was searching his mind for a word—a sentence. To-morrow, when he did not want them, he might think of hundreds; now, he could find none that would add force to his entreaty. He soon gave up the effort, and tried another tack:

"The Minister is rich, sir,—don't you think he might give or lend me two hundred guilders?"

Van Arlen looked straight at him. True, the Minister *was* rich, and what he refused Van Teuten he might yet be induced to grant to Van Arlen.

"If you would only speak for me, Mr Van Arlen,—I don't want to exalt myself—and yet, I believe—don't take it ill of me if I say so—I think my services are worth something—and if His Excellency would be willing to give me the money, I should be saved."

"Probably His Excellency would have the same reasons for declining as myself; but I cannot conceive, Mr Van Teuten, that there is not one of your colleagues who would be willing to help you out of a temporary inconvenience."

Would Van Arlen himself have found one so quickly?

"Oh! plenty!—but they want security—they want a guarantee; and . . . do you think His Excellency would become security for me?—or you, sir—your name will do anything you like."

"My good friend, you understand that I, in my position, cannot afford to get mixed up with any such affair, nor can the Minister either. Try and come to some arrangement with your landlord, but **don't** expect anything from *these* quarters, under such circumstances. We can't have anything to do with such matters."

Van Teuten bowed his head—he had exhausted his arguments, and all **to no purpose; he had** completely forgotten the eloquent address, thought out last night; **the** courage with **which he** had armed himself had oozed away— he went out silently. But suddenly he turned back.

"If it were *outside* the official circle, sir, could you **help** me then? I could get money at an interest **of one per cent. per** month—only I must have the security of one of the superior officials."

"I have told you, Mr Van Teuten, that I, in my position, cannot occupy myself with any matters of the kind. I am sorry for you, but I can do nothing."

The man with the fine hand went away, slowly and dejectedly, and Van Arlen was once more alone with—or rather without—his thousand guilders.

.   .   .   .

It is a mistake to suppose that, for the preparation of jugged hare, a hare is necessary. Mrs Van Arlen understood very well how to give a dinner, which, to the uninitiate, seemed the finest kind of "company" dinner, and yet consisted of the most commonplace everyday dishes. But there is an infinite difference between rice in a dish and rice in a mould—more especially when the latter is served with lemon sauce. The ham **was** prepared *à la mayonnaise*— Van Arlen was so fond of that dish,—he always partook **of** it when on those mysterious journeys of his; and then—you need not have a whole ham for it, a few slices are quite enough. Moreover, there stood, on the side-table, besides the never-failing ginger and cheese, a silver dish with ten little halfpenny tarts on it. It was quite a splendid dinner; papa and uncle had each a bottle to himself, and besides the ordinary wine glasses there were others of smaller size for the better wine.

But, with all this magnificence, a **certain gloom** prevailed among the Van Arlens. This is the way with the great ones of the earth; they enjoy wealth and ease without appreciating them.

Prigson, on the other hand, **was, as** usual, in excellent spirits. He felt in nowise overawed by the splendour of the feast, or the eight silk skirts which rustled round about him.

"You see, it's just our ordinary family dinner," said madame, with a pleasant little laugh. Prigson gave the obligatory answer, and paid no attention whatever to the material part of the dinner.

"Which of you girls are going out with me this evening?" he asked. "I can't take all seven—three is the maximum— or else your father will have to come too."

"You know, Prigson, my position is such that I cannot devote a single hour to mere enjoyment."

Madame sighed, and said, in a compassionate tone, that brother could form no idea of the life Van Arlen led.

"No doubt," said Prigson; "but I admit that it is far from appearing to most people what it really is." Prigson made the remark entirely without sarcastic intention, and went on, with a smile, "I would bet something that you haven't even read the paper yet, Van Arlen."

Van Arlen usually read his daily paper from title to imprint while taking his breakfast; but to-day he had entirely forgotten it.

"I haven't once looked into it; and here's the proof," he said, taking it still unopened from his pocket.

"So you haven't seen my advertisement?"

"Your advertisement?—no—did you insert one?"

"Do you remember our talk at your office?"

Van Arlen had not forgotten it for one moment, and if Prigson had paid more attention to him, and less to Caroline and Leida (who, in fact, were very pretty girls), he would have noticed that Van Arlen's looks continually took the vague direction which indicated that his mind was elsewhere. His wife, who noticed it, ascribed it to the responsibilities of his office; his daughters were thinking, this evening, more of their uncle than of him. Certainly papa was the very type of a handsome man, but uncle had something very distinguished about him—especially since Leida had told them about seeing him in the club.

"What advertisement is that, brother?" asked Mrs Van Arlen.

"Oh, my dear Hortense, it belongs to those matters which ladies can't understand; but if it comes to anything, and Van Arlen is willing to take a hand in it, he has only to say the word. You can make your fortune over it, Van Arlen."

The word "fortune" awakened in the Van Arlens a feeling which used to come over them day by day, and had as regularly to be suppressed. Now, however, they were able to give way to it for a moment, and Van Arlen himself—still under the influence of what he had endured that afternoon —looked at Van Noost Prigson with interest.

"How could that be done?" asked Mrs Van Arlen almost indifferently; while all the girls, holding their breath, looked at Prigson in order to form their own conclusions as to whether his project were practicable.

"In the first place, you would have to give up your situation; in the next, to leave the place; and in the third, to work rather harder than you do at present; but, on the other hand, you would earn six times as much money."

"You evidently don't know what the life of a Government official is," said Van Arlen, with a contemptuous smile at the mention of harder work than his.

"Oh, dear, no!" said his wife; and the daughters looked in consternation at the man who had dared to cast the slightest doubt on the extent and importance of papa's duties.

"Well, what now, Van Arlen?" said Prigson, seeing that his brother-in-law seemed once more lost in a brown study, "are you off to that office of yours again? You had better come to the opera with us this evening; that is to say, if these ladies are inclined to come."

A cold shudder—but it was one of delight—completely overpowered the self-control of Frederica and Marie. They scarcely knew the opera, except by name,—papa never went there,—and it was very long since they had been invited by any one else.

"The opera?" said Van Arlen, "I don't care about that; it's a sin against common sense."

"I beg your pardon?" asked Prigson, perplexed.

"Why, all the people there die singing—I can't get over that."

"Eh?" said Prigson, evidently much taken aback; "well, I never thought about that. But now I do think about it, I should say that the opera is the most natural picture of life. There are so many people that weep and wail all their lives; is that so very much more unnatural than that they should sing when they die? But, granting that it is as you say, let's go to an opera in which nobody dies. Isn't *Don Pasquale* on to-night, young ladies?"

"I think so, uncle," answered Frederica, blushing, for none of the girls even thought of looking at the theatrical announcements. What was the good?

"Yes, yes—*Don Pasquale*. Come, Van Arlen—that's a comic opera—just the thing for you!"

Van Arlen shrugged his shoulders. "I don't mind a comic opera—not if it's *really* comic," he said.

"Come along, then—you're sure to like *Don Pasquale*."

"No, I can't—another time, perhaps—I've too much to

do to-night," said Van Arlen, **absently** looking at the alabaster clock that did not go, but nevertheless seemed able to tell him that it was now *his* time.

"Yes," said his wife, "and if we're to go to the opera we shall have to dress."

"Hortense! Hortense!" said Prigson, with a mischievous glance.

"What do you mean, Prigson? Of course I can't let **the** girls go to the opera with a strange gentleman. **I've always** done my best, brother, to give my daughters **a** *good* bringing-up."

Prigson was too polite to answer; Van Arlen had **folded** his hands,—his wife did the same, and soliloquised in silence.

"Six of **the** ten tarts left **over** . . . perhaps the confectioner would **take** them back . . . **at** any rate, one might **try.** Leentje might go **and see.** . . . The opera . . . **that** has not happened in the last ten years—what **are we to do** about dresses?—we shall have to be quick about it . . . Amen."

Her reflections were brought to an abrupt conclusion, for Van Arlen had opened his eyes with a sigh, and once more saw Prigson before him. Oh! what would he not have given not to see him—to have opened his eyes in the consciousness that he had been sleeping! Sleeping, from the moment of meeting his brother-in-law in the street; sleeping, when the latter reminded **him of the** debt, when he had been **alone** after Prigson's departure, when Van Teuten stood over him; sleeping, too, that last quarter of an hour, when he stood before his desk after Van Teuten had left him. . . . But he had not slept—all, **all** was real . . . and then to go to a comic opera on the top of that!

"Excuse me, Prigson, but I must go back to work immediately, there are **some** documents wanted in a hurry."

"Oh! so things *are* sometimes wanted in a hurry at a Government office?" **asked** Prigson. "No, thank you—

take one of my cigars—real Havannah, fifteen cents—delicious—just try one."

"Oh, uncle, it's positively sinful!" said Leida, who had nearly forgotten etiquette so far as to hand him a light, which at a ceremonial dinner would have been highly unfitting.

"Sinful is it? . . . How old are you now, Leida."

"Eighteen next birthday, uncle."

"Good-bye, then—till later—no, don't apologise. But don't go to sleep, Van Arlen," Prigson shouted jocularly after his host, and then added, turning to Leida, "A happy time of life, Leida, I wish it were mine still;—but when I was that age, I didn't think fifteen cents too much to pay for anything I liked."

"How do you mean, uncle?"

"Just what I say, my dear girl. What is life, after all? isn't it always seeking for what you like, whether you understand by that the smoking of a good Havannah, or the consciousness of having done a good action? Enjoyment means just what people like—and the older they are, the more they want of it. It's unjust of old people to say that it's the young ones that always want to enjoy themselves—the old ones are just as set on it, but they get their enjoyment out of other things. Well, any man who can get himself one enjoyment for fifteen cents is certainly not cheated out of his money."

"But, uncle, must one always have money to enjoy one's self?" asked Leida, naïvely, but very much *à contre cœur*—for her whole life was in evidence to prove that, as a rule, one must.

"Certainly not, my very charming Leida," said Prigson, rising, and added, as he embraced his niece, "That's a treat for nothing, do you see?"

"Not for me, uncle," said Leida, laughing mischievously, as she ran out of the room.

"It's really a pity that Van Arlen's such a harlequin!" muttered Van Noost Prigson to himself, and then went to join his elder nieces at the window.

Van Arlen was once more in his room, and had locked the door—but he didn't go to sleep. He had his hand in his breast-pocket, and his fingers were clutching a little packet that seemed to burn them.

Borrowed? No—not borrowed; it was stolen—it was not his. And yet he was not a thief—he had already as good as put it back,—only the execution was awanting to complete his intention. He strained his ears listening for Prigson and the others to go out at the front door. As soon as they were gone, he would hurry to the office and put back the money! Why were they dawdling like that? If anything happened to prevent his going—if he were to find the lock out of order. Why did they not start? If there were a fire in a street he had to pass—if he were to meet with an accident. . . . Do be quick, Prigson! the money is burning me—if I start now, we shall be in the street at the same time—then I shall have to go with him, and he will have to walk slowly on account of the ladies. Which way shall I go? My hat—where did I put my hat? If Prigson were to take my hat by mistake—happily it has a mourning band on it. Why don't you go, Prigson? Have you given up the plan?

There was a knock at the door, and his wife entered.

"Are you going out, Van Arlen?"

"No, my dear, no."

"I thought you looked as if you were going to start."

"Certainly not, certainly not! Go now, make haste, or you'll be late."

"Perhaps you're going to give us a surprise."

"No, no—I've too much to do—and I don't care about operas, where people die singing. Good-bye, Hortense, good-bye! Don't let the girls come up, I'm too busy."

At last, at last, he heard the door close! and when Caroline, as the eldest available daughter, came to bring papa his cup of tea, his room was empty.

"Papa has surely gone too," she said, as she went down again.

"I don't think it's very nice of him if he has. Why, he said that if he went we should go too."

"Papa doesn't care for operas."

"Oh! *I* think he likes them well enough, really—only——"

She stopped herself just in time, keeping back the word, the great word, which might be thought, but never spoken, in the Van Arlen household.

When the family came home that night Van Arlen was even more silent than he had been at dinner, but his silence was a dull apathetic calm. The ladies had enjoyed themselves "*awfully*"; their flushed cheeks and dancing eyes spoke volumes for the effect of this unwonted gaiety.

"Oh, papa, you *must* go some time!"

"Was it comic opera?" asked papa.

"Oh, yes! indeed it was—awfully!"

"Yes—but *really* comic, *good* comedy?"

"Oh, yes, very good," said mamma.

Van Arlen's position was too important for him to let himself be guided by any chance person who chose to label an opera as comic. A thing must really be what it is given out for.

"I suppose you care nothing at all for tragedy, then?" remarked Prigson.

"Well, not altogether that, but a tragedy must be *really* tragic."

The conversation, of which some fragments are thus reported, will scarcely make the reader long to hear the rest. The Van Arlens consistently kept up their depreciation of sour grapes, to the great delight of Prigson, who amused himself by defending all sorts of paradoxes. But though the hands of the alabaster clock unchangeably pointed to half-past one, it was getting late. Uncle Van Noost Prigson prepared to take his leave, and Van Arlen made no great effort to detain him. He thought his brother-in-law a good fellow, and, under certain circumstances, an indispensable person; to-day, however, Prigson reminded him of so much that he would willingly have forgotten, that his presence became well-nigh intolerable. He breathed more freely when Prigson got up to go; and it was with a certain cheerfulness that he remarked, as he looked out at the front door at the stars, "I see you've a fine night."

"We'll hope so," said Prigson; "but now, business for a moment. I asked you for something this morning—not for the sake of embarrassing you, but of getting myself out of a hole. When can I have that money?"

"Will to-morrow evening do?" asked Van Arlen, with a sigh of thankfulness that it was no longer in his pocket.

"Don't let it be later than that—you know you've always told me I could have it when I liked, otherwise I shouldn't have asked at such a moment."

"Oh, it's no trouble to me!" said Van Arlen, though he was wondering all the time where the money was to come from.

"Now for my plan. I will guarantee that you get the money back three days after the King has signed this concession—but then you will have to work the Minister!"

"I?"

"No one is in a better position to do it; the business is honest enough, but, like all business, it has a shady side to it: and the authorities have a nasty way of seeing the black before the white. There *is* some black about it, I won't deny; but if you can manage to show up the white, we shall be that thousand guilders to the good."

"But I don't see——"

"No need you should, for the moment. Take the papers to your room, read them, think over them, and, once more, three days after the granting of the concession, your debt is no longer in existence."

"Prigson!"

"Van Arlen!"

"What you ask—can it be reconciled with an honest man's conscience?"

"What do you take me for, Van Arlen?"

Van Arlen was silent for a moment, and then said slowly, "For a man who wants to be rich."

"Quite right, my dear fellow, and you should do the same. With this concession your fortune is made. You will have a situation with a salary of ten thousand guilders." And with a cheerful "Good-night," Prigson departed, while Van Arlen went up to his room.

It was many hours before he rose from his chair. The sun was shining in at the window, but he had no inclination to sleep; he had been absorbed in the documents. He read from beginning to end, thought for a while, folded them up, and muttered—

"Heaven preserve me from it!"

Thoughtfully he went to his office that morning. He could find no solution to the Prigson question, and there was nothing to help him.

He was summoned to the Minister's presence, and found him extraordinarily amiable—a bad sign.

"Sit down, Mr Van Arlen, sit down," said His Excellency. Van Arlen obeyed.

"Mr Van Arlen—it is possible I may be mistaken—but it seems to me as if, just lately, you had shown—*passez-moi le mot*—less zeal for business than I formerly thought was the case with you."

"Your Excellency, I was not aware that I had felt less zeal for my duties than at any other time."

"Is there anything worrying you? Your health?"

"It is excellent, thank you."

"Domestic trouble?—it might be indiscreet to inquire—but I take an interest in all my subordinates. Is there perhaps any financial trouble? Just tell me freely. Our salaries are not high, I know, but, if I am rightly informed, you have some private means."

"At your Excellency's service," assented Van Arlen.

"I thought so, otherwise we might have thought of offering you some assistance in this respect. But as it is, I suppose the extent of your work is such that it presses too heavily on one man; and so I have been considering the feasibility of appointing one more official to my department, subject to His Majesty's approval of my nomination."

Van Arlen turned deathly pale; now he understood the Minister's friendliness, and the fate that lay before him; he understood also that the first offer was by way of gilding the pill. He had refused the gilding from pride, but had to swallow the pill all the same.

"I assure your Excellency that I do not know what work could be entrusted to such an official."

"That is quite a minor detail," said His Excellency, naïvely. "However, I wished to consult you first about the matter, and perhaps you will be so kind as to have the proposal drawn up. Baron Regenstein is the person meant."

"The son of your colleague?"

"I believe so; but he is a man of great acquirements, whose help will be extremely useful to you. I shall want the paper before two o'clock."

Van Arlen bowed and rose.

"Oh, as to salary, we shall give him eighteen hundred guilders."

"Your Excellency will allow me to remark, that in that case you will have exceeded the estimate for the department."

"Then we must see how we can manage with the

smaller salaries. Didn't some one die a month or two back?"

"Yes, an assistant secretary."

"Very good; and I just heard this morning that we've probably lost another. Van Teuten left town quietly last night."

"Van Teuten!" exclaimed Van Arlen, in consternation.

"Yes. Do you know anything in particular about him?"

"He came and asked me for two hundred guilders yesterday."

"Well, why couldn't you let him have an advance? or you might have sent him to me; if necessary, we could have helped him by getting up a collection. But you're too busy to attend to such things; it's a good thing we're going to have some extra help. Good-morning, Mr Van Arlen."

"That, too!" said Van Arlen, when he was back in his own room, and then called out to the messenger that he could see no one.

"A gentleman has been here; he said he would come back."

"Can't see any one to-day."

"Mr Van Arlen!" said a voice, just as the door was closing.

"Impossible, sir, the Minister is in a hurry."

The door was shut, and the voice—and all persons with whom it subsequently came in contact—were aware that there was "something up," perhaps a reorganisation of the whole department. . . . So much only was certain, that no one knew what it was but the Minister and Van Arlen, which still further increased the latter's importance.

But the drawing up of a proposal for the appointment of a supernumerary official was no joke. It was long since Van Arlen had such a ticklish document in hand, and the only reason it seemed to him that he could give was,—" Whereas it is our pleasure ... to supersede Van Arlen." At last, however, he found the way to do it. By noon the document was ready, and one of the copying **clerks**, in whose discretion he placed unlimited confidence, was sent for to prepare the mysterious paper for its high destiny, in Van Arlen's own room. At a quarter to two it was fairly written out, and Van Arlen presented himself before the Minister, who took the document, thanked him **courteously, and** glanced through it.

"You have forgotten the **date** when the new appointment is to begin,—the **1st of the** following month," said His Excellency, in a tone which clearly conveyed : " Really, Mr Van Arlen, your work is too much for you."

Van Arlen returned to his room with the paper in his hand, and found Prigson at the door.

" Good-morning, Van Arlen."

" Excuse me, Prigson ; I haven't a **moment to spare.**"

" What is it now **? Country** in danger ? **What's that** document ? "

" Ministerial business. . . . Where is Mr Zuigman ? " This to the messenger.

" Gone away, sir."

" Tell him to come here immediately."

But after his highly important activity in his superior's private room, the copying **clerk** Zuigman had understood that he was in need **of** some slight recreation, and, alleging a commission in town, he had gone off for a stroll round the square. His immediate superior had given him leave at once. One doesn't refuse modest requests like that **to a** man perceptibly high in **Van** Arlen's favour.

" What now ? " said Van Arlen. " My head is going round. Zuigman must come to my room the **very** first thing tomorrow morning."

" Can I help you, Van Arlen ? **What is** it has to be done ? "

"Writing, man, writing!—a proposal addressed to the King that will have to come before the Cabinet Council.... I don't know what to do."

"Can't you do it yourself?"

"I!" said Van Arlen, in consternation.

"Well, a good writing is not your strong point," laughed Prigson, "otherwise you never would have risen so high. The man with the worst hand gets on best, because they can't keep him on as a copying-clerk. Just give me a pen."

"But, Prigson, it's a great document! strictly secret—no one is to know anything about it!"

"I'll promise not to tell; let's have a look." And before Van Arlen could prevent it, his brother-in-law had already glanced over the paper.

"Heaven be good to us! a magnificent bargain!"

"A bargain?"

"Why, of course! Now-a-days it's not their own sons that ministers help forward; they do it for each other's. Regenstein is to get this, and your man's son has just been put into a good thing by his father's colleague. Splendid exchange! Did you draw up the proposal?"

"I have no time now, Prigson. Do be kind enough to let me alone."

Van Arlen rang the bell, and sent for one of the clerks. Van Teuten entered.

"Mr Van Teuten!"

"Sir, I have——"

"We'll see to that presently. Sit down, Mr Van Teuten, and write—here—recopy this page; but mind you put in the insertion! The first time a document of mine has been disfigured by an insertion! My head's going!"

Van Teuten wrote as he was told, and in a quarter of an hour the work was finished. He perceived, with visible complacency, how much better his writing was than that of his colleague.

"Two different kinds of writing! **Never** yet happened with a document of mine; **and** it's got to **go to** the King and the Cabinet Council!"

With these words Van Arlen rushed out **of the room,** leaving Prigson alone with **Van** Teuten.

"Can you copy decently?" asked Prigson.

"I venture to say, sir, that there isn't another hand like mine in this department."

"What **do you earn at** this work, now?"

"Six hundred guilders, sir. **Mr Van Arlen has perhaps told** you that I am financially in circumstances of great difficulty."

"Well, it is indeed **too** little for **a man who writes a hand** like that; **but surely you're out of all your troubles now?**"

"I?—I just wish I were!"

"Why, **a man who** knows all **about a** secret document like this need not be poor any longer than he likes."

"**Secret, sir?**"

"Most particularly so," said Prigson, turning away, while Van Teuten considered **with** himself whether it **could** really be the case, and whether, if so, he could **profit by it.**

Van Arlen came back, thanked the copying clerk, and recommended him to keep the matter secret.

Prigson stole a glance at Van Teuten, who was **now** convinced of the truth of his **words.**

"Do you want anything, Mr Van **Teuten?**" asked **Van** Arlen, for the man remained standing.

"May I venture to remind you of my request yesterday, sir? Perhaps you know that . . . that I . . . **yesterday . . .**"

"Yes, I know—nothing takes place in this department without my knowledge; but the Minister and I have agreed to take no notice of such ill-considered action on the part of a member of this department—provided, of course, it is never repeated."

"No, sir, I give you my word it shall not. Oh, if you had only known what I felt this morning, when I thought of my wife and children searching for me! I couldn't stand it any longer, sir, and I came back."

"The wisest thing you could have done."

"But that does not save me! I have obtained two days' respite; but after that—I am hopelessly lost, if no help comes. If you will allow me, sir, I will go before the court to-morrow."

"I'll do better for you than that,—I'll send a subscription list round the office, and let you have the amount. His Excellency is sure to put his name down too."

"And if there is any deficiency, I'll make it up," said Prigson.

"Certainly a State secret," thought Van Teuten, amazed and confused at the turn matters had taken,—which he ascribed entirely to the secret. He too was involved in it, —but, alas! he had read nothing, that was not his habit; A good copying clerk never reads—he only writes. "To begin on Aug. 1st,"—that was all he could remember. But it must be a secret of the highest importance,—and the stranger who seemed to have the principal share in the business was—yes, what could he be? Then he remembered that Talm had spoken of an English millionaire, introduced by him at the White Club, and somehow connected with Van Arlen;—but the millionaire, according to Talm, knew not a word of Dutch—it was for that very reason that Van Arlen had entrusted him to Talm's guidance; and now the secret document, and the unexpected help, and the change in his fortunes—had Van Arlen, perhaps, been raised to the ministry? . . .

Van Arlen and Prigson were left alone.

"Did you look over my papers?"

"Yes."

"And——?"

"I don't want to be in it; your business is not—not honest."

"What do you call honest, Van Arlen?"

"Perhaps I expressed myself rather harshly—it is not what it seems to be."

"*You* say that?" sneered Prigson. "Come, Van Arlen, *that* can be no reason for you to dislike a thing. But we'll grant that it is more profitable for the contractor than for the State—that's a matter of course. Do you think we're going to make the State presents, while the Ministers put their sons into all the fat Government places? Just tell me, on your conscience, Van Arlen, is that an honest business, that appointment? I bet something you had a heap of trouble to give the thing a decent appearance?"

Van Arlen nodded.

"Well, now, there's a present of eighteen hundred guilders being made to Regenstein. I suppose your Minister's son is getting double that? and am I to be fool enough not to get my share out of the 'Widow Woman' too? Let's be wise, and follow the good example set us."

Van Arlen was silent.

"Shall I tell you something? The functionary now being smuggled in—for whose coming you have been obliged to find the reasons—is really appointed in order to oust you. He is to do your work, and you are to become supernumerary, and then who knows how soon you'll be pensioned off?"

"Then I shall fall honourably."

"Cold comfort that; it's surely no dishonour to prevent the blow. Once more, I'll give you a receipt for that debt; I offer you a well-paid position, and if the concern comes to smash—for that *might* happen—I will guarantee that you shall lose nothing."

"So you admit that the thing is not honest?"

"My good Van Arlen, you're the very type of infantile innocence. If it were quite safe and certain to be profitable,

I could do without your help. One word more,—if you still refuse, Regenstein is a good friend of mine; he gets his appointment on the first, and within a month from that date I shall get what I want without applying to you. Just think over that."

"Prigson, you are a tempter."

"Van Arlen, you are a fool."

"If it should come out that I have been playing a double game?"

"If this Minister is still in office, just remind him of that appointment; if there is another, you can lay the blame on his predecessor, and the disorder occasioned by the unnecessary nomination of new officials."

"But—I took an oath——"

"And didn't the Minister do so too? Come, shut up shop for to-day, and come and dine with me."

"With you?"

"Why not? Yesterday I was your guest, to-day you are mine. I am staying at the Bellevue; but if there are too many princes there for your taste, we'll go and dine at the Badhuis restaurant."

"Impossible; I can't leave the office till four. If you'll believe me, Prigson, I envy the clerks, who can take their hats and go whenever they like."

"The burdens of greatness . . . So you're free at four, are you? Well, I'll drive round and fetch you."

Accordingly, at four, Prigson arrived in a cab, and conveyed not only Van Arlen, but his wife and Leida, to the garden restaurant at Scheveningen known as the Badhuis. They dined sumptuously, and did not even refuse champagne. This was an unheard-of event in their lives—but they were not paying the bill.

After dinner, as they were sitting on the terrace, they perceived Mr Talm. Mr Talm had on flesh-coloured kid gloves, and an eye-glass prominently fixed in his left eye, the cord waving in the wind like the **web of a** gigantic spider. Talm was quite presentable, and, being now **of** opinion that the Van Arlens were presentable also, he accosted them, and was honoured with an invitation to join their party.

Madame thought it would be nice to walk up and down the terrace, and Leida also showed herself pleased with the idea. Talm offered his escort, and Prigson was once more alone with his brother-in-law.

"The business is clinched now, isn't it?"

"No," said **Van** Arlen, "I have been thinking it **over**, and I must abide by my first answer."

"That's a pity," said Prigson—"a pity for **you—for, as I** said, the matter will have to be got into shape without you; but I should have liked to have you in it, because I'm heartily sorry for you. Just excuse me a minute," he went on, rising and signalling to a stranger, who was casting sinister glances at the teacups—"it **is** my friend Valtoucourt, one **of the** associate concessionaires. . . . I'm sorry, for I could have introduced you to each other—in fact, I shall have to do it after all,"—and Prigson, continuing in French, presented Baron de Valtoucourt to his brother-in-law, for whom he invented a high-sounding title on the spur of the moment. Van Arlen had never thought that his name would **sound** so well in French. But French was not his forte, and now his silence made him seem more solemn than ever; and he was convinced in his soul that Baron Valtoucourt thought **him** the pivot of all the home and foreign politics of Holland. Prigson did his best to strengthen this hypothetical opinion. "You see, my dear fellow," he said to the stranger, "if Van Arlen is willing, he can do anything, but he is fond of raising objections—*ce cher* Van Arlen."

The stranger muttered, with amazing rapidity, a long French sentence, of which Van Arlen could not seize **a** word. He therefore confined himself to ejaculating now and then "*oui*" or "*peut-être*," and at the close wrapped himself in a diplomatic silence. His wife and Leida returned with their cavalier; the stranger greeted them with a bow, as deep and solemn as though he were announcing her death-sentence to the Queen of Spain; he then bowed no less deeply to Talm, who, on his part, was not to be outdone, and, deeply impressed by the high solemnity of the occasion, made another low bow before Van Arlen. The latter, having witnessed the performance three times, involuntarily saluted his assistant secretary in a similar manner.

It was, in fact, most impressively solemn.

The stranger was a man who knew life, and could understand that a man might fill a highly important position without being an accomplished French scholar. He therefore slackened the flow of his words, and assured them that he should consider it a great honour to have Van Arlen as a director.

"But," said Van Arlen, "I never said that!"

"*Si, si,*" said the stranger, "we understand one another perfectly;" and then he pressed his hand and gave utterance to a friendly wish, whereat Van Arlen (unwilling to acknowledge even to himself that he did not understand) replied, "*Nous verrons.*"

Next morning he sent for his wife and Leida to his own room, and completely bewildered them, first by swearing them to secrecy with regard to a conversation they had neither heard nor understood, and next by completely losing his temper, when Leida innocently asked: "Why, papa, you frighten me—one would think it was high treason!" He was so violent that Leida went off into hysterics, the girls came up to see what was the matter, and Van Arlen left for the office in a very bad temper.

He found that Prigson had been there, and was coming back at three o'clock.

The Minister not only refused to have anything to do

with the subscription-list for Van Teuten, but hinted disapprobation of those who had got it up; and let fall expressions which tortured Van Arlen all the morning, making him wonder whether His Excellency had penetrated his secret. At last Van Teuten came, and he was forced to acknowledge his failure. The poor man, nearly in despair, was about to make a last effort, and ask the Minister to become security for him, when Van Arlen had a luminous idea.

"I will——" he said. Van Teuten was overwhelming him with thanks and blessings, when he interrupted him:

"On these conditions I will become security. First, the money must be here by two; secondly, you must borrow, not two hundred, but twelve hundred; thirdly, the whole matter must be kept secret."

Van Teuten was ready to promise anything,—he would willingly have made him a present of his soul into the bargain. Not long afterwards a former Government clerk, who was now "in business on his own account," was admitted to Van Arlen's private room. The money-lender was inclined to make objections—twelve hundred guilders was a large sum for a clerk whose income only amounted to the half of that sum.

"If I don't raise that difficulty," said Van Arlen indifferently, "I see no reason why you should."

"Yes, you see—but you are mortal like the rest of us; you might have to retire, or be put on half-pay—excuse my suggesting such things, but they're all possible."

"You're not lending money to me, but to Mr Van Teuten; if anything of the sort were to happen, he would find you a new security."

At last the matter was settled, at an interest of seven and a half per cent. The money-lender produced the twelve hundred guilders, and carried off the bill, duly stamped, and signed by Van Arlen and Van Teuten.

When the man with the handwriting was once more alone with his chief, the latter said, "Two hundred guilders are all you want for the present; I'll keep the rest for you, in case you should get into difficulties again. Never mind about the interest—I'll pay that."

Van Teuten was fairly dazzled by such liberality. There must be something behind it—probably the State secret.

The news went like wildfire through the department how that unlucky devil of a Van Teuten had been set on his legs again by Van Arlen! Zuigman knew what to think of it—*he* had seen documents; but he never spoke, and that his colleagues knew right well.

Talm, too, had his say on the subject,—Talm, who had introduced the millionaire, and had, yesterday evening, walked on the terrace at Scheveningen arm-in-arm with his chief's wife. Further and further spread the fire, and every one made his conjectures. Van Teuten's rescue remained the great event of the day.

It struck three, when Prigson was announced. Van Arlen was deep in his work.

"What zeal! But of course you want to leave the books in good order when you go!"

"I'm not thinking of going, Prigson."

"What do you say? And our agreement?"

"I have made no definite agreement; but, in so far as I have made any promise to join you, I withdraw it."

"What the deuce! Van Arlen, aren't you right in your head?"

"On the contrary, I have come to my senses. When one has been an honest man for thirty years, Prigson, one is thoroughly in love with honesty."

"Especially the way it is appreciated! The reward of all your honesty will be, that you fall from the tree, like an over-ripe fruit, and lie there till somebody treads you flat."

"Better so than trample on one's self."

"That is a gymnastic feat I would rather leave **to a Mün-**chausen. But you're mad, **Van Arlen—the matter is getting into** shape after all."

"Do you think **so**?" Van Arlen stood up, and looked his brother-in-law straight in **the face.** "Do you think I would ever allow it?"

"My good friend, you **won't** be asked. Regenstein is going to negotiate **the** business."

"Then I'll inform the Minister. The supernumerary will be on his guard."

"Like the dying gladiator—*moriturus salutat*—it's heroic, but comic **too.** I'd be more sensible, if I were you, Van Arlen."

"Prigson, when I came here this morning, with the feeling that I had broken my oath and betrayed my country . . . Oh! I couldn't stay here **a day—I couldn't live—I** should lay hands on myself."

"Treason—perjury—you do choose such fine words! and the real point is, whether you're going to depart from an old habit or not. Believe me, you're the slave of habit."

"I prefer to remain so."

Prigson looked at him, and saw that his mind was made up. But he had one resource left, "Well, I suppose you're your own master, and **can** do **as** you like. . . . But I'm sorry—I shall have to remind you of what I asked you for the other day."

Van Arlen put his hand **in** his breast pocket, and laid **a** small parcel on the table before Prigson, "Will you kindly see if that's all right?" he said.

Prigson **was** disappointed. He did not need the money —**in** fact, Van Arlen's utter inability to pay would have been worth another thousand guilders to him.

"I suppose it's all right," he said, glancing over the notes. "There, Van Arlen," he said, with a sudden change of tone, and a quaver in his voice, "give me your hand, old fellow!

you're better than most men. Good-bye! Stay as you are!"

He left the room, and Van Arlen, finding himself alone, felt like a man saved from shipwreck.

It is some weeks after the first of August. The new official has long been installed, and the Minister does nothing without consulting him. Everything passes through Mr Regenstein's hands.

It is Sunday afternoon. On Sunday afternoons, as a rule, it is too hot for a walk; or, if not too hot, it is too cold. If neither too hot nor too cold, it most likely threatens rain; and if none of these three atmospheric conditions prevails, —well, formerly Van Arlen always had urgent work to do. This Sunday, however, he is quite at leisure, and the weather is perfect, but—it is the anniversary of Aunt Cornelia's death.

Van Arlen looks over the blinds at the passers-by, most of whom are on their way to the Bosch. Here and there a quietly dressed lady, with a Bible in her hand, threads her way through the throng.

"I think I'll go to afternoon church," says Caroline. "Will you come, Frederica?"

"Oh, yes, Caroline," answers Frederica, with a little sigh, and they go.

Leida and Hendrika made a slight grimace.

"Papa really might go out for a walk with us."

"Oh, fie! girls!" said their mother, "that would not be at all proper on a day like this."

"Couldn't we keep the day just as well to-morrow, mamma?" asked Leida simply. "I don't see why we should have to keep it up for twenty years; I'm quite sure that Uncle Van Noost Prigson himself doesn't remember it now."

The name made Van Arlen look up.

"Oh, papa—have you heard anything more about the

situation uncle was talking **about at dinner that day?**" asked Marie.

"That's all come to nothing, dear child; I **have** been talking it over, but they say they can't do without me at the office."

"But, papa," asked Hortense, "if they can't **do** without you, how does it happen that you have less to do than you had?"

"Does the importance of a position lie in **the mere** amount of work?" asked Van Arlen, with dignity.

"Papa has this secret business now, you see," **said his wife,** anxious to help him out—she **was looking straight** before her. "This business **is,** by itself, **of tremendous** importance."

"Is that since Uncle Prigson was here?" asked Leida, going up to **her father,** and laying **her arm over his shoulder.** "You're not angry with me any more, are you, papa?—**you** know—since that morning?"

Van Arlen bent down to his daughter and kissed her on the forehead. "No, little girl,—I can't be angry with you."

"But you never travel now, papa. Has that part of your work been taken away? That's stupid!"

"The travelling has **come to an** end," said Van Arlen thoughtfully,—"come to an end for good and all."

The item "Travelling expenses," in the Van Arlen budget, was now replaced by another, which was, "Instalments and **interest** on **debt.**"

"That's a pity," said Caroline, "because now you can never take **two of** us with you, as you promised to do long ago."

"That plan has come to nothing too, child. Besides, I'm getting old."

"Oh, papa!—you old! that's the first we've heard of it. It must be since you gave up your glass of wine at dinner."

"Papa has to keep his head clear, you see," said Mrs Van Arlen. "That's the penalty of greatness, girls!"

She was silent, and they all followed suit. No one had anything more to say. If only a caller would come!—but since papa had entered on his important position as supernumerary in the office, callers had been scarce. So the dull Sunday wore away. The two eldest girls came home from church; the dinner hour drew near, and, still in silence, the Van Arlens took their places round the big table, on which a soup tureen was the only dish visible. It does not take long to eat soup, and the dessert, as usual, remained untouched. Already Leentje had stuck her shining Sunday face, and her hat with the flowers in it, through a crack of the door, to give notice of her departure—for it was her day out, and "it suited." The family were still seated round the table. Why should they rise?—the evening was long enough. Suddenly, however, they were startled out of their inertia by the front door bell. Leida went to answer it, and immediately returned with Van Noost Prigson. Van Arlen felt himself turn pale—was he to be tempted again?

His wife, too, was seized with panic—supposing Prigson had not dined! Fortunately, he set her mind at ease forthwith.

"I left the dinner-table before dessert, fearing that otherwise I should not find you at home. I suppose you're going to Scheveningen?"

"No; it's rather too crowded for me at the Badhuis on Sundays," said Van Arlen, feeling that it would not quite do to allege to the widower the anniversary of his wife's death as their reason for remaining at home.

"Crowded! The father of seven daughters ought simply to revel in crowds. What do you say, nieces?"

The nieces had no opinion to offer on that point.

"Really, Van Arlen," Prigson went on, throwing himself back in his chair, and surveying the seven girls, one by one, with a well-pleased expression,—"really, my dear fellow, you ought not to stay at home on Sunday evenings! At any rate you should send your daughters to church."

The younger ones looked mischievously at Caroline and Frederica.

"It has always struck me as strange, Van Arlen, that there are so many old maids at the Hague. What in the world is the cause of that?"

"Because the girls are rather hard to please, uncle," said Leida.

"Oh, that's the reason, is it?" said Prigson, with an air of simple faith. "I'm sorry to hear it—I've just come to look for a wife at the Hague."

"For Cousin Cornelius, uncle?" asked Leida. "I suppose he's about twenty now, isn't he?"

"Good for nothing, girl! And have you heard, Van Arlen?" he continued, turning to his brother-in-law.

"What?" asked the latter.

"Oh! you know well enough,—you're only pretending, because you want to make out it's a State secret."

"On my word, as an honest man——"

"That's worth something, as we know. So you haven't heard? Next week your Minister's going to resign."

"Prigson!"

"The day before yesterday, it was brought before the Cabinet Council, and His Majesty made as little difficulty over the matter as I should have done. He'll get the Grand Cross now, and perhaps be Minister of State—but *you'll* be rid of him!"

Van Arlen sat looking at his brother-in-law, without moving a muscle of his face, and the girls felt convinced that papa knew just as much about the business as Prigson.

"And the best of it all is, that your friend Regenstein has been doing his level best to pull His Excellency down! Well—reap as you've sown!"

"Prigson, we're not alone here."

"I see no earthly reason why your wife and daughters

may not know it. I hate these mysteries. They may shout the whole thing from the housetops, for all I care."

"But think of my position!"

"It will be greatly improved, Van Arlen. Regenstein has made his own terms, like a sensible man; but I'll tell you about that later. As soon as I heard that His Excellency was going to close his portfolio, I came to the Hague at once; last night I had a talk with him, and now my business is done. The Minister wasn't of the same mind as a certain fellow I know, when *he* found himself set aside."

"But, Prigson!"

"All men are not equally conscientious, my dear man. His Excellency had too much common sense to make difficulties,—but that's not to the point. Enough that the matter's settled! By Jove, but I'm sick of it! To Amsterdam yesterday—to Rotterdam this morning—but now I'm going to get some rest!"

Van Arlen shook his head doubtfully over such lack of principle.

"And are you remaining in town some days?" asked Madame, with distinction.

"That depends, Hortense. I've told you what I came for."

"Uncle is sorry for the Hague ladies," said Leida. "But remember, uncle, they're very hard to please."

"I think I shall have to run off with one. What would you do, Van Arlen, if a fellow ran off with one of your daughters?"

"Prigson, my daughters are far too well brought up, ever to be exposed to the danger of such a thing."

"But supposing a man comes and proposes in due form?"

"I think it's going to rain," said Marie.

"Dear me! isn't that picture hanging all on one side," exclaimed Hendriek, at the same moment.

"Mamma, have you noticed that the edge of the tablecloth is all ravelled out here?" asked Hortense.

Frederica rose to pick up her napkin, which she **had** dropped.

"Shall we have tea in the front or back room, mamma?" asked Antoinette, whose turn it was **to** see **to** the housekeeping this week; and they rose, followed by Caroline, who went over to mamma, to whisper a very confidential communication with regard to a ribbon in the latter's cap. Leida was lighting a spill for papa. "You might **as** well ask, uncle, what is the amount of the dowry papa is going **to** give us," she **said,** handing Uncle Prigson a light at the same time.

"**Pretty girls need no** dowry," answered Prigson.

"Thanks for the compliment to your nieces," said **Leida**, with a roguish curtsey, as she left the room.

Prigson and Van Arlen were once more alone.

"Prigson," said the official, "I must repeat to you candidly what I have already told you—you're not playing a fair game."

"Do you think I want to turn your daughters' heads?"

"I didn't mean that—your enterprise, which now seems about to succeed——"

"Say, which *is* going to succeed; but let that matter rest just now."

"Surely you have a conscience, Prigson?"

"**An** amazingly big one, Van Arlen; and, between ourselves, I think it's made of some elastic substance, most **likely** of the same material as your Minister's and your friend Regenstein's."

"Prigson! Prigson! a time will come——"

"**Dear** me! Van Arlen, what a platitude!"

"You're scoffing, Prigson; but listen, you set store by the respect of your fellow-creatures—mine, for instance; you told me once that I was better than many men."

"Well remembered; but have I forfeited that respect?"

"Not quite, yet—but still——"

"The greater part? Good. Now the proof of the sum; Van Arlen, I want to ask you for the hand of your daughter."*

"Prigson, do remember that we are discussing serious matters."

"But, Van Arlen, I'm speaking as seriously as I ever did in my life. Your Leida is a nice, pleasant, merry girl, with a good heart, and—excuse my having seen a little deeper into your domestic economy than perhaps you like—Leida knows how to keep house."

"Your age!"

"Do you reckon by the heart or the head?"

"You might be her father!"

"If I had six more daughters, like you, I wouldn't envy their position. I don't understand, Van Arlen, why you should make any difficulty about it; a father of seven girls ought surely to be glad enough to get rid of one of them."

"You forget that a daughter's marriage involves expenses too heavy for a household like mine."

"I will bear the cost of everything."

Van Arlen was silent, and reflected. He had just been calling Prigson a dishonest man,—was he going to give him his daughter? Could he answer for such a step to his own conscience? . . . But it was a good match after all . . . and then . . . seven daughters! And the outfit! But perhaps that was only a nominal present after all . . . ; perhaps Prigson only meant to reckon it as cancelling the money still due to him.

"Our debt——" he began.

"Cancelled on the wedding-day."

The prospect was, in truth, a seductive one; but how could he give his daughter to a man without a conscience? Suddenly there occurred to him a way of escape, which united in itself all possible advantages.

---

* This marriage would be legal in Holland.

"Prigson, with me everything must give way to my children's happiness; I have never forced any of them into a marriage" (in fact, the opportunity had never offered), "and I would not attempt to prevent a union which——"

Van Arlen paused—Prigson waited.

"Which may, perhaps, lead to your happiness—even your higher happiness, Prigson. The influence over you may have the power to inspire you with better feelings, with—let me speak plainly—more moral principles."

It was an inspiration of the moment,—but Van Arlen, by this time, was quite convinced that it was his principal motive in consenting.

"Will you let us hope so, Van Arlen?"

"But——"

"Well?"

"Would not Caroline, who is nearer your own age——"

"I am convinced that Leida's influence will act on me more powerfully," said Prigson, humbly. "What do you think of taking a drive out to the baths now? I shall have a better chance of getting a few words with Leida than here, where there are always six more of them sitting sorrowing that the offer was not for them."

"I do not think my daughters would take that view of each other's happiness."

"Come! we're getting on!—you call it happiness, do you? Will you have a fly ordered?"

"The nearest driver is a Roman Catholic."

"No, of course he must not drive us; that would begin to play the mischief with the moral principles at once. I'll go and find a Calvinist cabman."

That same evening Leida called her uncle by his first name; and in two months' time the Van Arlens were giving a ball in honour of the engagement,—a thing they had never done before,—with Prigson's money. Talm appeared at this festivity; and the man with the handwriting, who was accustomed to amuse his leisure hours with the clarionet (purely for the love of art, of course), also assisted—at a distance. He told his friends next morning that he had been one of the invited guests, and that Mr Talm would probably get a good piece of promotion before long, for he had been dancing all the evening with one and the same Miss Van Arlen—who, moreover, gave him her bouquet when he left!

The ball had important consequences, moreover, for five more of the Van Arlen girls; and the old man now lives on his pension, with his wife and eldest daughter. He often calls to mind his important position,—especially the time when he was entrusted with such very, very confidential business, of which no one knew anything at the time, and no one knows anything to this day.

GERARD KELLER.

ROUGH DRAFT OF A NEW SET OF REGULATIONS.

FOR THE BENEFIT OF SERVANTS AND THEIR EMPLOYERS.

THE milkman must be made to understand that it will not do to ring people out of their beds at seven in the morning, and make them catch cold at the front door.

Pianos are not to be locked by the family after using; the servants would like a little music now and then.

The master and mistress must consult the servants before subscribing to newspapers and magazines. The foolish choice that is often made in this respect is very trying to the feelings of the latter.

Another practice that cannot be too strongly reprobated, is that of carrying off books and magazines from the circulating library to people's bedrooms before the servants have read them.

Madame and the daughters of the house should always knock properly before entering the kitchen.

When visiting the servants' own rooms, they should always send some one up to announce them first.

When the housemaid is sent **to** order a cab, it by no means follows that she is **to tell the** cabman to drive her home by the shortest way.

If the master and mistress are medically attended by a Professor, it **will not** do **to let** the servants be treated by an ordinary doctor.

Stale bread will no longer be eaten.

When a serious misfortune is impending—*e.g.*, a bankruptcy or **the** like—the servants ought always to be warned in time.

If the family have a box at the theatre or the opera, the servants should **have the** full use of it.

The family should not speak French **at** table while the maid is in the room, unless it has been previously ascertained that she understands that language.

Tips **ought to** be compounded for, just as much as tithes.

Uilenspiegel.

THE STORY OF A BOUQUET.

ALFRED possessed two qualities **common to** many young men besides himself,—he was in love, and he had very little money.

His condition was therefore **a** sad **one ; but** he cherished the hope that the lovely Clara would not only make a good wife, but also put an end to all his pecuniary embarrassments. So he neglected nothing that he thought might please her.

Every one knows that homage when offered in the shape **of** flowers **is, as a rule,** well pleasing to ladies. But, unhappily, the world is at present so prosaically constituted, that even the perfumed children of Flora are not to be had except for money,—and this point constituted, as we have already seen, the Achilles sinew of our enamoured here.

Day and night his thoughts were occupied with this difficulty, and, when it did not keep him awake, his sleep was filled with uncomfortable dreams.

After one of these weary nights, another bright morning had dawned,—the larks were singing, the roses were in bloom, and Alfred was busy cleaning his pipe.

In the midst of this poetic occupation, he was suddenly inspired with a practical idea. He sketched out a plan which would have done no discredit to the most finished diplomatist, and executed it with an energy worthy of a worse cause.

He had been accustomed to sell his cast-off garments to a humble citizen of much experience in retail trading; and, considering the man's astuteness and eloquence, he had often been seized by a suspicion that he (Alfred) had not got the best of the bargain.

This must be put an end to. He broke off his commercial relations with the experienced dealer, and concluded a treaty with a nursery-gardener's boy, to whom he presented his worn-out clothes; in return for which the boy engaged to gather him a bouquet, from time to time, late in the evening, and bring it to him with the necessary discretion.

This plan answered well enough for a time. The boy brought the flowers, and received in return, gifts of equal value, —a hat, adorned with dints like a Homeric shield; a waistcoat, wofully stained down the front; and a coat, whose collar shone like a meteor; and furthermore, a pair of shoes, on which the cobbler's art could no further go.

On the morning of a bright summer day, the gardener's boy, being unable to come in person, sent up by another hand a magnificent bouquet of roses, which Alfred, without loss of time, despatched to his adored Clara.

THE STORY OF A BOUQUET.

Full of joyous hope, and sure of a friendly welcome, he sped the same evening to the house of his chosen one, but found, to his great disappointment, that he was received with decided coolness.

"You sent me a note this morning," began Clara, after an awkward pause.

"A note?" he asked, in astonishment; "I?"

"Yes, with the flowers——"

"YES, WITH THE FLOWERS——"

"Yes, I did send some flowers—roses——"

"Into which this note was stuck," went on Clara, freezingly. "Here it is—do you deny having sent it?"

And she handed the miserable man a piece of paper, on which he read, to his consternation—

"*Don't forget the old boots you said you would give me last week.*" *Uilenspiegel.*

"TO HOLD UP FOR THE KISS."

UNBIDDEN GUESTS.

I.

NOTARY VAN ELST generally comes home from his office about five in the afternoon, and his return to the bosom of his family is a pretty sight.

The Van Elsts' neighbour,—unsociable old bachelor that he was,—noticing how eagerly this return was watched for every afternoon and greeted with joyful acclamation, had a way of turning away his head, and muttering crossly, " I might have known that sort of thing too, if only——"

In the *bendy** sent to fetch Van Elst, the curly head of his eldest child was always to be seen; Nonnie and little Ada were always watching for him on the verandah steps when he drove up; and no sooner did the wheels crunch over the gravel than a pretty little wife would come flying out with the brightest, pleasantest face imaginable, which she never forgot to hold up for the kiss which was always forthcoming, unless the children interfered, clinging about him as they did, and clamouring for attention.

Then came an interval of peace. Papa went to dress, and mamma sent the little ones out for a walk; and when the old bachelor returned to his verandah,—having been away for his bath meanwhile,—he would see his gentle little neighbour seated at the tea-tray as placidly as if she had not been busy the whole day running here and there,—now urging a perverse "boy" to work, now disposing of a contumacious pedlar or unreasonable *lengànan*,† or, most frequent occupation of all, flying to soothe the children in the countless infantine woes and accidents which were always occurring.

---

* Two-wheeled trap or **dogcart** (a Malay word).
† Chinese trader.

"WHEN THE OLD BACHELOR RETURNED TO HIS VERANDAH."

It really *was*, and not merely in the old bachelor's fancy, a pretty sight.

The wife got all the newspapers and letters, and the master of the house innumerable cups of tea. He would retail all the items of news,—she, the children's pretty sayings and doings; and if she felt a craving to unburden herself of domestic grievances, she found him ready to listen, as far as appearances went, at least.

"Is there no news to-day?" she asks, when the little disturbers of the peace have been sent out, and her husband throws himself back luxuriously in his lounging-chair.

"Oh! yes, a great piece of news. **Just guess.**"

"Oh! come; do tell me. You know I hate guessing."

"Well, then, a letter from our cousins the Martendijks. Where on earth did I put **it?** Oh! here it is **in my coat** pocket. Well, there's not much in it, except **that they ask** if we will have them on a visit."

"The *Martendijks!*" Jo exclaims, her face lengthening. But immediately she recollects that they are relations of her husband's; and as this is rather a sore point with him, she hastens to add: "What do *you* say to it, **Max?**"

"Well, you see," answers Max, "I have been wondering whether we should not write that you are not yet strong enough for visitors."

Jo does not indeed look strong, with her fitful colour, and that languid droop of the eyelids, but, like most mothers of a family who know how ill they can be spared, she is loath to allow that she is not robust, and does her best to persuade herself and every **one** else that, once she has got over this or that, she will be perfectly strong.

"No; you must not do that. We can't let them stay on at that hot Soeka-Manies, especially with the bad season coming on. When do they propose to come?"

"On the 5th."

"Good gracious! the day after to-morrow! And I have

to put clean curtains on the beds! They might have given us longer notice, I think. Surely Emily knows as well as I do that there are always some arrangements to make in a busy household."

"Then am I to write that they are welcome?"

"Yes; we can't well do anything else. Another cup of tea, dear?"

Here follows a pause. Mr Van Elst puffs away contentedly at his cigar, while his wife begins to fidget a little. At last, laying her hand on her husband's, she says, hesitatingly, "Do you know why their coming is not very convenient just now, dear boy? the *godown* is nearly empty."

"Empty *again?* My dear Jo, what on earth becomes of the things?"

And as if this remark—a favourite one with married men, and generally as unjust as it is senseless—were not enough, he continues, in an aggrieved tone: "Good gracious, child! it is not three months since I ordered in a whole supply. Are the four boxes of wine finished? And all those tinned things? And all the casks of butter?"

"No, not yet. If no visitors were coming, we could easily hold out for another month; but you absolutely must order in a new supply now."

"A new supply! And the beer not paid for yet at the bazaar! It's all very well for you to talk, but you forget it's easier to order than to pay."

"Oh, Max! how can you speak so?" was Jo's only answer. She might, if she chose, have retorted that it was he who drank so much wine,—though certainly *she* required the stimulant more than he did,—that the tins were rarely opened except on the numerous occasions when he brought home friends to dinner, and that it was he who grumbled if the dinner ever chanced to be a little scrimp. But she made no remark, and merely turned a piteous little face to her husband, which resulted in his immediately **exclaiming**: "Well, dear! don't worry about it." **And** then he continued, impelled to vent his wrath on something,—"But living is so confoundedly **dear** here, that a fellow **is** at his wits' end to know what to **do**. And then come visitors to ruin you altogether. . . . They asked for an answer by wire," he added, after a pause.

"Well, **it** does cost a good deal **of money**," said Jo; "but, oh dear! if it is to please them!—"

When the morning of the 5th came, the Van Elsts' neighbour over the way congratulated himself on **his single** blessedness, remarking **to** his dog, "That's what comes of getting married." He relented after a little, however, when his cup of coffee had put him in a somewhat better humour, and added: "After all, Van Elst is not so much more tied than I am. It isn't often he's interfered **with. It's a marvel how** that woman always finds time for everything."

To-day, however, Mrs Van Elst found it rather difficult to fit in everything. She was dreadfully busy; and, as might be expected, lost her temper a little, got cross with the "boys," gave Nonnie a push, and Max a sharp answer, and then was stung with remorse, and said, resentfully, "that she could not understand **why** Cousin Martendijk had not written sooner; it was such short notice,—such a nuisance!"

It was indeed. For when Van Elst came home at **midday**, and she met him with the query if everything did not look **nice? he saw** by her flushed cheeks, and the dark rings under her eyes, that she had over-exerted herself.

"Yes, very nice indeed; but you have been doing far too much again," he said, reproachfully. "Do take a rest now," he added, pouring her out a glass of port.

"Thanks, dear; but I must go and dress first."

"Yes, yes, presently," he said, as he seated himself beside her on the couch, holding her back as she struggled to free herself, and then resorting to endearments and caresses which he well knew would retard her escape.

Presently a carriage drove up to the door. Jo sprang up in dismay, and made a bold attempt at flight; but she was caught in the act, and found herself face to face with the Martendijks! Very smart did Mrs Martendijk look in her white gown, flounced and embroidered; and Jo became painfully conscious of her own dishevelled hair, her soiled and crumpled *kabaja*, and old faded *sarong*.*

"My wife was just going to dress," remarked Van Elst, aware of her embarrassment; "we did not expect you before two o'clock."

"Yes, so we wrote; but we changed our plans. It would have made us so late for luncheon, and that does not suit my complaint, you see," said Martendijk.

"If you had sent me word, I'd have made a point of being ready," said Jo.

"Well, of course, I had not time to think of that with all the bustle of starting. How d'ye do, Njo?" †

Now the reader must know that Njo, to whom Mrs Martendijk addressed this remark, was the Van Elsts' pride and joy. They had two dear little girls besides—very fine children, too,—but Njo; their Njo! when *he* came into the room, the father's and mother's eyes wandered involuntarily in his direction, and instinctively they would pause in their conversation to allow their visitors an opportunity of expressing their admiration, and their amazement, over "Such a fine little fellow! Such a *huge* child!"

"Our Njo" looked perfectly charming to-day. Mamma had brushed the pretty brown curls herself, to do him

---

* *Kabaja* is a long loose jacket, and *sarong* the Malay petticoat, forming the usual morning dress of Dutch ladies in the Indies.

† *Njo* is the Malay title given to the eldest boy in a family (like *baba* in Hindustani); for a girl it is *Nonnie*.

justice in the eyes of her husband's relations; and it was with his most roguish expression, and his usual winning manner, that he held up his little face with a merry laugh for the new aunt to kiss. And Aunt said nothing but "How d'ye do, Njo?"

Max glanced at his wife; but she replied by a sign which was meant to convey some such remark: "You can't blame her **for it**; she doesn't **understand** children," **and** that checked Max's rising resentment.

All this time the poor hostess was sitting very ill at ease; she kept up the conversation for a few minutes, and then asked if her cousin would not like to be shown to her room.

But Mrs Martendijk preferred to drink **a glass of port** first, so Jo had **to** remain sitting in the *kabaja* and *sarong*, which seemed to her more soiled and **faded every moment.**

II.

It was doubly **annoying to the dainty little hostess to be** surprised in such slovenly attire, because **this was her first** introduction to the Martendijks, and **she had set her heart** on making a good impression on them.

Though Emily and Johanna now met for the first time, their husbands were cousins and old acquaintances. Van Elst had been **under some** obligation to Martendijk's father; and although he had not much in common with his cousin, he had always remained on friendly terms with him, **in** acknowledgment of his uncle's past kindness.

They had both gone abroad at the same time, and after the lapse of ten years they thus met again, both married —the one managing partner in a sugar factory, the other notary in a prosperous place in the eastern province of Java.

There was no resemblance, not even a trace of family likeness, between the cousins.

Max was a strongly built man of middle height, broad-shouldered, and remarkably robust, with clear blue eyes, fresh colour, a full beard, and a laughing mouth; while Piet Martendijk was one of those long lean men whose appearance suggests that they have not been over fed in their young days, with scanty whiskers and hair, a long neck, and alarmingly thin legs; his complexion was sallow, his eyes lack-lustre, and his lips without a smile, which made some ladies pronounce him interesting, others distinguished, and men declare it a sin that he should have such a fine-looking wife.

She *was* a good-looking woman, with her handsome and graceful figure, her regular features, her luxuriant mass of dark hair, and her tasteful dress. But, after a few days' acquaintance, one found oneself wondering curiously if there was nothing could call forth a change in the expression of her eyes,—so cool was their gaze, and so indifferent, that a warm heart involuntarily shrank before them. Impassive faces of that sort have sometimes a certain fascination,—one is ready to imagine that the well-controlled features mask some deeply hidden sorrow, some tragic secret, that there is warm blood in the pale cheeks, and a passionate heart beating in the seemingly placid bosom. But Mrs Martendijk's whole personality was so insignificant, her talk so trifling, and her smile so cold, that it would have been difficult for the most romantically inclined to find her interesting; and for the Van Elsts it was absolutely impossible, as they knew her whole history.

A most commonplace one it was. The eldest daughter of a man who had made his money in the cheese trade, she had known Martendijk for years without thinking of a tenderer relationship, and had got engaged to him by correspondence, after he had been some time in the Indies, and the idea suddenly occurred to him of winning her as his wife. As soon as the old cheesemonger had made satisfactory

"ONE OF THOSE LONG THIN MEN."

inquiries into the prospects of the sugar trade, all arrangements had been completed by letter, and she had "come out."

It was a childless marriage. Both professed themselves highly satisfied with this state of matters,—an assertion which usually suggests the old story of the fox and the grapes, but which might gain credence in this case considering the peculiar tastes and dispositions of the couple.

Fresh from her toilet, in her dainty white *kabaja*, with the faintest touch of colour lending a downy softness to her pretty little face, Mrs Van Elst stood in the verandah awaiting her guests.

With the self-complacency of an active housewife she let her eye rove over the tempting table, to the sideboard with its sparkling crystal, and to the side-table where the dishes stood ready to be handed round. "What a shame to let everything get cold," she said to herself, greeting Max as he entered with the query if the "boy" had not announced luncheon.

"Yes, and I have called them myself too," says Max, a little crossly, for he loves to have the curry served hot, "but they don't seem to be ready yet. How splendid it looks," he continues, and, with a furtive glance round to make sure that the children are out of the way, he helps himself from one of the dishes to a leg of roast fowl. He has abundant time to pick the bone leisurely before the guests appear, with the immediate request from Emily that the door may be closed.

"Oh, cousin," Max exclaims, "it will be so frightfully stuffy here!"

"Yes, but there's such a draught just now; and that's so dangerous for Piet's complaint, you see. So—if you don't mind?"

They seat themselves, and the "boys" begin to wait. Jo is glad to see that the cook has exerted herself to the very utmost, and throws a contented little nod across to her husband, as much as to say, " Now, haven't you a clever little wife?" to which he replies convincingly by helping himself very liberally from the various dishes.

All at once Jo discovers that Cousin Martendijk is eating away at *dry rice!*

"Won't you have some curry?" she asks; "or perhaps you would rather——"

"No, thank you, cousin, I often eat my rice dry."

"Do have a little piece of fricassee, then!" she exclaims in dismay, as he lets even that indispensable dish pass.

"No, it's so dangerous to eat fricassee. You never know what it's made of. And when one is a martyr to indigestion——"

"Oh, come," Max exclaims impatiently, "you don't need to be afraid of anything of that kind here. Jo always makes the fricassee herself, and most delicious it is, I assure you."

"Well, a small piece then."

Mrs Martendijk ate very little also; and Jo could not help noticing how Cousin Martendijk, who was rather short-sighted, gave a disdainful sniff every now and then at one or other of the dishes, and how his wife, without even honouring them with a glance, sent away one after another with a brief but decisive "*tida.*"*

My gentle readers will admit that this was a very trying experience for a hostess. Jo begins all at once to doubt her own domestic capabilities, and the painful conviction grows upon her that the fowl must be very tough, and the fish not fresh, and that there is a want of variety. A sort of dumb rage at the cook gradually takes possession of her,—she has such a trick of making the *sambalans* too hot; and she casts a vindictive glance at the "boy" when he forgets to hand round the pickles. And when the pickles are likewise smelt,

---

* "No."

and examined, and declined, she feels her face blaze, and her appetite vanish, and a wild longing comes over her for the moment when she can give the signal to rise from table.

"My dear cousin," began Emily the next morning, following Jo into the store-room, where she was busy giving out provisions, "I think you were rather hurt at our eating so little yesterday, were you not?"

"Well, to tell the truth——"

"Now then, to put it all right, I'll just tell you what was the real reason. You use cocoa-nut oil, don't you? and you don't make it at home! I tasted that at once."

"No, that is true; the cook has enough to do as it is."

"Oh, my dear! don't you pay any attention to a cook like that. They can easily get through all their work. And do you know why Piet ate so little? Everything was too strong for him. I'm just telling you, you know, so that you may manage things better another time."

"Yes, but that won't be so very easy," Jo ventured, "because—well, you see, my husband likes his food very highly seasoned."

"That *is* a pity. But," continued Emily, with an amiable little laugh, "I know what you can do. Have some *sambal** made separately for him, and he can mix it with his food. We must adapt ourselves to one another, must we not?"

"Oh, certainly," said Jo, "if there happens to be anything else you don't care for, or that is bad for Cousin Martendijk's inside——"

"Oh, no, thank you! We had a delicious dinner yesterday evening. Your cook is a capital hand. Oh, wait a moment, though, I had nearly forgotten. My good man is accustomed to have a cup of *bouillon* about eleven o'clock,

---

* *Sambal* answers to the curry of British India, and is as various in its composition.

and I a cup of chocolate—but it must be *chicken*-broth; he is not allowed beef-tea."

"Very well," said Jo, a vision immediately rising before her of the **wrath of** her **cook** when told that not only was she expected to make the cocoa-nut oil herself, but to **prepare** *kaldoe** and chocolate **at** the very busiest hour **of the** morning. It was enough to make her give notice on the spot.

Mrs Van Elst, to tell the truth, stood **in** considerable awe of this cook, who was highly proficient in **her** art, used little butter, and did not appropriate much of the marketing money; and, I appeal to you, what mistress would not tremble at the thought of losing such a **treasure?**

She paved the way, therefore, with some friendly remarks, and even went the length of promising a new *sarong* before she broached *the* subject; and flattered **herself** that all was going to end smoothly, when cook all **at once snatched up** a basket of potatoes with one vicious jerk, **and** with another laid hold of the rice, and closed the door of the store-room behind her with a bang that thrilled her mistress from head to foot. Jo knew what to expect.

For the rest, Emily supplied **a** ready answer **to** the **great** question which haunts Indian no less than Dutch housewives: what are we to have for dinner to-day? **It was** virtually she who proposed the *menu* every day. "**Do you** know what I'd make to-day?" she would remark to Jo;— "one of those dishes **of** macaroni, with ham and cheese." Or, "If you want to give Martendijk a treat, dear cousin, give him asparagus, he's wild about that." Or, "Do you never make tarts, Jo?—You do?—Well, **I have a** delicious recipe for one I can lend you if you **like.**"

It was really very kind of Emily, Jo thought; and she had little more cause to complain **of** her guest's want of

---

* Broth.

appetite, especially as **Mrs Martendijk** had taken upon herself to make sure that nothing came to table which might prove injurious to her husband's digestion.

III.

Visiting is more of a burden than a pleasure in Holland, where people are confined within such narrow limits, and where the usual routine of daily life must be gone on with as usual.

The Dutch host may express the hope that you will "make yourself quite at home," adding that you are perfectly free to do what you like; but when bedtime comes, he also informs you that they breakfast at eight sharp, and his wife asks you in the sweetest manner possible to be so good as not to keep the light burning; and both are rather hurt if you do not evince any great anxiety to cultivate the acquaintance of all their friends, and think it rather "strange" if you go out on your own account.

Only in the Indies can one "make one's self quite at home," and that undoubtedly accounts for the interchange of visits being so much more common there than with us, and for people who are barely acquainted beforehand finding it possible to stay weeks and even months with one another without inconvenience to host or guest.

Even in the Indies, however, much depends on whether or not the visitors are located in a detached part of the house. This is an arrangement which commends itself especially to those who have children with them. There are so many details to be attended to, and arrangements made in that case, that the close proximity to strangers is a little awkward, and the visitor has rather an anxious time of it in Holland. Every mother knows the haunting dread lest the baby should take it into its head to indulge in a prolonged fit of screaming in the middle of her host's mid-day nap, and she **is** painfully aware that childish freaks and misdemeanours may not always meet with sympathy in their new surroundings.

But in the Indies these fears and worries are unknown. The children are quartered **in** the detached part of the house, where they may romp and scream to their hearts' content ; and there is no risk of interference if punishment is required, nor need to blush for shame at one's powerlessness under the rule of a spoilt four-year-old tyrant.

Others, besides happy parents, have reason to be grateful for the Indian arrangement,—the young man with his late hours, the young lady with her delicate little traffic in *billets-doux* and bouquets, for instance. And it commends itself highly to many a young couple, when the husband takes a fancy to revive the days of courtship, or the young wife has set her heart on a charming blue dress in the bazaar,—so cheap, and blue is just the colour he likes her best in,—and so on. (We all know the sort of talk that goes on, and how it ends.) And should it happen—for such things **do** occur— that they have a slight disagreement, and the tender husband's tone waxes warm, and his sweet little wife has recourse to tears,—well, the courtyard is wide, and the host and hostess are totally unaware of any disturbance; so, presently they trip into the verandah as staid and as charming as if they never heard of " spooning," not to speak of squabbling. It is not at all unlikely that the host himself may have profited by their absence, "*pour laver son linge sale en famille.*"

The Van Elsts had a very nice visitors' room detached from the rest of the house, with a verandah opening on a pretty flower-garden. Jo was in the habit of having her visitors' breakfast set in this front verandah, chiefly because she liked to devote the morning undisturbed to her husband and children, and because, moreover, it was more convenient for all domestic arrangements.

But the very first morning after their arrival, Emily came, laughing, to say that they thought it would be so much more sociable to breakfast altogether, especially as Piet fancied it was a little damp over the way, and he had to guard carefully against damp on account of his complaint.

The Van Elsts thought it charming of their guests to be so sociably inclined, but it was a little awkward nevertheless; and Jo wondered, with some surprise, how Emily did not understand that, though it might be pleasanter for herself, it might be decidedly inconvenient for the mother of three children to have her visitors about her so early.

Jo had a great deal to do in the mornings, like all Indian ladies, though Dutch housewives, we know, are inclined to be sceptical on that point. The children had to be bathed, —an operation she liked to superintend in person,—the clothes to be looked over, the washing and sewing given out, the dinner ordered, and the thousand and one little domestic duties attended to; it was generally eleven o'clock before she was ready to sit down quietly.

There was, of course, more than usual to do with the Martindijks in the house, but Jo was ready at last, and having just about an hour to spare, she was anxious to finish the little frock over which she had been busy for some time, and which was only waiting for the buttons and trimming.

"I hope I'm not intruding, Cousin Jo?" said a suave voice, and Emily came in, and continued, regardless of the frock Jo held in her hand, "Look here! I have a skirt which doesn't hang well; do you think you can see what's the matter with it? I hear you are so neat-handed!"

Jo laid the little frock aside with a sigh, and began with deft fingers to examine the drapery. The fault was soon detected. The skirt must be unpicked, the folds relaid and pinned down; and in the middle of this process, Emily suggested sweetly that it was more than time Piet had his broth. Jo ran off with all speed to the kitchen, where cook received her with a withering glance, and when her mistress asked for the *kaldoe*, assumed an air of dense stupidity which checked all further inquiry. Only by dint of lifting one lid after another did **Mrs Van** Elst at length discover a fowl floating in tepid water.

Jo was not accustomed to yield,—not even to her invaluable cook,—nor had she forgotten how to work in the Indies; so, soon **she had** the *kaldoe* simmering **over a** moderate fire, and the chocolate all ready save **the boiling** water. But **to procure** boiling water seemed to require some magic quite **beyond the powers of an** ordinary **cook;** an immense **kettle, full to the brim, was** suspended **over a** low fire, the wood was apparently damp, the kitchen full of smoke, and not a single clean saucepan was to be found. . . . When Mrs Van Elst at last carried in the two cups, it certainly **was** not only the heat which flushed her cheeks and made her hands tremble!

Emily did not seem to notice her agitation; she thanked her cousin quite cordially for the trouble she had taken, evidently found the fragrant chocolate very much to her liking, tasted the *kaldoe* critically, and when Jo expressed the fear that it was not strong enough, she smiled goodnaturedly, and had no doubt it would be **better to**morrow!

Her next proceeding **was to** beg Jo to try on the altered skirt, so that she could judge better of the draping, and the time was spent in pinning and laying folds till the "boy" came to announce dinner.

Jo laid away the unfinished frock, hoping that perhaps to-morrow she might make up for lost time. But next morning Emily proposed a visit to the Chinese quarter, if her cousin would be so good as go with her,—she had some shopping to do. And the third morning, just as Jo had once more produced her work, Emily, who was sociably inclined, and did not care to be alone, came to beg her cousin to be so very kind as to explain to her how that lovely collar was made that she had on yesterday.

Oh, certainly! Jo would tell her,—so much embroidery, and lace, and . . . . "Wait a minute!" cried Emily; "I'll just fetch what we need, and you can help me; you are so clever at these things—much cleverer than I am! This is a splendid chance, Jo, for me to go over my wardrobe; it is so much cheaper to do up things one's self than to be always going to a milliner or dressmaker—and you *will* help me, won't you?"

IV.

"Just listen to this!" exclaimed Van Elst, reading the foreign telegrams at the tea-table that afternoon. "Russia has declared war against Turkey."

"Indeed!" remarked Martendijk indifferently. "Well, I thought it would come to that in the end."

"It's really terrible," Max went on. "How many wars does that make within our recollection? And in our much-vaunted nineteenth century too! I hoped they would have been able to avert this."

"Have your people Turkish or Russian bonds?"

"No; why on earth should you think that?"

"Oh, because you are so interested in that war. You would be in a bad way in that case. It is great folly. We don't have anything to do with that sort of thing either—do we, Emily?"

"No, indeed," said Emily. "As far as we are concerned, all Europe can go to war."

"Alas!" cried Jo, who had not been listening to this dialogue between the couple. "What terrible news, Max! To think of the waste of strong young lives, and all the wives and mothers who are left at home." And instinctively she drew little Jan towards her, and pressed him close.

"Well, there's no danger for *him* in the meantime," said Martendijk; and Mr and Mrs Van Elst glanced at one another, as they had so often done during the past few days, as if to ask what manner of people these cousins could be.

Mrs Martendijk was also glancing through a newspaper, and, suddenly turning to her husband, she exclaimed, "What did I prophesy, Piet? Van Dalem is in the bankruptcy court."

"Well, well!" said Piet. "After all, what else was to be expected. It's the last straw breaks the camel's back! It is the man's own fault. You must understand, Max," he continued, addressing his cousin, "this Van Dalem was a near neighbour of ours. He came into a splendid business, and might have been rolling in wealth in a few years; but you never saw such a spendthrift. He was always thrusting himself forward, always entertaining, always having visitors——"

"Yes," affirmed Emily; "and the worst of it was, while his wife was giving parties, he was lending money right and left,—standing security, advancing money to every beggar who came to him; he said he could not refuse."

"Real good-natured folk, then?" asked Van Elst.

"Oh, yes, good-natured enough as far as that went. I can't tell you how many widows he has given shelter to, how many little waifs she took in from the native village (they have no children of their own), how many forced sales he has put a stop to——"

"Poor fellow," cried Max, "I wish I could do something for him."

"It's easy to say that, Max," interposed Martendijk; "but," and he pulled his thin whiskers meditatively, "it comes to be a question if it is right to sympathise with people of that kind. Is it not their own fault that they have gone down in the world? Is it not inexcusable to run through one's money in that way?"

24

"Inexcusable? I don't agree with you there. At least he has run through it in a way which speaks well for his heart, if not for his good sense."

"I am anxious to see if people will help him in his turn," said Emily, in a tone which irritated Van Elst beyond measure.

"Of course they will," he said, curtly.

"Do you think so?" asked Martendijk, with some expression for once in his weak face. "People are, as a rule, more ready to look you up when they need you than when you need them. He certainly had a great many friends; but we know what that amounts to. In any case," he continued after a pause, "it is safest to make sure that you will never be dependent on any one's help."

"That is true," said Max. But as he spoke he left his seat abruptly, and went to have a look at the flowers with little Jan. Jo very soon followed him. It was very evident that he had lost his temper; and she was always ready in such an emergency to do her best to drive away the clouds as quickly as possible.

"What's the matter, dear?"

"Oh! nothing. Rather disgusted; that's all. How do you like the Martendijks, Jo?"

"Oh! not particularly. Perhaps it would be better to suspend our judgment of them for a little, Max."

"I don't see it," said Max, sharply. "But, Jo, do you know what we might do?" he added, hastily, seeing her shrink at his vehemence, "go for a drive just now; then Jan can go too."

"Oh! yes, papa," cried Jan, delightfully, "and sit on the box."

"My dear, the horses have been too far to-day already. Emily drove to the Chinese camp, and was out for more than two hours."

"*Indeed!*" said Max. "Well, then, for goodness' sake,

let us stop at home. That will be very nice too, won't it, Jan? and we'll build a fortress."

Jo was satisfied that the clouds were fast dispersing; she took her husband's arm, and exerted herself to be specially bright and charming, chattering to him about the children, and all sorts of interesting things, and finally assisting at his toilet,—a favour he particularly enjoyed,—and prattling all manner of pretty compliments to him.

Max was in high good-humour when he left her to go for a turn with Jan.

When Jo appeared, after a hasty toilet, she found their cousins in the verandah before her, busy with the illustrated papers.

That was a most innocent pastime certainly; but, alas! Martendijk had taken possession of Max's place and chair.

Now Mrs Van Elst was the most accommodating little person imaginable, and would have given up *her* chair to any one in the world; but she was quite different where *Max* was concerned.

"Oh! there's my husband coming," she exclaimed in a minute or two, as he came up the drive with Jan; and as Martendijk showed not the slightest disposition to take the hint, she added, as pleasantly as she could, "Martendijk, I'm sure you are not aware that that is Max's place?"

"Yes, dear cousin," said Martendijk, stretching himself with an air of contentment. "To tell you the truth, I was quite aware of the fact; but Emily chose this place for me, because there are such draughts everywhere else."

"Oh! I am sure Cousin Max will be glad to give up his place to you for a little,—won't you, Max?" Emily struck in.

To Jo's relief, her husband assented, and Martendijk made himself as comfortable as he could in his host's chair.

The children came in from their walk, and stayed as usual

with papa and mamma till bedtime,—a habit as pleasant for parents as for guests.

They formed a pretty group, the three innocent child-heads, and at the sight Max's and Jo's beaming eyes met, and at last the happy little wife could not refrain from the question,—

"Don't you two think our children are little angels?"

"Yes, darlings!" responded Emily. "So good and sweet-tempered; especially little Jan, he doesn't give you much trouble now."

"*Trouble!*" exclaimed Jo. "Oh! not one of them gives any trouble,—only a very little when they are ill. But as long as they keep well I have nothing but pleasure in them."

And she spoke the truth, for all cares and anxieties were light to her, because so willingly borne.

"I'd not mind having a boy like this, about three or four," Emily continued, drawing little Jan to her caressingly; "but a baby like *that*" (with a glance at "charming little Ada") "I consider *horrible*."

"*Horrible!*" Jo shrank from her in dismay, indignant that any one should speak so. But her anger was transient, for she immediately remembered that it was not poor Emily's fault that she had such strange ideas; she really did not know what it was to have children of her own.

V.

The Martendijks had been about three weeks with the Van Elsts, when the solitary bachelor over the way began to observe some change in his neighbours.

The notary began to go earlier to his office, and to come home later. The little wife, of whom he was growing rather fond by dint of watching her so long, did not take her walks so regularly; and when she played with the children in the garden in the morning, her laugh sounded less merry than it once did. When the old gentleman (who seemed to have assumed this privilege of observing his neighbours with special interest because it *might have been* his lot to have just such another family) noticed that **Mr Van** Elst **looked cross,** and his wife very wearied, he began **to** grow uneasy, and at last set on foot inquiries through the medium **of** his own "boys" and those **of** his neighbours, which resulted in the reassuring news **that** no one was ill. After that the old bachelor did not know what to make of it.

And **yet** the explanation was simple enough!

To be ousted from your favourite seat, to **have tasteless food set before you, to** see **your** delicate wife **tired to death,** your horses over-driven, your **store-room plundered, all this** is very easy **to** bear,—nay, **may even** be reckoned among the pleasures **of** hospitality, if your visitors are agreeable people, whose society compensates for the **lack** of the usual cosy *tête-à-tête*, and whose cordial **interest in all your** concerns proves that they like **you and appreciate the** friendship you show them. But, **when you see that your** guests regard you merely as **convenient people** to spend some time with,—that they take advantage of your hospitality, and honour you with no **special** cordiality in return, —**when** they remind **you,** by their treatment, of certain **fruits** you throw away **once** the juice is squeezed out, it **is** impossible **to** submit to the visitation **with a very** good grace!

That certainly was the case here.

Van Elst, moreover, with his warm temperament and strength **of** character, could **ill** brook his cold-blooded **cousin.** He liked **men** to be firm, **and** women tender-hearted; and Piet was so weak, and Emily so cold, and the two couples so directly opposed to each other in all their sentiments and opinions, that the most innocent conversations **often led to** collision. When, for example,

Van Elst brought home the news one day that one of their acquaintances had been suddenly taken ill, and Jo asked, with a quaver in her voice and tears in her eyes, if she could do anything to help the poor wife, Emily scarcely listened, and Piet only to inquire anxiously what was the matter—he hoped nothing infectious!

With regard to society, there was great diversity of opinion between the couples. Up country in the Indies it is possible to live on such terms with all the Europeans as to avoid giving offence, while at the same time one cannot be intimate with all. One comes across many people there who are wealthy, who entertain, and are to a certain extent admitted into society, but of so low a stamp intellectually and morally that it is impossible for respectable families to associate familiarly with them.

The Van Elsts had thus soon chosen their own friends, and to this select circle they had introduced their guests.

But the Martendijks struck up acquaintance with a family with whom they had no wish to become intimate.

"Good gracious!" said Max, who did not approve of this at all; "what is there in that man to take your fancy?"

"Not much," replied Martendijk.

"Surely his wife isn't the attraction, then?—a stupid insignificant creature like that!"

"Yes, she is very stupid," said Martendijk. "But she is a capital cook," he added, after a moment.

"Well, but they're not people to get so very intimate with. Perhaps you don't know that he has a very shady reputation,—it is well known that he got that factory into his hands by a very dirty trick. They say he made the former owner drunk, and then——"

"That's very likely true," interposed Martendijk coolly; "he looks to me just that sort of man. But that does not prevent his keeping capital wine, and being very generous with his help——"

"For any sake hold your tongue!" cried Max, suddenly turning his back on his guest.

But the most violent explosion took place one morning at the breakfast-table, when the conversation turned upon one of their aunts—a sister of Martendijk's father and Max's mother—who was in great poverty, and had been very unfortunate.

"I have not troubled my head about her for years," said Piet. "I may tell you I make a point of interesting myself only in my respectable relatives."

"You mean in those who have got on well in the world," observed Max. "Aunt Liza is a worthy respectable woman, whose only fault is her poverty."

"But she had no position at all in Delft," said Emily. (Martendijk was silent: he preferred not to argue with his cousin when Max's eyes flashed like that.) "She dealt in tea, I think, or knitting-cotton, or something of that kind."

"Yes, just so, in *tea*," said Max; "exactly in the same way as your husband deals in sugar, and your father in cheese. Good morning!"

"Good gracious, Jo, what a temper your husband is in!" exclaimed Emily, who was determined not to take offence, because she was very comfortable with Martendijk's relatives, and the building at their own place at Soeka-Manies —the real reason for their visiting—was still going on.

"Yes," said Martendijk, the courage of his opinions returning as soon as he heard Max drive away; "I don't see why on earth he should get so excited!"

What surprised the Van Elsts more than anything else, was the relation of the couple to one another. The same man and woman, who had not one grain of sympathy for the troubles of others, or for the most terrible national calamity, and who were totally impervious to the sufferings of even their friends and relations, were full of devotion to one another.

If Piet was not quite the thing, Emily was full of anxiety; and if she looked worried, Piet did his best to conquer his despondency. In short, disagreeable though they were in every other respect, they were a model couple. It was difficult for a third person to start any subject of conversation with them, because nothing interested them which did not affect themselves directly or indirectly; but they were never at a loss for a subject when by themselves, and their conversation was inexhaustible so long as they could devote themselves unreservedly to the discussion of their own affairs, bringing every effort of mind to bear on what concerned them alone.

Money was a favourite topic: how they could enjoy this or that together—it was always together!—without much expense; how to manage their domestic expenditure most satisfactorily; how to invest a small sum securely—and so on.

They spent so long over these interesting details, that it was impossible for outsiders to take any part in their discussions.

VI.

"Just look here a minute, Max; is it my fancy, or does Jan look a little pale to-day?" asked Mrs Van Elst one morning, as she went out to the verandah to see her husband off.

"Of course it is your fancy," said Max, who made a point of never allowing that any of the children were ill,—a device intended to calm their nervous mother, but which always had precisely the contrary effect. "Come here a moment, Njo; your mother says you're not well. Come, my boy, tell me what's the matter with you," he added less carelessly, as Jan, usually anything but slow to respond to his father's call, dragged himself listlessly towards them, and sank down upon a chair.

"Not comf'ble, papa—headache!" was all he vouchsafed.

Max took him on his knee, and glanced at his wife. Yes, the old story; she was pale, her lips trembled, and her eyes were bent tenderly and anxiously on the child. It was this readiness to take alarm which caused Jo more suffering than the patient, whenever her husband or children were ailing.

"Shall we just send for the doctor, dear?"

"No; did I ever!" cried Max. "The man would think we were mad. Because Njo has a little headache, forsooth! Come, my boy, go and play."

"*Play!* Good gracious! Max, just feel how hot his head is."

"Well, put him to bed then. You can do that at least," and he laughed, as it seemed to her, heartlessly, and called her "a silly thing"—a jocular remark which was met by none of Jo's usual repartees.

"Papa must come too," was Jan's command, and we know that no general is better obeyed by his soldiers than a sick child by its parents. So Max carried his boy first over one shoulder, then over the other, after which he had to creep on all fours round the room, roaring like a lion, before Njo would be laid down. The patient was not particularly disposed to go to sleep; he allowed papa to coddle him, and mamma to bring him lemonade, and did as many children do when much notice is taken of their ailments—made himself out much worse than he really was.

When it was really impossible for his father to remain longer, he coaxed and whimpered a little, and finally cried himself to sleep, so that Jo was free to enjoy a quiet hour by his bedside with her work-basket, for every available moment must be snatched to make up for the time lost through Emily's visit.

Their visitors had gone out very early that morning to call on one of their new acquaintances, a sugar manufacturer like Martendijk. It was so pleasant to come across some one in your own line, he remarked; they could discuss one thing and another while driving or walking together, and one got many a hint and idea in that way.

On their return home, the "boy" told them "Sinjo Jan" was ill.

"Oh, dear! that's always the worst of visiting where there are children," said Martendijk, as he sipped his *bouillon;* "there's always something wrong."

"Well, this would not be much to speak of," said Emily, "only I'm afraid it may interfere with to-morrow evening."

It must be explained that the Martendijks had talked so much about the attention shown to them on all sides as the Van Elsts' guests (and they certainly had not been slow to avail themselves of the social advantages of the neighbourhood), that Jo felt at last obliged to give a small party in acknowledgment of the courtesy shown to them.

Her guests need never know all it had cost her to talk Max over, and how, when one argument after another failed to win over her perverse lord and master, she had at last taken refuge in that weapon which loses its power when too often used, and is the very last resort therefore of a clever woman—I mean tears.

For, though Jo would hardly admit the fact even to herself, Max had not been just altogether pleasant to deal with of late,—indeed, he had really been quite disagreeable and cross, and very unwilling to acknowledge himself in the wrong.

His liver had been bothering him for some little time (no wonder he grumbled), and Jo, only too ready to find satisfactory excuses for his ill-temper, was glad enough to reiterate constantly to her visitors, who had also a good deal to stand from his bearish ways, how the liver affects the temper, and how wretched it makes one feel.

This did not prevent their cousins from assuring one another repeatedly, once they were safe in their own room, that Max was a disagreeable fellow, and that were it not for the comfortable quarters they were in, and the building going on at home, they would remain no longer. For so wrapt up were they in themselves and in one another, and so absorbing was their *egoïsme à deux*, that it was impossible for them to realise how actions and remarks like theirs affected others; therefore, of course, they blamed Cousin Max for the rather strained relations which had come about.

As soon as she had drunk her chocolate, Emily betook herself to the nursery to see what were the prospects for the party.

"Well, dear cousin," she began, making no attempt to lower her somewhat harsh voice, "what is this I hear? Is little Jan ill?"

"I am very much afraid he is," said Jo; "he is so restless in his sleep."

"A little feverish, perhaps," said Emily, taking the child's hand in her own for a moment. "I'd give him a good dose of quinine," she continued, "and he'll be all right by to-morrow evening."

"Why to-morrow evening," asked Jo, puzzled.

"Did I ever! Have you forgotten all about that? Why, it was to-morrow evening we were to have that party."

"Dear me, so it was," cried Jo. "I'd nearly forgotten all about it. But, of course, if he is ill it will have to be put off."

"Oh, yes, of course," said Emily, "if he is ill. But it's surely nothing serious. You always get frightened so quickly."

"Yes, I do, it is true; and it really can't be anything. But oh, Emily, he is such an angel, my Njo! and you always see that particularly sweet children don't live long."

The wet eyelashes and quivering lips were not without their effect even on cold Mrs Martendijk.

"Well, well," she said kindly, "I would not worry about that. Jan has his naughty fits just like other boys; and besides, if all the children were to die whose mothers consider them 'almost *too* good' for this world, there would not be many left."

Seeing how nervous Jo got, and how the event generally proved her fears groundless, Max was always making resolutions not to yield to such exaggerated anxiety another time. So when he came home at mid-day and found his wife still occupied with the child, he coolly carried her off to another room, and gently but firmly forbade her to leave it until she had rested for a few hours.

Jo was too tired to resist, and soon fell asleep. She did not awake till late in the afternoon, for which she could not forgive herself, though it was, in fact, the best thing that could have happened, considering the disturbed night she was to have. It did not need much persuasion to induce Max to send for the doctor next morning.

Emily took care to be in the verandah when he stopped to say a few words to Mrs Van Elst after his visit to the little patient.

"There's not much the matter is there, doctor?" she asked.

"No—at least I think not," was his reply. "It's not easy to predict in a case of illness, but, as far as appearances go, it seems to me an ordinary cold."

"There, you see, Jo, what did we all tell you? You do get anxious so soon!"

"Well, you see, I have so much to lose," said Jo deprecatingly.

"If it gives you any pleasure to worry," said the doctor, "you had better do so about yourself, and not about that sturdy little chap,"—and with a compassionate glance at the young wife, who had already been so often a patient of his, he took her hand in his own. "You're not looking so well as you did, Mrs Van Elst," he said. "You wear yourself out, and don't do enough to get up your strength. I shall have to scold in good earnest—or speak to Van Elst."

"Oh, no, for goodness' sake, don't do that!" exclaimed Jo, glad that Max was safe in his office. "How angry he would be!"

"Well, Jo," said her guest, when the doctor had gone, "that *is* a relief. An ordinary cold, it will be better in a day or two. Now **let us set to** work to get ready for the party."

"Oh, dear Emily, **what do** you think? Shall we not rather put it off?"

"Put it off? and why? **Come, Jo, what's** the matter with you? All the invitations are out already."

"I'd like to have it for your sake," Jo began again; "you know that, don't **you**? But I am *so* tired! I never closed an eye last night; and there is **so** much to be done—baking, and all that."

"Well," said Emily, "surely your maid can help you?"

"Siah? Oh, no; she must stay with Njo—she's his old 'baboe.'* No, really, it can't be managed. Oh, if you only knew how dead tired **I am**!" and the poor little woman sank into a chair, and closed **her** eyes as if to shut out the mountain of work that the mere thought of the party conjured up.

"If *I* undertook all the trouble," asked Emily, after a moment's reflection, "could we go on with it then?"

"Oh yes," said Jo, "if you would be so very good."

She was too much absorbed in her sick child to trouble herself much about the success **of** the party, else she would have been decidedly uneasy; for it had gradually dawned upon **her** that Emily did not know much of the noble art of cookery. Notwithstanding her great readiness to recom-

---

* The Javanese equivalent to "ayah."

mend dishes and to lend recipes, she had never yet concocted anything herself; and even when Jo had begged her to help with a few domestic duties on specially busy days, she had always tried to get out of it. To-day it was quite different, however.

She asked for the keys, and in ten minutes had all the "boys" and maids hard at work; while she herself was here, there, and everywhere, thinking of everything,—making cakes, planning the *menu*, and all with a deftness and briskness which were quite enviable.

"Oh dear!" thought Jo, when she saw her cousin's activity, "if she had only helped me like that sooner, how much nicer it would have been having visitors."

Jo arranged the flowers; Martendijk the card-tables; Emily superintended the supper; and by mid-day everything was ready.

Emily went to take a nap, while her hostess did the same, so as to be bright and fresh when the evening came.

And so probably she would have been, after a quiet undisturbed sleep; but the little patient grew worse about the middle of the day; and when his father came home, he saw at once that the child was feverish.

"Oh, dear Max," sighed Jo, "what a worry! A sick child, and that party in the evening!"

"*Party!*" cried Max, to his wife's great consternation. "It's out of the question. Did you think I'd ever allow that? Certainly not. What a mad idea to think of having people here to-night! Emily's at the bottom of that, I'll be bound."

"No, indeed, dear. I was quite anxious for it too," pleaded Jo, shielding her guest at the expense of her own truthfulness. "And oh, Max, Emily has been so good; she arranged everything, and I have had nothing at all to do."

"Of course she helps you now, as it's her party, and she

is bent on **having** her own way,—but **I'll soon** see who **is master** in my house. The party will *not* **go on**, I tell you. I'll have the people put off. Where are the **boys?**"

Van Elst had spoken so loud in his passionate outburst, that it needed no eavesdropping to find out his intentions; and perhaps that was the reason that Emily appeared so opportunely just then.

"Oh! **excuse me, cousin,**" he exclaimed apologetically, running against her in his hurry. "Do you know where the boys are?"

"They are round **at the back,**" said **Mrs** Martendijk, looking brighter and livelier than **he had** ever seen her. "Look here, cousin," and **she took his arm** confidentially **to** lead him to **the** back verandah, "have we not worked well to-day? Everything **is ready**——"

"But the party can——" began **Max.**

"And should you like to see what you're going to have to-night?" And in the same friendly manner **he** was conducted to the pantry. "Just look **at** that magnificent trifle. And are not the tarts a success? **But** the *pâtés* are *the* thing. They **look** just as if they **came** straight from the best confectioner's—do they not?"

"I am really sorry you have **had** so much trouble, and **I** must say it all looks beautiful; but the party cannot possibly go on," repeated Max, firmly.

"What do you say?"

"Yes; it's a great pity, and **I** can understand how annoyed you feel; but Jan is decidedly worse. . . ."

Emily **had** recovered **her** composure by this time.

"Jan **worse! My** word! **I had no idea** of that," she cried. "Gracious! cousin, if **I had** known that an hour sooner; and now the punch is made!"

It was now Max's turn to be disconcerted.

"What do you say?" he exclaimed.

"Well, it was time it was done, you see;" and Emily

seated herself. "One would really need to know everything beforehand," she went on, coolly; "then we should at least not have opened those fine wines and the expensive champagne. The supper will cost a great deal too, to be sure, and the money's all thrown away now; but we can eat everything some time or other among ourselves."

"The *punch* won't keep, I suppose?" asked Max.

"Oh no! it *is* a pity Jan is so ill."

"Oh, he's not so very much worse!" exclaimed Max impatiently. "But what a wretched amount of stuff," he added, after a moment, when he had made a rapid mental calculation of the needless expense, and realised how odious it would be to see Piet and Emily devouring all the dainties. "If only Jo was not so very tired."

"Yes; it would be very unfortunate if she were not able to appear. But we can always see how Jan is; and if she were to decide at the last moment to stay with the child,— well, I'd be glad to do the honours."

"For goodness' sake let it be, then," said Max; and as his guest made her escape as fast as she could, without prejudice to her dignity, he sent a wish after her which was more expressive than courteous.

Emily only enjoyed a little laugh at his helpless fury, congratulating herself on the success of her diplomacy, for on hearing about half-an-hour before that the child was worse, she had given orders to have the punch mixed; and when she stepped into the store-room, she was met with a request from Piet, who had been told off to superintend, to taste and see if the ingredients were right.

VII.

Jo did *not* appear that evening. Jan complained of sore throat; and the mother, in her dread of diphtheria, sent for the doctor at once, and remained at the child's bedside, in spite of his assurances that nothing was the matter. Emily did the honours, and appeared to enjoy it.

Though each of the guests had privately resolved not to stay late for the little boy's sake, it was two o'clock before the last had departed, and three before the house was quiet. **Indeed** absolute quiet there never was that whole night, for **Jo, as** she lay awake, heard **first** all sorts of unaccountable sounds proceeding from the guests' apartment, and **then an** excited calling out for **servants,** who either could **not or** would not hear, followed **by a** knocking **at her own door,** and an agitated demand for laudanum, and **a** confused story about salad and punch, which might be the death of people who suffered from **internal** complaints. **Tea must be** infused, and hot-water bottles filled; but **when Jo sprang** up eager to go and help, her husband held her back authoritatively. He had feigned to **be asleep all the** time, but when the door was shut, while the strange sounds continued to be heard, then he was seized with such an uncontrollable fit of laughter, that **Jo** was infected by his merriment, and lay in mortal terror lest Emily should hear them, or Jan be awakened.

But Jan was the **last to think of** awaking. He slept not only the whole night, but far into the morning. Max was not permitted to go to his office before he should awake, for just as she would have thought it "very alarming" if he had not slept at all, so it seemed to be "very alarming" that **he** should sleep so long.

At last, about nine o'clock, he opened his eyes. The rest seemed to have done him good, for not only did he demand bread and butter, but, **as soon** as his glance fell on the new box of bricks papa had bought for him the day before, he jumped out of bed, and seated himself on the floor to play, as if **nothing had happened.**

"How is the poor little throat?" asked Jo, as soon as she had recovered from her glad surprise.

"My throat?" repeated the child wonderingly; "my throat is not ill."

Max was so relieved, and thought it such a capital joke that he burst out laughing; even the Martendijks laughed; and Jo tried to join in, but the joy was too sudden after the anxiety she had undergone, and she broke into a hysterical fit of weeping instead.

"There you are now! I told you so—insisting on the party like that!" cried Van Elst, losing his temper completely.

"What kind of an outbreak is that?" asked Emily, forgetting the repairs at home for the moment, in order to give vent to her indignation.

"What is it? It is your fault, Emily, if she is laid up. I could have told you beforehand,—Jo is not fit for all that worry and fuss!"

Emily followed her husband from the room—the thought of the building recurring to her; while Van Elst led his wife away.

When the doctor came, he spoke of over-excitement, nervous strain, and prescribed strong beef-tea, absolute quiet, and keeping to her room. Jo submitted. Jan was nearly all right again; it had been a mere cold, and in her joy and gratitude for his recovery, she could have submitted to much; to remain in one's room, however, is a trial to appreciate which one must be the mother of three children.

"Your visitor can surely manage the house for a few days?" the doctor had said. But, strangely enough, now the party was over Cousin Emily seemed totally incapable of domestic duties.

So Jo lay listening to piercing cries from Nonnie, who was evidently tumbling downstairs, and hungry little Ada's wails would penetrate to her ears; or the maid would appear one moment, the "boy" the next, to ply her with questions. Worse than all were the fears she created for herself,—Jan would be sure to catch cold, or the children would venture too near the well or the cistern; who was to put away all the plate and crystal? and would not the servants appropriate all the remains of the feast?

Luckily Van Elst came home early; but he brought no balm to Jo's heart, for when he saw that she was no better, he began by scolding her, and then abruptly left the house.

This was the very opportunity his neighbour over the way had been watching for.

With apparent unconcern he sauntered across his own grounds, where he had lain in ambush for some time; for ever since he had witnessed the doctor's repeated visits, his curiosity had known no bounds.

"Well, Mr Van Elst," he began, feigning great surprise at meeting him there, "and how are you all at home?"

"Oh, first-rate," said Van Elst; "mother sick, child sick, and husband no longer master in his own house!"

"Bless me!" said Mr Smits. "Come, I'll walk up and down a bit with you. I understand how it is when the wife is ill, especially a wife like yours, but we'll hope she'll soon be herself again. And then things will be all right, won't they?"

This was very diplomatic on Mr Smits's part; he wanted to know about more than the wife's illness. It was a well-calculated move, for the whole story came out.

"*All right!* No, indeed, we shall not. What upsets my temper is those guests of mine. You will hardly believe, Mr Smits, what a tiresome, irritating fellow that Martendijk is, with his terror of infection, and his eternal complaints about his health. And what a heartless creature his wife is! But, above all, what studied egoists they both are!"

Mr Smits had to hear it all; how worn-out Jo was; how their guests had taken advantage of them; how he had been driven into giving that confounded party. "And if I could once for all just give them a piece of my mind—

but you see I can't, as they are my guests. My wife is always giving me nudges and winks to keep me quiet; and if I do break loose occasionally, I get nice little scoldings from her into the bargain. Oh, there's no standing the life I lead just now!"

"And is there no chance of their leaving soon?" asked Mr Smits.

"Oh, no! they talk of remaining another month at least," replied Van Elst, in so despairing a tone, that his neighbour pitied him from the bottom of his heart.

"But if there are unwelcome guests in one's house, it's surely easy to find some way of getting rid of them?"

"I don't know any way. They are not particularly sensitive on some points."

"You may ask what old Smits has to do with it," began the bachelor; "but you must remember I have gradually grown to take an interest in you and your wife."

"Take care, Mr Smits, I am jealous," cried Max, who had totally recovered his good-humour now he had unbosomed himself.

"Absurd! an old fellow of sixty!" said Mr Smits, not a little flattered. "But what I wanted to ask you was, may I try to devise some plan for your deliverance?"

"Oh, yes; and if you succeed I'll be grateful to you all my life."

The first thing put into Van Elst's hand next morning, when he sat down to his early coffee in the verandah, was a carefully sealed note from his old neighbour over the way. It was concise, and to the point.

"FRIEND,—Your wife is feverish. Your cousin has a dread of infection. Is there any danger of typhus?—Yours,
"SMITS."

With a heartier laugh than he had indulged in for a long

time, Van Elst sprang to his feet. "**The** very thing! What a capital idea!" He would take steps at once.

"How is Cousin Jo?" asked Emily half-an-hour later at the breakfast-table.

"No better," said Max gravely; "I would not go near her if I were you, Cousin Emily; I think she's asleep."

The doctor came, and pronounced the patient convalescent; so he sat chatting sociably with her for some time, and then left her, prescribing a tonic.

Scarcely was he gone when Max joined his cousins in the front verandah.

"What a long time the doctor stayed," Emily remarked. "It's nothing serious, is it?"

Van Elst preserved an ominous silence.

"Cousin Jo **will** soon be going about again, I hope?" asked Martendijk, with some concern; for domestic affairs had not gone **so** smoothly, nor had they, personally, fared so well, since Mrs Van Elst had been laid up.

Max's face assumed a very serious expression. "Going **about!** No, indeed, not for a while yet."

"What do you say?"

"Well, you see—h'm—after all," said Max, as if making a sudden resolve, "I think **it's** best to tell you frankly, **the** doctor is afraid of typhus **fever.**"

"*Typhus!*" shrieked Martendijk. "Good Heavens! Emily, d'ye **hear?**"

"Yes," said Emily, and, to her credit, we must confess that her first thoughts flew to the poor husband and children, who, if the worst should happen, would lose so devoted a wife **and mother.** "Alas! Cousin Max," she said, "how terrible."

"Was the doctor quite sure of **it?**" asked Martendijk, his face blanched with mortal terror, the remembrance of which long remained an unfailing source of amusement to Van Elst.

"No, not at all certain; he thought it might perhaps be small-pox," he replied.

Martendijk stared at him in the wildest consternation.

"Good God!" he stammered, "that's no trifle either. Small-pox and typhus fever! One every bit as infectious as the other!"

"Yes," said Max, "small-pox especially. Well, I'm off to the office," he concluded. "Good-morning, you'll go and see after my wife every now and then, won't you, Emily?" he asked, as he sprang into his *bendy*.

"No, Emily, indeed you'll do nothing of the kind, I hope," cried Martendijk, as soon as Van Elst was beyond earshot. "You might bring back infection, and——"

"Ah! Piet, you really are rather a coward in that respect."

"Yes; but, Emily, *small-pox!* Just fancy if you were to take it——"

"Well, of course; but you need not be so ready to accept it as a fact. If Max were sure of it he would not have been so calm about it."

"Dearest," and Piet's voice was as meek as any child's, "I hope you agree with me, we must get away from this *at once*."

"What would people say if we left Jo——"

"Oh! my dearest wife, do not agitate me with all these objections!"

"It looks so cowardly, Piet. And the climate here agrees with you so well. And the building is not finished yet."

"Well, we must just make the best of it. Anything rather than remain in this infected atmosphere. Oh, Emily, dearest Emily, have you no more affection for your husband? O Lord! the pain, the pain! The shock has set it going again!"

.   .   .   .

When Van Elst came home from his office at mid-day, his "boy" brought him another letter. It was not from Smits this time, however, but from the Martendijks.

"Dear Cousins (it ran),—You will quite understand our haste to get away, now your house is attacked by such a terrible epidemic. We would willingly have remained much longer, and it is our intention to repeat our visit soon.

"In the meantime accept our cordial thanks for the hospitality you have shown to us.

"Though your behaviour to us has not been all it might have been, dear Cousin Max, we do not bear you the slightest grudge, and are quite ready to excuse it, knowing what a bad effect the liver has on the temper.

"We wish dear Jo a speedy recovery, and earnestly trust that she may be spared to her husband and children.—With our kindest regards, your affectionate cousins,

"P. & E. MARTENDIJK."

"Hurrah!" exclaimed Van Elst. "Hurrah! Jo! our guests are gone!"

Though Jo received the news with considerable consternation, and thought it disgraceful and inexcusable in Max to joke about anything so terrible as typhus fever (in which Max agreed with her penitently), it was amazing how rapidly she sprang out of bed,—the departure of her guests proving more effective than all the doctor's tonics.

So when their old neighbour strolled past the Van Elsts' house a little later, with an air of indifference, and Max rushed out to tell him the glad news, and to thank him for his friendly and timely help, he found Mrs Van Elst in the verandah, as bright and merry as ever, ready to assure him—though she insisted on thinking it a disgraceful proceeding!—that he had done her a great service by his lucky inspiration.

An invitation to a quiet dinner on the following day was the result; and the dinner was so good, the host in such excellent spirits, and the hostess so sweet, that the solitary old bachelor caught himself thinking, as he always did when a spectator of the Van Elsts' domestic bliss, "I might have known this sort of thing too, if only——"

ANNIE FOORE.

BIOGRAPHICAL INDEX OF WRITERS.

BUNING, ARNOLD WERUMEUS, born at Uithuizen (Groningen), in 1846, and served in the Dutch navy from 1861 to 1876, when he was forced by ill-health to retire on a pension. He then settled in his native town, but afterwards removed to the Hague, where he now lives. He is the author of a great number of short stories, mostly more or less naval, and one or more novels, of which the principal is "The Burgomaster's Inheritance" (Leyden, 1873), and frequently contributes to *Eigen Haard* and Elsevier's *Geillustreerd Maandschrift*. He is not remarkable for the subtleties of humour, his genius being more akin to the rattling fun and boisterous spirits of such writers as Captain Marryat and the late Henry Kingsley. But he can be touching too, and there is unaffected pathos as well as fun in the little volume, "Marim-Schetsen," from which our extract is taken. The education of the orphan boy by his father's old mate, "The Red 'Un," who trains him up with unsparing rigour in the way in which all good sailors should go, is good in both ways; so is the sketch (in *Verschillende Ouwe Heeren*) of old Jan Hallema, the Hilligermond pilot.

CATS, JACOB,[*] born at Brouwershaven, in Zeeland, 1577; died September 12, 1660; and was buried in the Kloosterkerk at the Hague. He studied law at Leyden, and then travelled in France and Italy. Returning, he practised as a lawyer in his native town for some years. His health gave way, and he visited England in order to consult Dr William Butler, at Cambridge, but received no benefit. He went home to die, but was unexpectedly cured by a strolling alchemist. He then settled at Middleburgh, and married. His profession seems to have left him abundant leisure for poetry, and for enjoying the society of his family at his country place of Grypskerke. It was during this period he produced his "Emblems of Fancy and Love," "Galatea," "Mirror of Past and Present," and "Marriage" (Houwelick). In 1621 he was appointed Pensionary (stipendiary magistrate) of Middleburgh, and in 1623 transferred to the same office at Dordrecht. In 1627 he was sent on a diplomatic mission to England, and knighted by Charles I. After his

---

[*] *See* Introduction.

return he lost his wife, and dedicated to her memory the *Trouw-ringh* ("Wedding Ring"), published in 1635. In 1636 he was chosen Grand Pensionary of Holland, resigned his office in 1651, and in 1657 went on another unsuccessful embassy to England, where he delivered a Latin oration before the House of Commons. On coming back to Holland he retired to his villa of Zorgvliet, near the Hague, where he devoted himself once more to farming and poetry, and died at the age of seventy-three. He has always been a most popular writer in Holland, his mixture of canny morality and shrewd homely wit being in thorough accordance with the national genius, which found his long-windedness no drawback. His reputation for "soundness," and his tendency to preach also, no doubt secured his popularity among a nation peculiarly suspicious of heterodoxy, frivolity, and anything "without a moral at the end," though it must be said that his notions of propriety appear to be somewhat large when judged by present-day standards. It may seem difficult to believe, after all this, that he possessed the faintest spark of humour; but his shrewd mother wit makes him sometimes amusing, even to an outsider, and now and then he records a touch of that "detached outlook in life, which goes to the making of a real humorist." Southey, who read Dutch among other things, and was probably introduced to a great deal of Dutch literature by the poet Bilderdijk, has a highly complimentary reference to him in the epistle to Allan Cunningham:

> ... "Father Cats,
> The household poet, teacheth in his songs
> The love of all things lovely, all things pure.
> Best poet, who delights the cheerful mind
> Of childhood, stores with moral strength the heart
> Of youth, with wisdom maketh mid-life rich,
> And fills with quiet tears the eye of age."

Cats' works used to occupy in Dutch households the position of the "Pilgrim's Progress" and Fox's "Book of Martyrs" in old-fashioned English ones. He is still popular, not only among his Protestant countrymen, but even in Belgium, and a complete edition of his works has lately been issued at Antwerp. It includes a large collection of proverbs, some of the qainter ones being given in the text. A translation of some of his "Zinne-Beelden" was published, under the title of "Moral Emblems," by Richard Pigott, in 1860, in a large and handsome volume, with reproductions of the original woodcuts.

CREMER, JACOBUS JAN, born at Arnheim in 1827, is now living at the Hague. He devoted himself for a time to painting, but in time entirely abandoned the pencil for the pen. He is most successful in his village stories, the best being located in his native "Betuwe," which he calls "The Paradise of Holland." The list of his works, which include novels, short stories, and sketches (published in serial collections), and plays, is far too long to reproduce. Like Dickens, he was at one time conspicuously successful in giving readings and recitations from his own works.

DEKKER, EDWARD DOUWES, best known by the pseudonym of *Multatuli*, was born at Amsterdam, March 2, 1820. He went to Java in 1840 or 1841, with his father, the captain of a vessel, and shortly afterwards obtained a Government clerkship. After a succession of appointments in different places, at one of which he made the acquaintance of the lady who afterwards became his first wife,* he became "Assistant Resident" at Lebak,—a post which he threw up in 1856, because the Governor-General would not listen to his representations with regard to the extortion and tyranny practised by the native chiefs, and (indirectly) by the Dutch Government. Coming home, he embodied his opinions and experiences in the novel of "Max Havelaar," which, crude and formless as a literary production, startled the reading public with its origin and audacity, and, having regard to the effect it produced, may fitly be called the Dutch "Uncle Tom's Cabin." For some time after landing in Holland he and his family were in the greatest distress, as through his hasty resignation he had forfeited the pension which would have been due to him in another year or two. He obtained some grudging help from his wife's relations, who offered to provide for her entirely if she would leave him, and were righteously indignant at her refusal. With the appearance of "Max Havelaar" his success as a literary man was assured, and from thenceforth he was able to live by his pen, though continually harassed by debts (he was careless, generous, and extravagant, and had a constitutional incapacity for accounts), controversies, and quarrels, well or ill founded, with friends or

---

* She was Everdine Huberte, Baroness Wynbergen, a portionless orphan of good family, whose property, seized by rapacious relatives, afterwards cost him a series of lawsuits. Having picked up a lady's handkerchief at a ball, he chose to interpret the initials worked on it as "Eigen Haard Wel Waard" ("A hearth of one's own is worth much"), and at once declared his intention of finding and marrying the owner. She is the *Tine* of "Max Havelaar."

foes. After the death of his first wife, he was married a second time—to Mej. Schepeles—and made his home in the Rhineland, first at Niederingelheim, and then at Wiesbaden. He died at Mainz, in February 1887. Perhaps his best work is to be found in the *Ideen* (filling in the collected edition of his works some seven volumes). They are a kind of continuous rambling *causerie*, contributed to a Dutch daily, the *Dageraad*, and ranging over every possible topic, full of aphorism, paradox, epigram, and with an occasional story woven in here and there. The most important of these is the delightful fictitious biography of Wouter Pieterse, which, though certainly not an autobiography, incorporates many of the experiences of his childhood and youth. It was never finished, and proceeds in a most capricious manner, being frequently interrupted by digressions for dozens of pages together, and then suddenly taken up again. Some extracts are given from this and other parts of the *Ideen*. Most of his other works, except the dramas "The Bride in Heaven" and "The School for Princes," are of a more or less occasional and fugitive character. But Multatuli's position is not to be measured by the mere number and extent of his works. He is a distinct force in modern Holland, and a name to conjure with to the younger generation of Dutch readers.

EEDEN, F. VAN, is the editor of the *Nieuwe Gids*, and author of novels, sketches, critical articles, &c., besides the poem "Ellen," and some plays, including the comedy from which our quotation is taken, and a farce, "The Student at Home."

FOORE, ANNIE, is the pseudonym of Mevrouw W. J. F. Ijzerman, whose maiden name was Francisca J. J. A. Junius, daughter of a learned theologian, the minister of Tiel. She was born at the latter place in 1847, and married an engineer, at Padang, Sumatra, in 1873. Her principal works are the novels, "The Colonial and his Superior" (1877), "A Family Secret," "Florence's Dream," and several volumes of short stories. The specimens in the present volume are taken from "Family Life in the East Indies." She has great power of observation, a fine sense of humour, and an easy flowing style of narrative, though sometimes her stories are defective in construction. Her pictures of colonial life are admirable. For the translation of the story "Unbidden Guests," I am indebted to Miss Margaret Farquharson, of Selkirk.

HUYGENS, CONSTANTIJN, born 1596, at the Hague. His godfathers were the Admiral Justinus von Nassau and the City of Breda; he was named after the "constancy" shown by the latter to the House of Orange. He enjoyed a singularly complete and brilliant education, studied law at Leyden, and became, in 1625, private secretary to Prince Frederick Henry. He was on friendly terms with Hooft, Cats, and the beautiful and talented daughters of Roemer Visscher, —Anna and Tesselschade. Like Cats, he had visited England (in 1618), where he made the acquaintance of John Donne, whose poems he afterwards translated, and whose influence is visible in his writings. He was knighted by James I. in 1622. He married **in 1627, and** the loss of his wife, ten years later, was the great **affliction of** his life. He had four sons, the second being **the** celebrated mathematician, Christian Huygens, and one daughter. He continued his political activity till 1672, when, being to a certain extent superseded on account of his advanced age, he devoted himself to literature and (like most Dutch gentlemen) to gardening at his villa of Hofwijk, near the Hague; he died there in 1687. His works are of various kinds,—didactic and descriptive poems ("Batava Tempe"), satires ("The Costly Request"), epigrams (we give a few translations), the frightfully coarse farce of "Trijntje Cornelis" (taste of the times again!), &c. His best poem is **"Oogentrost"** (Eye Comfort), dedicated, **in** 1647, **to** a friend, **Lucretia** van Trello, who feared **she** was going blind. He also **wrote a** Latin autobiography, under the title "De Vita Propria Sermones." He published his collected poems under the title "Corn Flowers." Personally he seems to have been in every **way** worthy of respect, and is described **as** "one of the most lovable men that ever lived."

KELLER, GERARD, born at Gouda, February 13, **1829**. He was **for** some time stenographer to the Dutch parliament, and afterwards editor of the *Arnheimsche Courant*. He is a clever journalist, and voluminous writer of fiction, in which latter department he would appear to have been influenced by Dickens. His earliest novel, "The Tutor's Family," appeared in 1857; "Overkompleet," the sketch from which our extract is taken, appeared in a volume with other short stories in 1871, but has been reprinted in a complete edition of his "Novellen," of which three volumes have already seen the light. Among his other novels we may mention "The Mortgage on Wasenstein" (1866), "The History of a Halfpenny, and other Stories" (1872), "Off the Rails" (1872), &c. He is also the author of several volumes of travel-sketches, among which we may mention four illustrated quarto volumes, "Amerika in Beeld en Schrift," and a lively description of a tour in Scotland ("Een Uitstapje naar de Schotsche Hooglanden"), which has appeared quite recently. Keller acted as a newspaper correspondent in France during the Franco-German War, and his experiences there resulted in two books, "Paris Besieged" and "Paris Murdered." Besides all this he has written several comedies, and numerous contributions to periodical literature, and is now, we believe, the editor of the monthly magazine, *Vreemd en Eigen*, having previously edited, at different times, *Kunst Kroniek* and the *Geldersche Almanach*. His style has a lightness of touch, perhaps due to French influence, and conspicuously wanting in all but some of the most recent Dutch authors, with the exception of Multatuli.

LAMBERTS-HURRELLBRINCK, L. H. J., is a young writer, living at Leyden, who has published more than one collection of short stories, mostly dealing with the province of Limburg and its people. His first volume, "Limburgsche Novellen," was reviewed, with perhaps undue severity, in *De Gids* for July 1890—a judgment which, it is said, was not altogether uninfluenced by party spirit. A later volume is "Van Limburg's Bodem." The sketch in the text appeared in *Elsevier's Maandschrift* for September 1892, and is to a certain extent founded on fact.

LENNEP, JACOB VAN, one of the best known of modern Dutch writers. Belonging to a literary family, he was born at Amsterdam in 1802, studied at Leyden, and took a law degree in 1824, and settled as a lawyer at Amsterdam. In 1854-56 he was a member of the Second Chamber of the States-General. He died at Oosterbeek (Gelderland) on August 25, 1868. His literary industry was so prodigious that we cannot attempt to give a list of his works, which were chiefly poems, novels (published in a collected edition of 19 vols.), plays, and historical studies. Perhaps his best novel is "Klaasje Zevenster," from which the bit of description we have quoted is taken. We give his comedy, "The Village on the Frontier," entire.

SEIPGENS, EMILE ANTON HUBERT, born at Roermond (Limburg), August 16, 1837. He was at first in the brewing business, but is now a teacher of German language and literature in the "Rijks Hoogere Burgerschool" of his native town. He has written several plays, some of them in the Roermond dialect, and two or three volumes of short stories, most of them strongly "Limburgsch" in local colour. The extract here given is taken from the volume entitled "In en om het klein Stadje" (Amsterdam, 1887). Another collection is entitled "Langs Maas en Geul." He is an occasional contributor to the monthly magazine *De Gids*, and also to Elsevier's "Illustrated."

LIBRARY OF HUMOUR

Cloth Elegant, Large Crown 8vo, Price 3/6 per vol.

VOLUMES ALREADY ISSUED.

THE HUMOUR OF FRANCE. Translated, with an Introduction and Notes, by Elizabeth Lee. With numerous Illustrations by Paul Frénzeny.

"From Villon to Paul Verlaine, from dateless *fabliaux* to newspapers fresh from the kiosk, we have a tremendous range of selections."—*Birmingham Daily Gazette.*

"French wit is excellently represented. We have here examples of Villon, Rabelais, and Molière, but we have specimens also of La Rochefoucauld, Regnard, Voltaire, Beaumarchais, Chamfort, Dumas, Gautier, Labiche, De Banville, Pailleron, and many others. . . . The book sparkles from beginning to end."—*Globe* (London).

THE HUMOUR OF GERMANY. Translated, with an Introduction and Notes, by Hans Müller-Casenov. With numerous Illustrations by C. E. Brock.

An excellently representative volume.—*Daily Telegraph* (London).

"Whether it is Saxon kinship or the fine qualities of the collection, we have found this volume the most entertaining of the three. Its riotous absurdities well overbalance its examples of the oppressively heavy. . . . The national impulse to make fun of the war correspondent has a capital example in the skit from Julius Stettenheim."—*New York Independent.*

London: WALTER SCOTT, LIMITED, 24 Warwick Lane.

THE HUMOUR OF ITALY. Translated, with an Introduction and Notes, by A. Werner. With 50 Illustrations and a Frontispiece by Arturo Faldi.

"Will reveal to English readers a whole new world of literature."—*Athenæum* (London).

"Apart from selections of writers of classical reputation, the book contains some delightful modern short stories and sketches. We may particularly mention those by Verga, Capuana, De Amicis. . . . Excellent also are one or two of the jokes and 'bulls' which figure under the heading of newspaper humour."—*Literary World* (London).

THE HUMOUR OF AMERICA. Selected, with a copious Biographical Index of American Humorists, by James Barr.

"There is not a dull page in the volume; it fairly sparkles and ripples with good things."—*Manchester Examiner.*

THE HUMOUR OF HOLLAND. Translated, with an Introduction and Notes, by A. Werner. With numerous Illustrations by Dudley Hardy.

VOLUMES IN PREPARATION.

THE HUMOUR OF IRELAND. Selected by D. J. O'Donoghue. With numerous Illustrations by Oliver Paque.

THE HUMOUR OF RUSSIA. Translated, with Notes, by E. L. Boole, and an Introduction by Stepniak. With 50 Illustrations by Paul Frénzeny.

THE HUMOUR OF SPAIN. Translated, with an Introduction and Notes, by S. Taylor. With numerous Illustrations.

To be followed by volumes representative of ENGLAND, SCOTLAND, JAPAN, etc. The Series will be complete in about twelve volumes.

BOOKS OF FAIRY TALES.

*Crown 8vo, Cloth Elegant, Price 3/6 per **Vol.***

ENGLISH FAIRY AND OTHER FOLK TALES.

Selected and Edited, with an Introduction,

By EDWIN SIDNEY HARTLAND.

With Twelve Full-Page Illustrations by CHARLES E. BROCK.

SCOTTISH FAIRY AND FOLK TALES.

Selected and Edited, with an Introduction,

By SIR GEORGE DOUGLAS, BART.

With Twelve Full-Page Illustrations by JAMES TORRANCE.

IRISH FAIRY AND FOLK TALES.

Selected and Edited, with an Introduction,

By W. B. YEATS.

With Twelve Full-Page Illustrations by JAMES TORRANCE.

London: WALTER SCOTT, LTD., 24 Warwick Lane, Paternoster Row.

IBSEN'S PROSE DRAMAS.

Edited by WILLIAM ARCHER.

Complete in Five Vols. Crown 8vo, Cloth, Price 3/6 each.
Set of Five Vols., in Case, 17/6; in Half Morocco, in Case, 32/6.

"We seem at last to be shown men and women as they are; and at first it is more than we can endure. . . . All Ibsen's characters speak and act as if they were hypnotised, and under their creator's imperious demand to reveal themselves. There never was such a mirror held up to nature before: it is too terrible. . . . Yet we must return to Ibsen, with his remorseless surgery, his remorseless electric-light, until we, too, have grown strong and learned to face the naked—if necessary, the flayed and bleeding—reality."—SPEAKER (London).

VOL. I. "A DOLL'S HOUSE," "THE LEAGUE OF YOUTH," and "THE PILLARS OF SOCIETY." With Portrait of the Author, and Biographical Introduction by WILLIAM ARCHER.

VOL. II. "GHOSTS," "AN ENEMY OF THE PEOPLE," and "THE WILD DUCK." With an Introductory Note.

VOL. III. "LADY INGER OF ÖSTRÅT," "THE VIKINGS AT HELGELAND," "THE PRETENDERS." With an Introductory Note and Portrait of Ibsen.

VOL. IV. "EMPEROR AND GALILEAN." With an Introductory Note by WILLIAM ARCHER.

VOL. V. "ROSMERSHOLM," "THE LADY FROM THE SEA," "HEDDA GABLER." Translated by WILLIAM ARCHER. With an Introductory Note.

The sequence of the plays *in each volume* is chronological; the complete set of volumes comprising the dramas thus presents them in chronological order.

"The art of prose translation does not perhaps enjoy a very high literary status in England, but we have no hesitation in numbering the present version of Ibsen, so far as it has gone (Vols. I. and II.), among the very best achievements, in that kind, of our generation."—*Academy*.

"We have seldom, if ever, met with a translation so absolutely idiomatic."—*Glasgow Herald*.

LONDON: WALTER SCOTT, LIMITED, 24 WARWICK LANE.

Crown 8vo, about 350 pp. each, Cloth Cover, 2s. 6d. per vol.
Half-polished Morocco, gilt top, 5s.

COUNT TOLSTOÏ'S WORKS.

The following Volumes are already issued—

A RUSSIAN PROPRIETOR.

THE COSSACKS.

IVAN ILYITCH, AND OTHER STORIES.

MY RELIGION.

LIFE.

MY CONFESSION.

CHILDHOOD, BOYHOOD, YOUTH.

THE PHYSIOLOGY OF WAR.

ANNA KARÉNINA **3s. 6d.**

WHAT **TO DO?**

WAR AND PEACE. (4 VOLS.)

THE LONG EXILE, AND OTHER STORIES FOR CHILDREN.

SEVASTOPOL.

THE KREUTZER SONATA, **AND** FAMILY HAPPINESS.

Uniform with the above.

IMPRESSIONS OF RUSSIA.

BY DR. GEORG BRANDES.

London: WALTER **SCOTT, LIMITED,** 24 Warwick Lane.

BOOKS AT 6/-.

VAIN FORTUNE. By GEORGE MOORE. With Eleven Illustrations by MAURICE GREIFFENHAGEN.

MODERN PAINTING. A Volume of Essays. By GEORGE MOORE.

PEER GYNT: A DRAMATIC POEM. By HENRIK IBSEN. Translated by WILLIAM and CHARLES ARCHER.

AMONG THE CAMPS; OR, YOUNG PEOPLE'S STORIES OF THE WAR. By THOMAS NELSON PAGE. (Illustrated.)

THE MUSIC OF THE POETS: A MUSICIANS' BIRTHDAY BOOK. Edited by ELEONORE D'ESTERRE KEELING.

THE GERM-PLASM: A THEORY OF HEREDITY. By AUGUST WEISMANN, Professor in the University of Freiburg-in-Breisgau.

London: WALTER SCOTT, LIMITED, 24 Warwick Lane.

DRAMATIC ESSAYS.

EDITED BY
WILLIAM ARCHER AND ROBERT W. LOWE.

Three Volumes, Crown 8vo, Cloth, Price 3/6 each.

Dramatic Criticism, as we now understand it—the systematic appraisement from day to day and week to week of contemporary plays and acting—began in England about the beginning of the present century. Until very near the end of the eighteenth century, "the critics" gave direct utterance to their judgments in the theatre itself, or in the coffee-houses, only occasionally straying into print in letters to the news-sheets, or in lampoons or panegyrics in prose or verse, published in pamphlet form. Modern criticism began with modern journalism; but some of its earliest utterances were of far more than ephemeral value. During the earlier half of the present century several of the leading essayists of the day—men of the first literary eminence—concerned themselves largely with the theatre. Under the title of

"DRAMATIC ESSAYS"

will be issued, in three volumes, such of their theatrical criticisms as seem to be of abiding interest.

THE FIRST SERIES will contain selections from the criticisms of LEIGH HUNT, both those published in 1807 (long out of print), and the admirable articles contributed more than twenty years later to *The Tatler*, and never republished.

THE SECOND SERIES will contain selections from the criticisms of WILLIAM HAZLITT. Hazlitt's Essays on Kean and his contemporaries have long been inaccessible, save to collectors.

THE THIRD SERIES will contain hitherto uncollected criticisms by JOHN FORSTER, GEORGE HENRY LEWES, and others, with selections from the writings of WILLIAM ROBSON (The Old Playgoer).

The Essays will be concisely but adequately annotated, and each volume will contain an Introduction by WILLIAM ARCHER, and an Engraved Portrait Frontispiece.

London: WALTER SCOTT, LIMITED, 24 Warwick Lane.

Crown 8vo, Cloth, Price 6s.

MODERN PAINTING.

By GEORGE MOORE.

SOME PRESS NOTICES.

" Of the very few books on art that painters and critics should on no account leave unread this is surely one."—*The Studio.*

" His book is one of the best books about pictures that have come into our hands for some years."—*St. James's Gazette.*

" If there is an art critic who knows exactly what he means and says it with exemplary lucidity, it is 'G. M.'"—*The Sketch.*

" A more original, a better informed, a more suggestive, and let us add, a more amusing work on the art of to-day, we have never read than this volume."—*Glasgow Herald.*

" Impressionism, to use that word, in the absence of any fitter one,—the impressionism which makes his own writing on art in this volume so effective, is, in short, the secret both of his likes and dislikes, his hatred of what he thinks conventional and mechanic, together with his very alert and careful evaluation of what comes home to him as straightforward, whether in Reynolds, or Rubens, or Ruysdael, in Japan, in Paris, or in modern England."—Mr. Pater in *The Chronicle.*

" As an art critic Mr. George Moore certainly has some signal advantages. He is never dull, he is frankly personal, he is untroubled by tradition."—*Westminster Gazette.*

" Mr. Moore, in spite of the impediments that he puts in the way of his own effectiveness, is one of the most competent writers on painting that we have."—*Manchester Guardian.*

" His [Mr. Moore's] book is one that cannot fail to be much talked about; and everyone who is interested in modern painting will do well to make acquaintance with its views."—*Scottish Leader.*

" As everybody knows by this time, Mr. Moore is a person of strong opinions and strong dislikes, and has the gift of expressing both in pungent language."—*The Times.*

" Of his [Mr. Moore's] sincerity, of his courage, and of his candour there can be no doubt. . . . One of the most interesting writers on art that we have."—*Pall Mall Gazette.*

London: WALTER SCOTT, LTD., 24 Warwick Lane.

WORKS BY GEORGE MOORE.

Crown 8vo, Cloth, Price 3s. 6d. each.

TWENTIETH EDITION.
A MUMMER'S WIFE.

"'A Mummer's Wife' is a striking book—clever, unpleasant, realistic. . . . No one who wishes to examine the subject of realism in fiction, with regard to English novels, can afford to neglect 'A Mummer's Wife.'"—*Athenæum*.

"'A Mummer's Wife,' in virtue of its vividness of presentation and real literary skill, may be regarded as in some degree a representative example of the work of a literary school that has of late years attracted to itself a great deal of notoriety."—*Spectator*.

EIGHTH EDITION.
A MODERN LOVER.

"It would be difficult to praise too highly the strength, truth, delicacy, and pathos of the incident of Gwynnie Lloyd, and the admirable treatment of the great sacrifice she makes."—*Spectator*.

SEVENTH EDITION.
A DRAMA IN MUSLIN.

"Mr. George Moore's work stands on a very much higher plane than the facile fiction of the circulating libraries. . . . The characters are drawn with patient care, and with a power of individualisation which marks the born novelist. It is a serious, powerful, and in many respects edifying book."—*Pall Mall Gazette*.

Crown 8vo, Cloth, Price 6s.
VAIN FORTUNE.

With Eleven Illustrations by MAURICE GREIFFENHAGEN.

A few Large-Paper Copies on Hand-made Paper, Price One Guinea net.

A VOLUME of ESSAYS by GEORGE MOORE.

Crown 8vo, Cloth, Price 6s.
MODERN PAINTING.

Crown 8vo, Cloth, Price 5s.
THE STRIKE AT ARLINGFORD.
PLAY IN THREE ACTS.

London: WALTER SCOTT, LIMITED, 24 Warwick Lane.

COMPACT AND PRACTICAL.

In Limp Cloth; for the Pocket. Price One Shilling.

THE EUROPEAN
CONVERSATION BOOKS.

FRENCH   ITALIAN
SPANISH   GERMAN
NORWEGIAN

CONTENTS.

Hints to Travellers—Everyday Expressions—Arriving at and Leaving a Railway Station—Custom House Enquiries—In a Train—At a Buffet and Restaurant—At an Hotel—Paying an Hotel Bill—Enquiries in a Town—On Board Ship—Embarking and Disembarking—Excursion by Carriage—Enquiries as to Diligences—Enquiries as to Boats—Engaging Apartments—Washing List and Days of Week—Restaurant Vocabulary—Telegrams and Letters, etc., etc.

The contents of these little handbooks are so arranged as to permit direct and immediate reference. All dialogues or enquiries not considered absolutely essential have been purposely excluded, nothing being introduced which might confuse the traveller rather than assist him. A few hints are given in the introduction which will be found valuable to those unaccustomed to foreign travel.

London: WALTER SCOTT, 24 Warwick Lane, Paternoster Row.

www.ingramcontent.com/pod-product-compliance
Lightning Source LLC
Chambersburg PA
CBHW020544300426
44111CB00008B/785